Fictions of America

Narratives of global empire

Judie Newman

Routledge
Taylor & Francis Group

LONDON AND NEW YORK

First published 2007
by Routledge
2 Park Square, Milton Park, Abingdon, Oxon OX14 4RN

Simultaneously published in the USA and Canada
by Routledge
270 Madison Ave, New York, NY 10016

Routledge is an imprint of the Taylor & Francis Group, an informa business

© 2007 Judie Newman

Typeset in Baskerville by
Bookcraft Ltd, Stroud, Gloucestershire
Printed and bound in Great Britain by
Antony Rowe Ltd, Chippenham, Wiltshire

British Library Cataloguing in Publication Data
A catalogue record for this book is available from the British Library

Library of Congress Cataloging in Publication Data
Newman, Judie.
   Fictions of America: narratives of global empire / Judie Newman.
      p. cm.
   Includes bibliographical references and index.
   1. Literature and globalization. 2. American literature—Foreign
influences. 3. American literature—History and criticism.
   4. Literature, Comparative. 5. Multiculturalism in literature.
   6. Culture and globalization—United States. I. Title.
PS157.N49 2008
813.009'355—dc22   2007028586

ISBN10: 0-415-33383-0 (hbk)
ISBN10: 0-415-33384-9 (pbk)
ISBN10: 0-203-41405-5 (ebk)

ISBN13: 978-0-415-33383-2 (hbk)
ISBN13: 978-0-415-33384-9 (pbk)
ISBN13: 978-0-203-41405-7 (ebk)

Fictions of America

internet has had a huge impact on channels of communication and
rmation, reaching across time and space to connect the world through
lisation. In this internet-led world, story links to story, windows open
v stories and no overall authority establishes priority. This sense of
ation has raised many questions for contemporary American novel-
imarily the usefulness or redundancy of narrative and its potentially
tive function. What are the right stories for such a broadband world?
do contemporary American novelists respond to issues such as the
ence of the multinational corporation and its predecessors, human
imperialism, the literary work as a marketable commodity, transla-
s betrayal, data overload and the implosion of the virtual into the
phe e? Is globalisation inevitable – or is it a fiction which fiction turns
to ea ity?

tio s of America explores these questions and looks at the ways in which
I China and Africa can be said to have underwritten American culture,
litе rature has been marketed globally and how novelists have answered
power with resistant fictions. Judie Newman examines a wide range
ion from the mid-nineteenth to the twenty-first century, including the
ational adoption narrative, short story, historical novel, slave narra-
ernational bestseller and Western to illustrate her argument. Looking
at authors such as Bharati Mukherjee, John Updike, Emily Prager,
Crafts, Zora Neale Hurston, David Bradley, Peter Høeg, and
McCarthy, Fictions of America provides a bold response to the crucial
s raised by globalisation.

Judie Newman (Professor of American Studies, University of Nottingham,
Fellow of the English Association) is the author of seven books on American
and postcolonial literature, a past President of the British Association for
American Studies, and recipient of the Arthur Miller Prize in American
studies.

This book is dedicated to the memory, and to all the descendants, of Laura Finch, Thomas Golding, William Herringshaw, Elizabeth Taylor, Mary Walker, George Young (63rd Foot), Honour Fox, Elizabeth Roberts, Mary Rudd, William Telford, John Wilson, Matthew Davidson, Margaret Bell, Eliza Wykes, Deborah Harper, Sam Cooper (RA), Emily Jane Hurst, Mary Ann Benton, Sarah Embury, Ellis Smith, Joseph Cross, Thomas Wilson, Thomas Smith, Saul Newnham and Cordelia Jane Bladen.

Contents

Acknowledgements

In writing what follows I have incurred many debts, too many indeed to name individually here. The responsibility for any errors is of course entirely mine.

I am grateful especially to my colleagues in the School of American and Canadian Studies, University of Nottingham, and to the students in my 'Fictions of America' course in the last three years. Among individuals who helped with specific queries, suggestions, criticism and support I take this opportunity to thank William Andrews, James Annesley, Vicki Barnaby, Celeste-Marie Bernier, Rachel Bowlby, Janice Burrow, Susan Castillo, Gloria Cronin, Pil Dahlerup, Michelle Drew, Val Fraser, Mick Gidley, Richard Godden, Paul Grainge, Cindy Hamilton, John Howard, Graham Huggan, Yvonne Jerrold, Maha Marouan, Sarah Meer, Peter Messent, David Murray, Dragana Obradovic, Kirsten Holst Petersen, Prem Poddar, Monika Reif-Huelser, Kirsten Thisted, Graham Thompson, Dennis Walder. Liz Thompson has demonstrated infinite editorial patience, as the project was interrupted by a succession of academic, medical and criminal events.

I should also like to thank the editors of *Foreign Literature Studies*, *Journal of American Studies*, *Journal of Literary Studies*, *Journal of the Short Story in English*, *Modern Language Review*, and *Spring: Tidsskrift for moderne dansk litteratur* for the opportunity to try out pilot versions of material which is developed in the book. Similar thanks go to James Yerkes as the editor of *John Updike and Religion* (Grand Rapids, MI: Eerdmans, 1999). I am also grateful for invitations to lecture at the Georg Brandes Skolen, University of Copenhagen; the School of American and Canadian Studies, University of Birmingham; the Department of American Studies, King's College, University of London; Shanghai International Studies University; the Open University Staff Seminar; American Literature Association Symposium on Contemporary Fiction; American Literature Association Annual Conference; African American Literature and Culture Society Conference; Annual Conference of the Association for the Study of the New Literatures in English;

International Centre for the History of Slavery Conference. I gratefully acknowledge financial support from the University of Nottingham Research Committee, the Dean's Fund and the British Academy for funding attendance at conferences and research time. I am particularly grateful to the Research Committee of the University of Nottingham for paid research leave. A special debt is due to the staff of the Hallward Library, University of Nottingham, particularly the Inter Library Loans staff, for invaluable assistance in tracking down materials. Thanks go once again with feeling to Alice and Cash Newman, Chris Revie and James Revie for their encouragement and support.

Introduction
The West Coast Offense

In Bharati Mukherjee's novel *Desirable Daughters* the Bengali-born narrator and author, Tara Chatterjee, is in an implicit contest with another writer, her ex-husband Bish, a writer of software programs who enjoys semi-mythological status among Indians as the Stanford college student who, with his equally penniless friend Chet Yee, made a fortune overnight in computer bandwidth routing technology (recalling the story of Sabeer Bhatia, inventor with his Stanford friend Jack Smith of Hotmail, subsequently sold to Microsoft for $400 million). As Amitava Kumar comments, 'It is the software writers from India rather than the fiction writers who are wired to the circuits of global production.'[1] Bish's discovery is prompted by watching a football game in which the players exploit the 'West Coast Offense', a tactic in which short passing plays among designated receivers replace the running game, to stretch the field and control the ball – a process appropriately invented by Bill Walsh of the Cincinnati Bengals,[2] so named after a Bengal tiger in the Cincinnati zoo. The system, called CHATTY, is 'about width, using the whole field, connecting in the flat, no interference, a billion short passes linked together'.[3] It also exemplifies the method of Mukherjee's novel. In interview Mukherjee said that

> The aesthetic strategy of the book was using the width of the field – of history, geography, diaspora, gender, ethnicity, language – rather than the old-fashioned long, clean throw.[4]

The reader is thus passed from story to story across a broad geographical and historical sweep; the narrative passes from one receiver to another, with the story moving forward through side-passes, as a narrative based on descent and filiation is replaced by a model which involves side connections, sibships and horizontal or lateral moves.

This is also (though in more prosaic fashion) the method of the present study, which eschews the long, clean throw in favour of passing the global argument across a broad field, to interrogate the relationship of contemporary American fictions to globalisation. Before the reader cries 'foul', it is important to establish that this tactic makes particular sense in relation to the topic of globalisation, itself dispersed and diffuse. Paul Harris has argued that, while the contraction of the globe is self-evident, with information passing instantaneously across it, at the same time the individual finds himself experiencing dispersion, being in several different orders of space simultaneously, with an inevitable impact on how we read and write texts. 'Reading narratives that relate a single storyline has been displaced by the subtle art of pointing and clicking.'[5] The suggestion lingers that the ball will pass to the software writers, as narrative declines in importance. Harris, however, argues that the reverse is true. In the globalised world the human need for stability becomes more acute, and narrative becomes more essential as a means to tune worldly discourse into a coherent resonance, to help make sense of the world. 'Narrative ultimately becomes a tuning into the world which rediscovers and re-establishes our place, our home in it.'[6] Harris's domestic metaphor is worth noting; globalisation affects the reader's perception of 'home' – nation, family, affiliations – in complex ways. For other critics, however, the relation of the novel to a flattened world seems more problematic. One perceived risk is that novels about globalisation may also participate in it, confirming its myth. James Annesley highlights the dangers of representing globalisation as 'an irreducible reality that the novel is powerless to either interrogate or resist'.[7] Even less optimistically the novel may be envisaged, not merely as incapable of resistance, but as actively propagating the phenomenon itself. Thomas Peyser argues that 'novels themselves may have a crucial role to play in the very process of globalization.'[8] They may thus become fictions in the service of a fiction, since the existence of globalisation as a new and real phenomenon is both contested and open to multiple definitions.

Globalisation suffers from an exceptionally fuzzy brand identity. The reader sensitive to the s/z distinction will notice the variant spellings of the term in different critical registers. It has more than one brand image, depending on who is using the term, and what feelings or ideas are being associated with it. A fair working definition is offered by David Held and his collaborators: 'A widening … and speeding up of interconnectedness in all aspects of contemporary social life from the cultural to the criminal, the financial to the spiritual.'[9] Alternatively, Anthony Giddens describes it as 'The intensification of worldwide social relations which link distant localities in such a way that local happenings are shaped by events occurring many miles away, and vice versa.'[10] As a sociopolitical and geographical phenomenon, globalisation has become a major focus of research in cultural studies and the social sciences. In literary studies, the recognition that the object of knowledge is situated in a vast network of intertextual and intercultural relationships has prompted fresh exploration of 'transnational' writers; the remapping of literary periods, influences and areas; and consideration of the connections between national literatures and postcolonial studies, border studies, diasporic culture and even scientific models. (Giddens's definition subliminally invokes the butterfly effect, from chaos theory.) For the wary, globalisation represents a form of literary appropriation, swamping autonomous cultures, in a conquest of the world by an Anglophone, internationalised aesthetic, in a condition of borderless culture. For other readers, the ball is passing in the other direction, to end American exceptionalism and produce a fundamental alteration in the character of its 'national' literature.

Daniel O'Hara argues that globalisation has emerged as a new master term of criticism, following in the footsteps of culture, power or gender, implying 'specific realities that everyone at the moment already knows (or is presumed to know) and yet [it] sounds suggestively vague enough to hold for a while a mysterious resonance'.[11] As O'Hara argues, everyone is supposed to know that the end of the Cold War means that capitalism is no longer tied to the social institutions of any one culture, or the customs of any particular people. Large TNCs can manufacture in China, centralise distribution in Memphis, advertise in New York and feed the markets of the Pacific Rim. 'Globalization refers specifically to this free-floating quality, this differential sense of the freedom to move anywhere at any time, from one locale to another around the world.'[12] Moreover, the term itself enacts the very process it inscribes; it travels easily, floating freely between different discourses, serving different interests. Stuart Christie construes this fuzziness in sinister terms.

> The term globalisation has always struck me as vague and woolly, grabbed (because of its implied internationalism) by the corporate would-be masters of the universe to cloak their own sinister 'free trade' agenda.[13]

Yet the vagueness of the definition is an opportunity as well as a danger. Globalisation is a travelling concept. In the humanities Mieke Bal characterises as travelling concepts those terms which 'do' rather than remaining static, which are often condensed theories in themselves, rather than definitive labels, travelling between disciplines, scholars, historical periods and academic communities. Hybridity, for example, a term from biology which usually implies sterility, has been enthusiastically adopted in cultural criticism to suggest an idealised state of postcolonial diversity. The nomadic concept enjoys a productive power to reconfigure phenomena in new ways –

to stretch the field by passing the ball sideways. Bal uses the example of the term 'subject' as it might be used by a philosopher, a psychoanalytic critic, a narratologist, an architectural scholar and an art historian, who might respectively understand it as relating to the rise of the individual, the unconscious, the narrator's voice, the human being confronted with space, or the subject matter of a painting. For Bal, 'the travelling nature of a concept is an asset rather than a liability' though she enjoins as a result the necessity for very rigorous and close readings of any chosen cultural objects.[14]

As it travels globalisation comes to mean very different things to economists, politicians and social scientists, not to mention anarchists and neoconservatives. On the one hand the term is invoked to celebrate the potential for economic and social liberation, greater human integration and the extension of democracy.[15] In this incarnation, a subset of terminology (most memorably Michael Ignatieff's 'Empire Lite') concerns itself with human rights imperialism, intervention on humanitarian grounds in other people's countries, in a new form of imperial tutelage.[16] Oddly, given the usual views of its adherents, this type of 'One World' globalism is closest to nineteenth-century Marxism, in the idea that politics are merely 'superstructural reflections of underlying economic relations', as if a single worldwide economic system can emerge to issue in an era of peace and prosperity.[17] The suggestion that there might be competing forms of globalisation (sinicisation in the East as opposed to anglobalisation) is rarely entertained. This brand of globalisation easily elides into associated ideas of 'liberal empire', notably in Niall Ferguson's argument that the world needs more US rule, rather than less, to underwrite the free international exchange of commodities, labour and capital; the rule of law; fiscal stability; and decent infrastructure.[18] In Ferguson's version of Pax Americana the real problem is that globalisation is not global at all. It is its absence or inhibition which condemns Third World countries to economic penury. Nor are the Americans enthusiastic imperialists; in his analysis they are keener on Social than National security, on building shopping malls rather than nations, and so distinctly unwilling to function as settlers beyond the First World as to lack all will-to-power. Chalmers Johnson, however, moves the terminology from empire to militarism, arguing that the will of the American people is largely irrelevant to their political masters, with most of US imperialism a 'stealth imperialism' operating well below the sightlines of the American public.[19]

For antiglobalists, one response is to cry 'Globaloney', and to decry globalisation as an invention or illusion – a form of self-fulfilling prophecy, or ideological device to advance the cause of certain Western financial interests. As Arvind Rajagopal notes,

The name itself carries its connotations, performing what it is meant to presuppose ... it describes an inexorable process but does not prescribe any particular values other than the acceptance of its own inevitability.[20]

In this argument there is nothing new about globalisation, which is merely empire (or capitalism) by another name, involving the cynical domination of the poorer regions of the world by the richer. Are today's globalised TNCs any different in reality from the web of international companies established in the 1930s and 1940s under the Third Reich, or such precursors as the Holy Roman Empire, the Hanseatic League or the Abbasid Caliphate? For those antiglobalists who accept the term as characterising a real event, it is a rallying call for resistance to homogenisation, capitalist exploitation, consumerism and media monopolisation. Its own technologies of instant communication can be used to coordinate acts of mass protest. In more everyday terms Arjun Appadurai argues that ordinary people may 'consume' mass media in ways which similarly embody resistance, selectivity, localisation and agency, in their everyday social practices of imaginary projection.[21]

In literary terms the recognition that America has been worlded has tended to translate globalisation into ethnicity. As David Nye has argued, Janice Radway's famous presidential address to the American Studies Association in 1998, saluting the inclusion of ethnic, gendered and racial minorities in the field of American studies, essentially reduced the question of American empire to the mistreatment of minorities as colonised others within the United States.[22] These are not of course negligible advances, and Radway's stance was distinctly preferable to any exceptionalist or nativist rhetoric. As Arif Dirlik, however, contends, the question is not merely to bring the world into America, but also to bring America into the world.[23] The translation of globalisation into ethnicity fails to recognise that America is not an exceptional land of immigrants, but merely 'one node in a postnational network of diasporas',[24] not a closed space in which to stoke the melting pot or assemble the multicultural salad, but a nation containing delocalised transnations with live links back to their nations of origins, just like many other nations in a globalised world. Ethnicity cannot be taken as a contra-globalist virtue in itself; it can also be mobilised in the service of globalisation.

What is incontestable is that globalisation is as much about the perception of globalisation as it is about the phenomenon itself.

What is new – startlingly and even shockingly new – is the sway that the idea of globality holds over the imagination, the force with which the processes and consequences of globalisation impinge upon the individual mind.[25]

O'Hara has called attention to the new pathological affect which makes the global condition recognisable to the modern individual, harassed by cell phones, bleepers, internet and media, creating the condition which Bruce Robbins calls 'feeling global'. Can the individual cope with the sensation of the 'Sweatshop Sublime', a consciousness of the inadequacy of the imagination, unable to grasp the idea of a whole and overwhelmed by the sensation of a myriad of interdependent agents in the production of the object?[26] The contemporary reader who Googles E.M. Forster's refrain in *Howards End*, 'Only connect!', will turn up an article on 'computer-mediated association and community networks'.[27] Google John Donne's 'No man is an island' (Meditation XVII) and up comes 'No man is an island; daily e-mail marketing advice'.[28] The fear of human isolation has been replaced by the anxieties of connectivity.

Globalisation is a term which dissolves and transforms, associating itself with topics as diffuse as terrorism, tourism and transnationalism, in addition to empire, neocolonialism and corporatism. It has awkward family relatives in glocalisation and modernity, and associated master narratives in the triumph of democracy, Manifest Destiny and the end of history. The present exploration follows ideas across textual sites which may seem heterogeneous, in novels which consider the long chronology of globalisation, TNCs, data overload, human rights imperialism, forcible globalisation and racialised modernity, militarism, spurious determinism and the anxieties of connectivity, as the writers under consideration revise the canon, create new genres, resist the commodification of literature and construct their own priority narratives. Obedient to Bal's close-reading agenda, the present study sticks to what Gilbert Ryle called, in an ethnographical context, 'thick description', allowing a text to be considered with full respect to its specificity. The ball may cross a broad field, but the individual passes need to be precisely judged. The texts considered here strike different variations on globalisation, passing it through different conceptual fields, but they remain complex, literary narratives which speak for themselves. Their very particularity is in a sense a resistance strategy, rebutting homogenisation. While appropriate reference is made to theorists (of globalisation and of literature) the study proceeds on the assumption that American fictions have in themselves the interpretive power more commonly ascribed to the literary critic.

At the risk of attenuating some of the surprises, a brief outline is probably useful. Appropriately the book begins with novels that establish a long chronology. The multinational corporation replicates in many respects an earlier institution of imperialism, the chartered company, authorised by an imperial nation to exploit and govern a foreign territory, with a division of profits between the national government and private investors. Chapter 1 examines the fictional treatment of the early antecedents of today's corporations, as exemplified in the English East India Company (1600), and makes explicit links between Puritan America and India. The argument focuses on two rewritings of an American classic, *The Scarlet Letter*, underlining the extent to which the canonical text and its cultural authority is underwritten by the American trade with the East. In its frame tale, Bharati Mukherjee's *The Holder of the World* excavates links between seventeenth-century Massachusetts and precolonial Moghul India through the quest of a 1990s asset-hunter for a lost diamond, the Emperor's Tear. In the inset tale, Indians (Native Americans) are replaced by Indians (from the subcontinent) as the heroine (based on Hawthorne's Hester Prynne) moves from New England to the Coromandel coast and the court of Emperor Aurangzebe. Transactions between cultures are at the heart of the novel, which calls attention to the trade between Colonial America and the East, reversing the direction of exploration and discovery. Mukherjee moves beyond the boundaries of the conventional historical novel, marrying *The Scarlet Letter* with virtual reality techniques, creating a fictional space which corresponds to her conception of transnational identity. The novel therefore both restores the history which Hawthorne occluded in *The Scarlet Letter* and in the frame tale implicitly questions the neohistoricist assumption that an increase in information will lead to an increase in the determinacy of meaning. In *S.*, his reconfiguration of Hawthorne's tale, John Updike brings the story into the present, transporting an Indian cult, fleeing religious persecution, to a twentieth-century neocolonial settlement in the heart of America. Where Mukherjee follows Weber in envisaging religion as the handmaid of capitalism, Updike turns the tables to emphasise how global capitalist networks can propagate mall religion. While *S.* offers the cautionary spectacle of the East depending upon its formerly exploited Others for self-definition, it also highlights the new imperialism of transnational corporatism, in the portrayal of the religious cult as a non-located capitalist enclave with a marketable alterity.

Chapter 2 moves further east, from India to China, to engage with what has become known as human rights imperialism, the justification of intervention in other people's countries by the appeal to a humanitarian mission. Where Updike and Mukherjee focus on the role of Indian trade and plunder in the construction of the canonical American work of art, exploring its imaginative genealogy through the family metaphor of intertextuality, Emily Prager is concerned with issues of modernisation and development, represented through mother–daughter relationships and focusing specifically on transnational adoption and the exploitation of the bodies of Chinese girls. Transnational adoption is a new phenomenon and transnational adoption narrative a new genre with its own conventions and recurrent motifs; *Wuhu Diary* explores how to tell a story which will take adequate account of the historical and political complexity of the issues. Prager's 'A Visit from the Footbinder' challenges a readerly politics of Western domination, in relation to the portrayal of China as underdeveloped, barbaric or timeless, challenging Julia Kristeva's *About Chinese Women* with the critiques of Rey Chow and Gayatri Chakravorty Spivak. The theme of footbinding is intimately related to issues of development, modernisation and globalisation, and extends into Prager's *Roger Fishbite*, as Chinese slippers turn into the sneakers made by bonded child labour. *Wuhu Diary* moves to the present and a sharpened sense of Western complicity in relation to transactions involving children. Transnational adoption has been both defended as a humanitarian rescue mission, justifying foreign intervention, and condemned as a biopolitical transaction dealing in human beings as commodities, in a trade regulated by laws of supply and demand. Prager's account unfolds against the backdrop of the American-led NATO intervention in Yugoslavia in 1999 which effectively produced a humanitarian disaster for those whom it was designed to protect, the Albanian majority in Kosovo, and included the disastrous bombing of the Chinese embassy in Belgrade, a dark shadow to Prager's own rescue mission.[29]

Chapters 3 and 4 turn back to history, to a very different trade in bodies, moving from Asian-American to African-American concerns. Globalisation is often taken to refer, narrowly, to the deregulation of capitalist markets in the last decades of the twentieth century, or (more broadly) understood as the result of new technologies of communication and transportation in the twentieth century, leading to people becoming increasingly interconnected across national borders. Yet the process may go through different phases, involving different areas of the world in different ways and at different times. Among those who found themselves forcibly globalised were the first black Americans. In the last decades of the twentieth century there was an explosive growth in numbers of novels which are generally termed 'neo-slave narratives': fictions which dramatise the slave experience, modelling themselves, often very loosely, on the classic slave narratives of the nineteenth century. Arguably the sudden resurgence of this particular literary form is as much a phenomenon of a globalised world as it is a response to a preglobal past. As Liam Connell has argued, texts which contain an implicit critique of global power may be circulated through the very economic and cultural systems which support and maintain existing global power.[30] Paul Gilroy's notion of the 'Black Atlantic', the region bounded by Europe, Africa and the Americas, has been enormously valuable in rewriting the history of modernity to include slavery and its racist ideology, and to highlight the fashion in which interactions between Black-American, -British, -West Indian and

African cultures have created a distinctive circum-Atlantic culture, a global culture to be prized.[31] But does the 'Black Atlantic' model, with its broadening out of the history of African-American slavery to include a wider time frame and a larger geographical extension, amount to a form of globalisation of African-American culture, in which genre floats freely across the racial divide? Is there a global commodification of the slave's story, as is suggested by the examples of Margaret Atwood's *The Handmaid's Tale* and Hannah Crafts's *The Bondwoman's Narrative*? In the latter example, the breathtaking speed of canonisation, the characteristically modern intermingling of global and informational features with the fictional narration (websites, media events, corporate sponsorship) and a heavy emphasis on genealogy and authenticity make the narrative a creation of our own times, as opposed to the 1850s, the putative date of composition. Is resistance to this commodification possible? Anachronistically yet decisively, Zora Neale Hurston provides a critique of the process of appropriation, as exemplified in the gift-exchange paradigm of *Their Eyes Were Watching God*, which emphasises a positive cultural internationalism. Alternatively the local can also be a defence. Paul Gilroy has emphasised the ambivalence experienced by Black Atlantic peoples in relation to modernity and to Western ideas of progress, constructing in response a counterculture of modernity to contest European blindness to the connections between slavery and modernity. In Chapter 4, David Bradley constructs in *The Chaneysville Incident* a story of slavery which explicitly rejects the analogy between slavery and economics, in favour of an emphasis upon imaginative truth. The narrative strategy is focused upon surrogation, the act of substituting one person for another, analysed incisively by Joseph Roach in *Cities of the Dead*. Bradley's story is emphatically local, carefully based upon the history of the Underground Railroad in Bedford, Pennsylvania, but at the same time stakes its claims on the primacy of the imagination over Enlightenment rationality. Where modern communications produce death and a mistransmitted story, Bradley's performative narration and creative surrogation construct a narrative which resists the dominating death metaphors of modernity.

Translation might be said to lie at the heart of any transnational fiction, which moves across cultures and languages. Readers may be comfortable with the desirability of opening up American fiction to other cultures, when these cultures are already to a considerable extent part of America, represented by Asian- or African-Americans. What happens, however, to fiction from minority cultures when it enters the American bestseller lists, and is linguistically and/or culturally translated? Gayatri Spivak argues that the foreign text 'gets translated into a sort of with-it translatese, so that the literature of a woman in Palestine begins to resemble, in the feel of its prose, something by a man in Taiwan'.[32] The phenomenon, ironically christened 'Mactranslation' by Emily Apter, suggests the spread of a de-contextualised, dehistoricised literature, variously described as Globlit, or World Bank literature, designed to offer a safe exoticism to the Anglophone reader.[33] Chapter 5 considers a non-American novel without an obvious 'home' audience, which is explicitly concerned with the means of resisting cultural hegemony through language. Peter Høeg's *Smilla's Sense of Snow* appears to exemplify that flexibility and adaptation which characterises the global – a flexibility of form which serves the interests of the trade in ethnic differences, and which informs the various degrees of complicity between local oppositional discourses and a global late capitalist system.[34] But can this flexibility and adaptation also be subversive? As Høeg's reference to the work of Michel Serres suggests, translation may imply interference with the message but that interference may also be part of the message. Moreover, the idea that a Danish novel has nothing to do with American global domination will not stand scrutiny. Høeg's novel, partly set in Greenland, revolves around a secret criminal operation at the American bomber base in Thule, and thus has a particular relevance to the critique of American impe-rialism. Chalmers Johnson has argued that neocolonial domination can as easily be militaristic as economic, based for example on military forces stationed in foreign countries. In 1954 the American government secretly forced part of the indigenous population of Greenland (a Danish colony) to move, in order to expand Thule air base, some 24,022 acres disguised since the Second World War as a weather station, but actually a refuelling base for bombers, and later a critical location for American ballistic missiles. Johnson argues that the American empire is founded on just such military bases, of which in 2006 he counted at least 737 in more than 130 countries outside the United States, in Central and South America, the Philippines, Japan, Guam, the Caribbean, Western Europe and the Middle East, a 'planet-spanning baseworld' of foreign enclaves which function as parasitical microcolonies, completely beyond the jurisdiction of the occupied nation.[35]

Adaptation and evolution are a frequent focus in contemporary narra-tives, exploring the human capacity for resistance and survival in a fast-moving world. Evolutionary hypotheses loom large in the last two chapters. Cormac McCarthy's *Blood Meridian* (Chapter 6) challenges the equation of American imperialism with destiny, in a mock evolutionary scenario, sati-rising pseudo-scientism and popular ethology. McCarthy's neohistoricist Western engages with the beginnings of modern American imperialism in the 1840s, beginning at the moment when 'America' forms itself, assuming its modern shape. Globalisation has much in common conceptually with Manifest Destiny; each relies heavily on an inbuilt determinism founded on notions of technological or evolutionary progress. *Blood Meridian* is a novel which primarily engages, however, not with the recent past, but with prehistory, in an explicit critique of the employment of a global genealogical scenario as an exculpatory fiction. As preceding chapters have indicated, the twentieth century is overpopulated with geneholics. Global flows of information and people have created both the desire and the resources for genealogical constructions, a process which McCarthy carries to its logical, and ironic, end, in a plot which deliberately reverses the tide of American history, sending empire reeling backwards.

The final chapter of this book returns to its opening pages, engaging with the ways in which 'the implosion of the virtual sphere of information into the biosphere is perhaps the definitive characteristic of globalisation', changing the texture of human lives, and the ways in which human beings react to these changes in imaginative narrative.[36] In an internet world, story links to story, windows open on new stories, and no overall authority establishes priority. For the novel, the central question concerns the usefulness or redundancy of narrative in a globalised world, its adaptive function. In the optimistic scenario, enhanced connections overcome national prejudices and enhance individual experience. Electronic communication bypasses normal 'gating' categories such as ethnicity or class, opening the way to greater pluralism, diversity and freedom. But the growth of internet crime and cyberterrorism tells another story. Bharati Mukherjee's *Desirable Daughters* explores the underside of new communications technology, as an Indian Bill Gates and his family are threatened by identity theft. Mukherjee uses the dynamics of a group of sisters to explore the way in which a story is claimed, transmitted or denied, how even in the apparent homogeneity of three almost identical sisters divergent roles are created, and what the political consequences are of a place in a sibship – envisaged as a literary and social model largely replacing 'vertical' lines of descent. As the chapter demonstrates, 'the work of the imagination ... is neither purely emancipatory nor entirely disciplined but is a space of contestation in which individuals and groups seek to annex the global into their own practices of the modern.'[37]

1 Red letters

Hester Prynne in India and
Arizona

Nathaniel Hawthorne's *The Scarlet Letter* is set between 1640s Puritan America,
the colony which became an empire, and a nineteenth-century introductory
narrative, thus eliding the eighteenth-century trading empire based upon
Salem and the Far East, which was the foundation of Hawthorne's family
fortunes and of the economy of maritime New England. Two rewritings of the
novel explore the economic conditions and consequences of transnationalism,
whether in the recreation via cyberspace of the Salem Indies trade on the
Coromandel coast (Bharati Mukherjee, *The Holder of the World*) or the transformation of an Oregon valley into an Indian Utopian ashram (John Updike, *S.*).
Both novels are the focus for an exploration of the instrumentalisation of
culture in the organisation of corporate and transnational workforces, the
status of neohistoricist revisionism and the use of historical source material in
the discussion of the 'long chronology' of globalisation in earlier imperial practices. In both, the problems of handling information and the human sense of
domination by data are key emphases.

Bharati Mukherjee is a writer who has never seen her 'country', Bangladesh, the ancestral home of her father, was brought up in Calcutta, moved
successively to Iowa, to a long residence in Canada, and finally back to the
United States where, in 1988, she became an American citizen.[1] *The Holder of
the World* sketches a similar transnational trajectory – only in reverse. In its
frame tale, the American narrator, Beigh Masters, a twentieth-century asset
hunter, is engaged in a quest for a lost Moghul diamond, the Emperor's
Tear, and in the process excavates links between seventeenth-century Massachusetts and precolonial India. In the inset tale, Indians (Native Americans)
are replaced by Indians (from the subcontinent) as the heroine, Hannah
Easton, moves from Puritan New England to the Coromandel coast, and the
court of the Emperor Aurengzebe. (The title is the translated form of
Alamgir, another name for Aurengzebe.) Along the way there is a torrid
affair with an Indian lover, a rajah, and Hannah returns to America with his
child, Pearl Singh. Mukherjee was inspired to write by a pre-auction viewing

in Sotheby's in New York of a seventeenth-century Indian miniature of a woman in elaborate Moghul court dress – a woman who was Caucasian and blonde:

> I thought, 'Who is this very confident-looking seventeenth-century woman, who sailed in some clumsy wooden boat across dangerous seas and then stayed there? She had transplanted herself in what must have been a traumatically different culture. How did she survive?'[2]

A second inspiration occurred to her in relation to the character of Pearl, Hester's daughter, described by Hawthorne as leaving America for an unknown destination, whence she sends exotic presents to her mother, with heraldic crests that cannot be decoded. Eurocentric criticism has assumed that Pearl went to Europe. But, as Mukherjee pointed out in interview, had that been the case, the crests would have been identifiable.[3] These were devices from a non-European world. Transactions between cultures are therefore at the heart of the novel, which reveals in its closing pages that Hannah Easton, the 'Salem bibi' – the white mistress from Salem – was the original for Hester Prynne, the heroine of that most canonical of American novels, Nathaniel Hawthorne's *The Scarlet Letter*. Mukherjee's novel therefore takes its place in a well-established tradition of rewritings or 'revisionings' of the so-called classics of the past, from *Wide Sargasso Sea* to *Foe* or *Water with Berries*.[4] In most cases the 'pre-text' is an emblematically colonial discourse, which almost singles itself out for contestation, whether it involves a Caribbean madwoman in Jane Eyre's attic, Caliban or Friday on their islands, or Turtons and Burtons in Forster's India.

But why rewrite *The Scarlet Letter*? More than one reader failed to see the relevance or necessity of this pre-text to Mukherjee's novel. As Vivian Gornick complained, the connection looks like

> a highly arbitrary explanation for one of the most mysterious figures in American Literature. She might just as easily have turned out to be the governess in *Anna and the King of Siam* as Hester Prynne.[5]

Indeed, although there are clues for the alert reader, the connection only becomes overt in the closing pages, when the reader is informed that Hannah knew one of Hawthorne's ancestors, who passed on the story which became 'his morbid introspection into guilt and repression that many call our greatest work',[6] a work which bears little relation to Mukherjee's version of historical 'truth'. 'Who can blame Nathaniel Hawthorne for shying away from the real story of the brave Salem woman and her illegitimate daughter?' (p. 286). Readers will recall that in Hawthorne's novel, set between 1642 and 1649 in Puritan New England, Hester Prynne is condemned to wear a scarlet letter on her chest as a badge of shame. Her husband, Roger Prynne, who adopts the name of Chillingworth, has been missing, presumed drowned, though he is actually held in captivity by the Indians. In his prolonged absence Hester has yielded to temptation with Dimmesdale, the local minister, to whom she bears a child, Pearl. Social ostracism sets her free from the narrow constraints of Puritan ideology and she transmogrifies to some extent into a freethinker and an emblem of passion and rebellion. As far as American criticism is concerned, the jury is still out on the degree to which Hawthorne endorses Hester's views. As Philip Rahv put it, 'The dark lady is a rebel and an emancipator; but precisely for this reason Hawthorne feels the compulsion to destroy her.'[7] In the novel's outcome, Chillingworth succeeds in defeating Hester's attempt to escape with her lover by sea, Dimmesdale confesses and his guilty flame is promptly extinguished by death, Pearl returns to the Old World, and Hester eventually ends her days in gloomy Boston, still something of a walking sandwich board against sin. As this thumbnail plot summary indicates, the connection between Mukherjee's Hannah and Hawthorne's Hester is considerably less obvious than that between, say, Bertha Mason and Jean Rhys's Antoinette Cosway.

Mukherjee's novel also raises other questions, transgressing the institutional and nationalist boundaries within which most literary critics still operate. Is Mukherjee a postcolonial writer or, as she has claimed, an American immigrant? For many reviewers, Mukherjee's apparently tenuous linkage of Hannah/Hester represented a means of self-aggrandisement, of laying claim herself to a place in the American canon. Fakrul Alam describes the novel as 'designed to secure for herself a place in the great tradition of American fiction'.[8] It is a view which also gains support from Mukherjee's own robust declaration of her identity as immigrant.

> I am an American. I am an American writer, in the American mainstream, trying to extend it. … I am not an Indian writer, not an exile, not an expatriate. I am an immigrant.[9]

In this sense, rewriting *The Scarlet Letter* is not so much an act of counter-discursive contestation as a claim to a place at the table with the canonical elite. Mukherjee's self-identification as immigrant may get her out of the ghetto of 'minority' writing, but it also suggests the adoption of a conventional American alibi-identity. One thinks of the persistent American Puritan myth of origins as that of a beleaguered band of immigrants fleeing persecution for freedom (as opposed to the first permanent Anglo-American settlement, further south in Jamestown, which was a straightforward colony). Mukherjee's novel apparently exploits the Puritan myth in its opening description of Hannah's life as an immigrant's daughter in Massachusetts, the survivor of a notorious Indian massacre in King Philip's War, a traumatised orphan who is adopted and brought up in Salem until marriage to Gabriel Legge transports her overseas. Strikingly, Mukherjee advances the clock from Hawthorne's 1640s to Hannah's birth in 1670, to allow Indian (Nipmuc) savagery to occupy centre stage (scalpings, killings, a game of football with a decapitated head) and to recreate the sense of beleaguerment in a hostile environment.

Geographical manipulation is also a factor here. Hester Prynne is disgraced in Boston. In shifting the scene to Salem, Mukherjee could hardly have selected a more emblematically Puritan locale. Largely courtesy of Arthur Miller, the town is almost synonymous with Puritans and conjures up immediate images of gloomy divines fanatically expunging all evil from their midst. Indeed in the manufacture of the American past Salem has a privileged status as an *ur*-location. The tourist who visits Salem today will find the town pandering wholesale to its reputation as 'the witch city'. At one point the town fire brigade, for example, had this title embossed on its engines, together with a rather nippy image of a hag on a broomstick. In the centre of town the Salem Witch Museum commemorates the 1692 witch craze with a full multimedia programme, sound and light show, tour of a recreated dungeon and live re-enactment of a witch trial. ('Children love this macabre exhibit', according to the publicity leaflet.) Farther afield a second historic site offers 'Pioneer Village', one of the earliest historical theme parks built in America. No sound and light show here, but thatched cottages, wigwams and dugouts, as built by the early settlers, an insect-infested pond with ducking stool and periodic displays by pikemen, sweating to death in full costume. It is a more primitive experience, in more ways than one.

There is, however, a third site in Salem, or rather a whole complex of buildings, the Salem Maritime National Historic Site, which commemorates a different Salem – the town whose material prosperity was entirely founded on the trade with the East. Here, along with Hawthorne's birthplace, the 'House of the Seven Gables', which supposedly inspired his novel of that name, and the Custom House where he worked, is the Peabody Museum, with its enormous collections of Asian art, porcelain, textiles and precious objects from India, China and Japan. In the days of its prosperity Salem was not 'the witch city'. Its city seal bore a palm tree, a Parsee and a ship, with the motto 'Divitis indiae usque ad ultimum sinum' (To the farthest port of the rich East).[10] As Luther S. Luedtke has amply demonstrated, between the 1780s and 1830s Salem was a major international port for the East Indies and China trade – silk, tea, chinaware, textiles and especially the pepper trade, of which Salem had a virtual monopoly. By 1799 41 Salem vessels had called at Calcutta, Madras and Bombay; 21 at Batavia and Sumatra and the Dutch East Indies; and five at Canton. Salem ships bore such names as the *Arab, Bengal, Borneo, Ganges, Grand Turk, Hindoo, Malay, Tigris* and *Zenobia*. So extensive were Salem's contacts in India and the East Indies that some traders actually believed 'Salem' to be the name of a sovereign nation. It was probably the richest American city *per capita* in 1790. Trade was so profitable that there was no need to rely on making a profit on the outward voyage; ships were often simply sent out in ballast. In 'Old News' (1835) Hawthorne himself noted the luxury of the Salem merchants' town houses, their silk beds and hangings, damask tablecloths, Turkish carpets, ivory, china and cashmere shawls. Indians also visited Salem, from the 'Lascars' of ship's crews to the bearded Sikh who is recorded in much the same terms as a museum exhibit, and inspired almost as much astonishment as the famous elephant imported from Bengal in 1796.[11] A Salem pastor wrote that 'No young man of Hawthorne's time considered his education finished before he had visited India, China or the Malay archipelago.'[12] If this was something of an exaggeration, it is none the less true that the young men's social life revolved around the Salem East India Maritime Society, with its exhibition hall and meetings. On festive occasions such as the annual dinner, its members dressed as Mandarins, Rajahs or Sultans and paraded through the streets. Salem's subsequent decline, the result in part of Jefferson's embargo, was hastened by the development of new deep draft clipper ships, which could only be outfitted in deepwater ports such as Baltimore, Boston or New York. By the 1830s the golden age of Salem trade was waning, and in 1846 the last pepper ship from Sumatra entered the port. In the intervening years, however, Salem had made a fortune out of the East.

This was a trade with which Hawthorne had intimate connections. Hawthorne was born in Salem, the son of an East India captain who died in Surinam in 1808, leaving the three-year-old Hawthorne to be brought up by the family of his mother, Elizabeth Manning. His father had sailed to the East half a dozen times, and left behind logbooks and journals, including that of a trip to Bengal in 1796, and to Madras, on the Coromandel coast, in 1800. Nathaniel was brought up in the Manning household on Herbert Street, close to the wharves. He himself found employment in the Boston Custom House, 1834–41, and then as Surveyor for the district of Salem and Beverley, 1846–9, losing his job as a result of Zachary Taylor's election and the manoeuvrings of pork-barrel politics. Hawthorne's paternal ancestry included William Hathorne, 1607–81, a persecutor of Quakers, and John Hathorne, 1641–1717, notorious for his presence at the 1692 witch trials – both Puritans in the gloomiest stereotypical mould. (Hawthorne hid the shame of his ancestry behind a letter – inserting a 'W' into his own surname.) All five of John Hathorne's sons, including Hawthorne's grandfather Joseph, went to sea. The Mannings were a mercantile family with extensive business interests. As Gloria Erlich notes, however, most biographers of Hawthorne have been much more interested in his Puritan forebears than in the tradesmen and sea captains who actually dominate the family history.[13] Mukherjee's project, then, of restoring connections between Hawthorne and India takes its place in an honourable tradition of filling in the gaps in history, correcting and amplifying the record and curing that amnesia which (as Gore Vidal reputedly remarked) is America's second name.

Curiously, although the canon of American literature has been extensively revised, expanded and rewritten in recent years, particularly by neohistoricist critics, there has been an echoing silence on the topic of Hawthorne and the East. The attempts of a generation of 'New Americanists' to restore the unacknowledged agency of the historically marginalised in shaping a dominant tradition, have tended to focus on the role of African-Americans, women and, to a lesser extent, Native Americans.[14] Historicist attempts on *The Scarlet Letter* have gone through various manoeuvres, emphasising the historicity of Hawthorne's novel (originally one of the planks in the ahistorical romance theory of American literature) either in its setting or as relating to the moment of its composition. Walter Benn Michaels, for example, translates economic forces into generic structures, examining how Hawthorne's anxieties about the fluctuation in value of American real estate relate to his deployment of the romance genre, opposing radical fictionality to the socially implicated forms of the novel. In his introduction to *New Essays on* The Scarlet Letter, Michael J. Colacurcio describes all the essays as 'significantly historical' in their approach.[15] His own is devoted squarely to the history of the Puritans and its presence in the novel in references to the works of Winthrop and Mather. Increasingly desperate attempts have been made to establish a connection with anxieties over slavery, despite (or perhaps because of) the fact that Hawthorne was famously dismissive of abolitionism and supported the Compromise of 1850. Attention has focused on issues of vexed paternity and miscegenation, the frequent references to blackness as evil and the concern with psychological slavery in the characters. Jean Fagan Yellin skilfully detects the iconography of abolitionism, used against itself.[16] In addition, the novel has been read as a response to fear of red revolution (1848) or, in its Civil War setting, as engaging with the American sense of civil division.[17] Even at high-school level the most determined attempts are being made to make Hawthorne historically 'relevant' and drag his novel towards political engagement. A textbook for high-school students devotes chapters to such issues as illegitimacy, single mothers, corporal punishment, child custody, witchcraft and the adultery of TV evangelists, and includes in its topic lists such instructions as 'Compare and contrast the cases and characters of Dimmesdale and

Jimmy Swaggart'; 'Do a campy stage production of [Wigglesworth's] Day of Doom'; and 'Stage a witch trial'.[18] Nothing in any of this about the East.

In creative writing there is a silence almost as deafening as the critical elision of the imperial space.[19] Maryse Condé's *I Tituba* sees the black slave Tituba's story as part of Hester's imaginative inspiration, though her Hester hangs herself, pregnant in prison, and the story is that of the slave. Christopher Bigsby's *Hester* and its sequel *Pearl* are squarely focused on the seventeenth century, establishing connections with Civil War England in texts fairly bristling with information on Norfolk emigration history. John Updike rewrites *The Scarlet Letter* three times, in *A Month of Sundays*, *Roger's Version* and *S.*, telling the story successively from the viewpoint of the adulterous minister, the wronged husband and the heroine. Although in modern dress, the Puritan heritage is very much to the fore in the trilogy's interest in conflicts between sexual passion and religious repression. Only the third volume, *S.*, re-orientalises its heroine and makes an Indian connection, as this chapter will explore. Popular film focuses on the Puritans but picks up political cues from the cultural climate – particularly in relation to slavery, Native Americans and the persecution of women. Those who have undergone the ordeal of watching Demi Moore in *The Scarlet Letter* (1995) will have noted that the film is knee-deep in Indians (Native Americans) to whom Dimmesdale is pastor, includes a witch scare and has a well-endowed black female slave featuring prominently in a bath. In the denouement it is rather as if *The Last of the Mohicans* had been crossed with *The Crucible*, as Hester is rescued from the scaffold itself by the Indians, led by Dimmesdale on a charger. In other words, in both critical and creative work, where Indians do feature it is as Native Americans; where the 'Other' is invoked it is as African-American or as woman.

The splendid exception to this consensus is Luther S. Luedtke, who in 1989 (just as Mukherjee was observing her Indian miniature) published *Nathaniel Hawthorne and the Romance of the Orient*, which discusses the history of Salem, the seafaring background and the presence of 'Oriental' material in Hawthorne's works. Luedtke concentrates his attention on the dark 'Oriental' heroines – Zenobia in *The Blithedale Romance*, who bears the name of the Syrian queen vanquished by Aurelian in AD 272; Miriam in *The Marble Faun*; and Hester, described by Hawthorne in *The Scarlet Letter* as having 'a rich, voluptuous, Oriental characteristic, a taste for the gorgeously beautiful'.[20] He also traces the source material of 'Rappaccini's Daughter' to the poison damsel tales of Indian mythology, catalogues Hawthorne's extensive reading of firsthand accounts of the East (whether tales of seraglios or more respectable travelogues), his essays on Eastern topics, and the influence of the 'Oriental tale' upon him (in Voltaire's version, particularly). He concludes that traditional moral, historical and symbolist readings of *The Scarlet Letter* have not fully realised the cultural dialectic of the Puritan pastor and his 'Oriental' other, or their failure to make a universe of their separate 'spheres' (to use one of Hawthorne's dominant metaphors). Hawthorne describes Hester's letter as 'her passport into regions where other women dared not tread' (p. 199), for it has accustomed her to a 'latitude of speculation' (p. 199) altogether 'foreign' (p. 199) to her compatriots. The journey of exploration is figured none the less as a pointless 'wandering ... in the dark labyrinth of mind; now turned aside by an insurmountable precipice, now starting back from a deep chasm. There was wild and ghastly scenery all around her' (p. 166). The connections between known/unknown, native/outlandish, New England/ the East remain essentially unforged. For Luedtke

> what we experience as the genius of *The Scarlet Letter* is not the rich domestic life of 17th century New England alone, but the counterweight which that culture provided to Hawthorne's Oriental flights of imagination.[21]

It is, in short, the tension between foreign and domestic which gives the novel its power.

For all the strength and originality of this argument (which has been quite passed over by most critics) it does pose problems in that it concentrates on the East as 'Orient', as an imaginative stimulus, and remains thin on actual connections to the Eastern trade. It might readily be objected that Hester is Oriental only in the stereotypical sense (dark and sexy) and that she could as easily come from Italy, like Beatrice Rappaccini, or the Azores, like the lady of 'Drowne's Wooden Image'. Luedtke strains the argument in places in order to demonstrate an Oriental connection which may simply not be there. The more interesting question – and the one addressed by Mukherjee – is *why* is it not there? Why, when Salem was steeped in the Indies, when Hawthorne himself worked in the Custom House, when his whole family were connected to the trade with the East, did Hawthorne choose to concentrate almost entirely in his novel on the Puritan moment?

That 'almost' needs glossing. It is well here to call attention to the structure of Hawthorne's novel, in which the tale of Hester is preceded by an introductory sketch or preamble entitled 'The Custom House' – a sketch which many readers still skim over. As Christopher Bigsby puts it, the sketch 'is different in tone from the rest of the book and has its pleasures but, if it should pall, stay with it for ahead lies a remarkable story'.[22] Writing in 1850 in 'The Custom House' Hawthorne's emphasis is squarely on decline and degeneration. He alludes briefly to the fact that Salem was once a prosperous port, but what he describes, in some detail, is a scene of decay, of dilapidated warehouses and grassy overgrown pavements. The past vigour of Salem trade is relentlessly downplayed. In his account, the merchants feature only as geriatrics: 'old King Derby', 'old Billy Gray' and 'old Simon Forrester' (p. 28); their empire is a mere temporary aberration in the historical record. Simon Forrester's head is described as scarcely in the tomb 'before his mountain-pile of wealth began to dwindle' (p. 28). When Hawthorne includes an account of his own ancestry he ignores the Mannings and seafarers in favour of an account of William and John Hathorne, noting that after these stern Puritan divines, the rest of the family sank from public view: 'From father to son, for above a hundred years, they followed the sea' (pp. 10–11), he comments dismissively. He then describes his research as poking about in the pointless rubbish of history, 'reading the names of vessels that had long since foundered at sea' (p. 29) and of merchants whose names were already fading off their tombstones. According to Hawthorne, he has made a decent effort to reanimate that past, 'to raise up from these dry bones an image of the old town's brighter aspect, when India was a new region, and only Salem knew the way thither' (p. 29), but the material turns out to be quite unrewarding. What he does find, however, the one piece of the past to quicken his curiosity and set off his imagination, is the small piece of mouldering cloth, the scarlet letter, which is the catalyst for the tale that follows. In his preamble, therefore, Hawthorne deliberately distances himself from the mercantile trade of Salem and effaces his commercial background in order to leapfrog the reader over the years of India trade to a tale of Puritans. The evidence of real history is left behind in favour of a fictional pre-Revolutionary artefact and a myth of origins. As a result Hawthorne leaves a conspicuous space between the Puritan 'beginnings' in the mid-seventeenth century and the era of decline in the nineteenth – a space which Mukherjee sets out to fill. Hannah Easton returns to America in 1701, lives on until 1750 and together with her daughter becomes an inspiration for the American Revolution. What I want to suggest here is that Mukherjee spots the gap in the story, the space in between the Puritan tale of origins and the decline which Hawthorne describes – the space of imperial expansion and Eastern plunder which was the foundation of New England fortunes, the sphere of activity of Hawthorne's own family and (as the development of this argument will indicate) a major contributor to specific forms of cultural authority in America. Where Hawthorne refuses to make connections, Mukherjee's novel reveals, in the words of its narrator, 'a hunger for connectedness, a belief that with sufficient passion and intelligence we can deconstruct the barriers of time and geography' (p. 11).

It is important to recognise that Mukherjee's novel does not merely offer the Salem trade as a latent context, or Hawthorne's novel as a belated afterthought, but as literal articulation. In rewriting the letter, Mukherjee establishes specific parallels and connections in which reinscription is a dominant focus. In *The Scarlet Letter* Hester is noted for her embroidery, and transforms the badge of shame into an ornate sign of defiance. Hannah is similarly skilled with her needle, and both women are reputed for their nursing skills. Mukherjee combines the two: Hannah goes in for an early form of skin grafting, a violent suturing together which is an apt image for the method of Mukherjee's novel, making reparative connections to remedy past violence – whether the scalpings of the Indian wars or the injuries sustained in the final battles of the novel between Muslim and Hindu. Hannah's husband's actions are rather the reverse. Where she pieces together, he inscribes violence. Hannah is tempted to adultery when Gabriel is reported lost at sea. (He is actually in 'savage' captivity, like his original.) She, however, does not succumb, and Gabriel returns to beat up the hapless suitor. Where Hester was forced to wear an 'A', Gabriel carves a blood-red 'F' for fornicator on the suitor's forehead, a scarlet letter of a different type. Later, when Gabriel in his turn is sent off on business by his superior, Cephus Prynne, who has designs on Hannah (shades of David and Bathsheba), Gabriel murders him, carving an 'H' on the corpse's forehead (for Hannah, presumably). Both erotic guilt and textual violence are ascribed to men.

Mukherjee also takes pains to invoke the Manning past. Hannah's best friend is Hester Manning, who lives on Herbert Street and drowns in mysterious circumstances when jilted by Gabriel Legge. The description of her corpse, fished out by Gabriel with a hooked pole, centres upon the lips twisted into a 'gaping O' (p. 66) and upon the rigid, outstretched arms. The scene refers explicitly to the death of Zenobia in *The Blithedale Romance*, hooked out and impaled by Hawthorne's narrator (in some readings her destroyer). Rigidity, violence and the inscription of that violence in letters are the province of Gabriel Legge, as opposed to Hannah's embroidery, which is imaginative and reparative. Hannah herself has a reputation for 'spells' or fits, and is kept as something of a recluse by her adoptive parents, who hold young men at bay. Hawthorne's mother, Elizabeth Manning, was given to similar fits of illness, and was also reclusive. Though a young widow, she never remarried. Hannah's mother is discovered at the close of the novel also wearing a letter, 'a shameful I boldly sewn in red to her sleeve' (p. 284). It means 'Indian lover'. When the Nipmuc attack Brookfield, Rebecca takes the opportunity to stage her own death to escape with her lover, by whom she has not one but five illegitimate children. Hawthorne's Manning ancestors also wore a letter I, but for a different reason. Gloria Erlich notes that in 1680 the wife of Nicholas Manning accused him of incest with his sisters, who were convicted, whipped and exposed in church with their sin writ large in capitals on their heads.[23] Mukherjee's narrator playfully notes the extent to which Hannah is sequestered by her family and comments 'Incestuous, obviously' (p. 61). Again, Mukherjee's reinscription of the letter emphasises female escape from social constraints, and associates a guilty past with the Manning name.

Other connections between the two novels are more obvious – both Hannah and Hester have black-eyed, illegitimate daughters called Pearl, both are associated with physicians, Hannah with Dr Aubry in London and the Venetian Antonio Carreri in India, Hester with her husband, also a doctor. Hester plans to escape from Salem on a rather dubious privateer, potentially a pirate ship. Hannah escapes by marrying Gabriel, who eventually trades in his job as an East India Company factor for an equivalent career in plunder, as a pirate. Hannah's story comes to light in a parody of Hester's, when Beigh Masters finds, in a dusty box in a museum of maritime trade near Salem, a set of Indian miniatures of the Salem bibi. The links between the two novels criss-cross in a tissue of connections, complicated by name changes and transfers. (Hannah, for example, is renamed Mukta or Pearl by her servant Bhagmati. She renames Bhagmati Hester, after the friend she has lost. The Salemites rechristen her 'White Pearl' and her daughter 'Black Pearl'.) Elleke Boehmer has commented on the transferability of empire's organising metaphors, citing as her example the name 'Indian', used for native peoples from the Maoris to the Caribs.[24] Mukherjee's achievement is to send the name ricocheting back, passing it from America to India, from one Bay Colony (Massachusetts) to another (the Bay of Bengal), one group of Indians to another, and even, in the examples of the Puritans and Aurengzebe, one ascetic religious group to another. In the process, all names become bundles of relationships, forcing the reader to think always in terms of multiple rather than monolithic referents. Every letter has its alternative meaning, or meanings; reinscription is embedded at every level of the novel.

Mukherjee also generalises the case of the canonical text as cultural authority, by her frame tale, which extends the connection from the single classic text and writer to the institutions which create canonicity. It is no accident that the frame narrator, Beigh Masters, is a Yale graduate, that Mukherjee's Fort Saint Sebastian is located in the outskirts of present-day Madras, or that the plot involves the early years of the East India Company and the pursuit of a famous diamond. Gauri Viswanathan has noted that the funding history of at least one major university in the United States, Yale, has its roots in the mercantile activities and imperial politics of the East India Company. Elihu Yale (to whom Mukherjee refers in the novel, p. 129) made his vast fortune as a nabob in Madras by a combination of legitimate trade and more questionable activities. He was responsible for the financing of Yale College in its early years, primarily by a gift of a shipment of textiles – muslins, poplins, silks, calicos and other merchandise which was turned into hard cash in the Boston market. As soon as this arrived in 1718 the trustees changed the name of their college to honour Yale. The goods netted them £800, the largest private donation to Yale for at least a hundred years and thus

> established the closest links between Yale College and the spoils of British imperialism, the plundering careers of East India Company men merging ... with the pragmatic aspirations of colonial America's new brood of educators and theologians.[25]

The American colonists had approached Yale directly in terms which exploit the interchangeability of India and America in order to extract cash, and yoke together the two as similar areas of colonial exploitation. Cotton Mather wrote obsequiously:

> There are those in these parts of Western India, who have had the satisfaction to know something of what you have done and gained in the Eastern, and they take delight in the story.[26]

What Yale had been doing in 'Eastern India', as Viswanathan establishes, was to create a personal fortune by any means at his disposal, including the acquisition of a private fort, trade on his own behalf independently of the Company, extortion of taxes from the indigenous inhabitants of 'Black Town', ruthless repression of the townspeople's revolt, the hanging of English 'pirates' in public as a warning to his competitors and a great deal of experience as a diamond merchant. (Yale sold the King of Siam false rubies at one point and swindled him out of a considerable sum.[27]) Gabriel Legge, we may note, is involved in local repression, executes offenders and eventually sets up on his own account, with his own private fort. He sends his plunder to New York. Viswanathan highlights two major issues implicit in Yale's career – the way in which one cultural authority (Yale's in India) translates into a new form of cultural authority in America (Yale College), and the economic transformation from British mercantilism to full-blown imperialism and the circulation of wealth in a global economy. These are issues vital to any consideration of canon-formation (as cultural authority) and its economic connections (in transnational, global, institutional practices). Just as the exploitation of India establishes the fortunes of Yale College, so it is implicated in the creation of America's canonical classic *The Scarlet Letter*. Mukherjee's novel deliberately brings the two 'spheres' together – postcolonial and American literature – upsetting institutional authorities in the process, crossing boundaries and renegotiating the spaces of cultural authority. As the example of Yale indicates, canonicity is not the property of the work alone, but of the processes of its transmission, in educational and economic institutions.

But here, it is worth pausing for a moment. Up to this point the argument has been proceeding (in good neohistoricist fashion) to argue that Mukherjee restores our awareness of the gaps and absences in the official record, the absences in history that (if we are to believe Pierre Macherey) are what the text is all about. In doing this, Mukherjee is in good company. Anthony Ilona, for example, has noted a spate of historical novels published contemporaneously with *The Holder of the World*, including David Dabydeen's *Turner*, Abdulrazak Gurnah's *Paradise* and Fred D'Aguiar's *The Longest Memory*. Ilona poses the question – is this quest for roots and history a backlash against notions of dislocation, fragmentation of identity, ambivalence and mimicry? Or are these merely warts on the commercial face of publishing, with issues of imperial history fostered by publishing establishments keen to retain the rules of division, of 'then and now', 'here and there', 'them and us'?[28] Like Hawthorne in his Custom House, it may be tempting to consign these topics to some distant, misty past, to write of slaves and trade, the Indian Mutiny or convicts at Botany Bay, rather than contemporary racial conflicts or forced globalisation. New historicist writing offers a potential solution to the problem, in its determined crossing of temporal borders, its circulation and exchange of different time frames, tracing the commerce between past and present. Mukherjee, for example, presents Hannah's story through the present-day narrator, who draws explicit parallels between the boom on the Coromandel coast in the 1680s and that on Wall Street in the 1980s. Mukherjee's brief sketch of the economics of the Coromandel establishes strong connections between India and America. Following the abrogation of the East India Company monopoly in 1688, the period of the 1690s was one of deregulation, a form of 'late-stage capitalism such as America saw in the 1890s or the 1920s, or ... the late 1980s' (p. 101).[29] The Coromandel is described as like Manhattan in the 1980s, with every 'interloper' (independent trader) the equivalent of a real estate agent, art dealer, arbitrageur, stockbroker, corporate lawyer and investment banker, all of them in the middle of the biggest real estate boom, jewel auction and drug emporium of the last 500 years (p. 107). Dutch, Portuguese, Danish, French and English trading posts stretch up the shore 'like Condos on the Florida coast' (p. 102). Far from escaping from her own time and place, Mukherjee offers in this respect an example of how a culture thinks about itself in a particular historical moment, highlighting the cultural interplays and mergers that take place in America, its polyethnicity and syncretism, whether in the seventeenth or the twentieth century.

But problems remain. Patrick O'Donnell has commented that the desire for the concrete, material, factual and artifactual pervades contemporary literary studies and that new historicism partakes of this amalgamatory desire. In this sense we are all, in a way, seeking the Emperor's Tear. The novel risks ceding its imaginative power to the attractions of history – just as *The Holder of the World* closes with its narrator enjoying (courtesy of virtual reality techniques) total immersion in the sensations and images of that last Indian battle. O'Donnell takes as his example Walter Benn Michaels's discussion of Hawthorne and notes the inordinate amount of fact referred to by the neohistoricist. There is, he argues,

> the implicit assumption that an increase in information will lead to an increase in the determinacy of meaning … [Benn Michaels's] method is a piecing-together of material from, seemingly, randomly-selected realms of being, as if to prove the overwhelming presence of the forces moving behind land speculation wherever one looks merely because bits of information can be gathered and juxtaposed in a certain way. Such an arrangement creates the illusion of inevitability that foregrounds a version of the will to meaning, a desire to get 'at' the material and the supposed reflective relation between social force, authorial intention, and the signs projected within discursive structures.[30]

In piecing together her novel from a mass of material – East India Company records, the history of Salem, Hawthorne's biography, tales of pirates, the history of the Puritans, the development of medical knowledge, Indian wars, to name but a few of the sources which she researched for eleven years – Mukherjee similarly brings together a mass of historical data, but does aesthetic pattern emerge? Susan Koshy, for one, complained of the 'fatal clutter' of the novel, of it having too many props.[31] If amnesia is one problem, so is hypermemorialisation; a novel is not a museum.

It is in this respect that the full originality of Mukherjee's novel becomes evident. Mukherjee's strategy is to guard against the danger of over-historicising by using a frame tale which explicitly cautions against the neohistoricist belief in the primacy of information. Indeed, the problems of handling data are a thread which runs through the whole novel. In the frame tale a computer programmer, Venn Iyer, is engaged with the problem of creating an interactive model of historical reality, inputting a mass of data to recreate the experience of one particular day. Venn is as deterministic as a manic neohistoricist. For him design is all; there are no accidents: 'every-thing in history is as tightly woven as a Kashmiri shawl' (p. 189). In its opening pages the novel sets out the dichotomy between restoring history, or drowning meaning in data. Venn 'animates information' (p. 5); he is intent on the restitution of historical density and texture. 'The past presents itself to us, always, somehow simplified. [Venn] wants to end that fatal uncluteredness' (p. 6). The process involves a randomly chosen date, 29 October 1989, for which the research team are supposedly ingesting all the world's papers, weather patterns, phone directories, satellite passes, arrests, TV shows, political debates, airline schedules, cheques written and credit card purchases so that when the database is complete, interaction with a personality will be possible, enabling any of us to insert ourselves 'anywhere and anytime on the time-space continuum' (p. 6). In theory this restoration of clutter looks highly desirable. Venn's method fuses history and cultural studies. Beigh's profession in asset retrieval reveals a similarly cultural-materialist bent. She describes her job as 'Uniting people and possessions; it's like matching orphaned socks, through time' (p. 5). A warning note is struck, however, by the congruence of their two fields, both implicitly materialistic. Venn's metaphors are commercial: 'History's a big savings bank ... we can all make infinite reality withdrawals' (p. 6). It appears, however, that restoring the density of experience may not be so easy for Third World locales. 'Because of information overload, a five-minute American reality will be denser, more "lifelike", than five minutes in Africa. But the African reality may be more elemental, dreamlike, mythic' (p. 7). Just in case the reader has missed the ironies of which Venn seems blissfully unaware, Mukherjee underlines the implicit exoticism by presenting the potential time-travellers as historical tourists. 'Time will become as famous as place. There will be time tourists sitting around saying, "Yeah, but have you ever been to April fourth? Man!"' (p. 7). (The phraseology irresistibly suggests the overlander on the hippie trail, outdoing his interlocutor in his access to exotic locations.) The subjectivity of the process is also emphasised. Because it is interactive, no two time-travellers will access the same reality. What we withdraw will depend upon what we invest. Every time-traveller will answer 1,000 personal questions from which a 'personality genome' will be created.

> By changing even one of the thousand answers, you can create a different personality and therefore elicit a different experience. Saying you're brown-eyed instead of blue will alter the withdrawal. Do blonds really have more fun? Stay tuned (p. 7).

The point connects explicitly to Mukherjee's rewriting. By altering one or two elements in the 'original' story of Hester Prynne, Hawthorne creates a very different personality. At the close of the novel, when Venn's team input the data from Coromandel and allow Beigh an immersive experience of virtual history, Hannah turns out to be blonde. Mukherjee's rewriting certainly allows her more 'fun' than Hawthorne allows his dark lady.

The virtual reality experience therefore establishes a vital difference between Mukherjee's novel – also a reanimation and connection of historical data – and history. Importantly the action of the novel questions the role of data in two ways: firstly in foregrounding the Puritan settlement as motivated by the retreat from data, a retreat which ended in defeat, and secondly by foregrounding the insufficiencies of data. In the information era literary critics have yet to address the political problems of handling mountains of data. To take the first point, history may be 'a billion separate information bytes' (p. 7), but Venn's approach to it exemplifies exactly what causes concern in neohistoricism, the deployment of fact as institutional capital. Mukherjee's portrayal of the Massachusetts Bay Colony is strongly marked by Andrew Delbanco's *The Puritan Ordeal*, which argues that far from leaving Britain with an idealistic 'errand in the wilderness', the settlers were retreating from what they feared they were becoming, a people overinvolved in balance-sheet realities and the pursuit of economic advantage by the new capitalist rules. Their American quest was therefore backward looking, to a purer time ruled by reverent feeling and the sense of miracle, rather than by discipline and calculation. The journey to America was therefore part of an effort to conserve the conviction that sin was not an entity in the soul, but a temporary estrangement from God, that 'space was the stuff of desire', an escape from pettiness and busy-ness, for those whose lives were drowning in details.[32] Their tragedy was that they evolved into what they fled; they lost the struggle against the idea of self-interested reciprocity and material exchange as governing the structure of experience. For the first settlers, a real transformation of the soul from calculation to mercy was attainable only by feeling (love, compassion, loving kindness) rather than by days spent over balance sheets, and nights filled with planning and with the weighing up of good and bad deeds. For their descendants, discipline took over and with it the idea of sin as an entity, 'sin as excrescence, disease, the threatening other – against which the community of purist selves builds barricades'.[33] In Delbanco's thesis it is a belief which underlies American politics, literature and the sense of self.

Fairly obviously Mukherjee picks up on the Delbanco thesis in her portrayal of the Puritans as evolving towards business and balance books, in Hannah's own translation to the ledger-book world of the East India Company and in her final appeal to Aurangzebe in terms of love and mercy. In the depiction of seventeenth-century Massachusetts, Mukherjee delineates the conflict between a life of feeling and beauty, and that of submission to order, reason and facts. An age-old battle is staged here between reason and imagination. One group of emigrants are described as middle-aged 'discontented city-dwellers' (p. 22). Hannah's grandfather, Edward Easton, is one such, formerly an East India Company clerk in London, a 'fact-fevered scribe hunched over ledger books, letters and memoranda' (p. 23). A random sample of his factual memoranda is provided (p. 24). Beigh wonders whether Edward Easton's mind had become so demented with details that he fled to the wilderness (p. 24). Easton is clearly a man of imagination – he dies while reading *Paradise Lost*. But it is his fate to be consigned to that very world of details which he fled. He becomes a fact, a footnote in Beigh's Yale thesis. Conversely Rebecca Easton is drawn in terms of art, beauty and reverent feeling. The description of her psalm singing emphasises 'her neck long and arched, her throat throbbing with song. A voice so strong and sweet that it softens the sternest spiritual phrases into voluptuous pleas' (p. 27). Attack by the Nipmuc offers Rebecca the choice of escape to 'the fecundity of an unfenced world' (p. 27). In witnessing this escape, however, and in keeping its secret, Hannah is described as witnessing 'the birth of sin itself' (p. 30). As the Puritans flee into fortified enclosures, so the garrison mentality with its demonisation of the Other gains the upper hand.[34] 'The secret dynamic of Puritanism had at last taken flesh. *Now we know* ... they really *are* devils, the woods really *are* evil, *it's true, it's true*' (p. 37). Hannah is moved to Salem, with its raucous wharves and its mercantile world, in which French, Spanish and English coins circulate equally, a culture which no longer recognises commonality (p. 40). Now that 'purity was no longer valued as the end of human effort, or the goal of social structure' (p. 40), class distinctions are emerging. In short, Hannah is back in the world which Easton fled, a world of exchange, trade, reason – a world of data. Even her suitor's letters to her family proposing matrimony are concerned only with financial facts and figures rather than with affective ties.

Hannah herself, however, retains the connection to her mother's vision, though, Philomela-like, she celebrates the beauty and plenitude of the world in needlework rather than song. One scene is emblematic. Hannah's voluptuous nature is expressed in the sampler which she sews entitled 'The Utmost Parts', an embroidery of an exotic world which is described as 'the embodiment of desire', the verse emblazoned 'in colours so tropical that the threads Hannah used had to have been brought from a mysterious place with a musical name: Bander Abbas, Batavia, Bimlipatam' (p. 44), together with an image of palm trees, black-skinned men casting nets, schooners and bright green foliage. The title refers to Psalms 2:8. In the novel Hannah's stepbrother reads to her in the Bay Psalm Book version: '*Aske thou of me, and I will give the Heathen for thy lot; and of the earth thou shalt possess the utmost coasts abroad*' (p. 43). Hannah, however, acts 'to correct the deformation of love' and goes back to sources in the Bible, an earlier, more erotic version: '*Desire of me and I shall give thee the heathen for thine inheritance; and the utmost parts of the earth for thy possession*' (p. 43). The fate of the sampler is, however, representative. Framed in wood left over from a chest made for John Hathorne, it becomes commodified 'collectible' art, and hangs in the Bel Air home of a schlockfilm producer. Hannah's art none the less stands in strong contrast to

Puritan norms. Her friend Hester reads to her from Mary Rowlandson's captivity narrative, the book which everyone is reading (p. 51), a sensational account of Indian captivity which inspires Hester to fantasies of being abducted in her turn, fantasies described as 'the devil himself whispering into the pillow at night' (p. 52). As Hester reads her favourite passage about Mary Rowlandson's 'obscene afflictions', her voice suggests the moral 'Guard yourself against aliens' (p. 53). In Hannah's mind, however, far from encouraging rape fantasies, the book recalls memories of a mother who loved an actual Indian. Rebecca has taught Hannah an alternative alphabet of revolt which substitutes for the gloomy Puritan hornbook ('A is for Adam's Fall') a rewriting which alters all the signs. 'A is for Act, B is for Boldness, C is for Character, D is for Dissent, E is for Ecstasy' (p. 54), an alphabet which Hannah completes for herself: 'I is for Independence' (p. 54). In this early Puritan upbringing, therefore, Mukherjee constructs a past for Hannah which offers two potential futures for America, a mercantilist trading world of ledger books, the recording of data, the garrison mentality and the demonisation of the Other, or a world of imagined beauty and sensuality, connecting across time and space, based upon mercy and love – the beliefs which inspire Hannah's embrace of her Indian lover, her final appeal to Aurangzebe for peace and her belief in independence, which is handed on to the future.

Hannah's India is similarly double, divided between the East India Company fort with its strict rules and regulations, and its focus on money and records; and the India beyond it. The dialectic of wilderness/garrison is replicated in that of jungle/trading factory, the latter also with its customhouse, and eventually even a 'New Salem' named in Hannah's honour. When Hannah lands at Fort Saint Sebastian on the Coromandel coast, she wanders off towards the jungle as if to make good her escape into the forest, 'as had her mother years before in Massachusetts' (p. 109), but is recalled sternly by the Company officials. What went wrong in the 'New World' is now corrected in the 'Old' as Hannah traces a reverse trajectory from ledger-book realities, the control of feeling and capitalism writ large, to an Indian lover, in her turn. As the narrator comments, 'It is the story of North America turned inside out' (p. 160). And from her experiences in the Old World she takes back a corrective vision of freedom to the New.

Hannah's transition from Puritan daughter to the wife of a pirate is also a representative one. When Gabriel turns pirate, Hannah sees his trade as a normal outgrowth of the conditions of plunder and violence that were otherwise condoned and even lauded by the Company and its factors. Gabriel Legge is impatient with the Indian lack of interest in *using* money. He laments 'its utterly useless wealth, employed to no end, ignorant of investment' (p. 77). Where Hester Prynne's husband was unavoidably detained by the

Indians, it is strongly suggested that Gabriel stages his reported death not merely to test Hannah's fidelity, but also her capital value: 'he wanted to know if she was prized' (p. 89). Exchange realities dominate the sphere of Eros. On the Coromandel coast 'the most profitable factories – trading posts – were those that enforced the rules of order and cleanliness' (p. 99). Hannah is exhorted to control her emotions and not to yield to self-indulgence (p. 110). On the Coromandel, 'The value of every commodity was suddenly reassessed with an eye to its resale potential, a meter was put on everyone's time' (p. 102). Calculation goes hand in hand with a manic recording of data. The East India Company enjoins the keeping of diaries on its servants, and both Hannah and Gabriel keep journals. Hannah's is frugal in detail, impersonal in style, with notation of the weather patterns, the arrival of various ships and the landing of goods. The interesting point here, however, is that the major meaning of the diary is detectable only in its gaps and omissions, its silences. The entry for 10 January 1695 records the arrival of Captain John Bendall on his ship, the *Pride*; on 17 January he is carried off the boat, dangerously ill, and on the 30th Gabriel Legge has gone to speak with Mistress Bendall to obtain power of attorney from her. By 14 February the captain is dead. On 20 March Hannah notes that Prynne is holding the widow accountable for the Captain's debts and 10 days later Eliza Bendall is married to John Harker, who undertakes to pay them off. On 10 April Hannah records the fact that Mrs Higginbotham is wondering whether to tell the new bride that John Harker made all his money from a secret marriage to a native bibi. On 16 May the diary records in parentheses the death of Eliza ('having met with an accident month last', p. 124). The reader may presume that with Gabriel's connivance, Eliza was sold in marriage to meet her family's debts, learned of the native wife and objected, and came to a sticky end. Beneath the official state of repression and order Fort Saint Sebastian conceals a parallel world of emotion. Each man has a bibi, though their existence is entirely silenced. As the diary comments, 'No Englishman here accepts any connection with Mr Harker's keeping a Bibi and Eliza's falling off her horse' (p. 125). Historical records are not nearly as important as readerly and imaginative skills. The bibis are entirely absent from the historical data,[35] despite the enormous amount of it available, from the meteorological observations of Mir Ali, to the customs officials who log the contents of every ship, the sales receipts of every store in the fort, the official diaries and consultation books of the Chief Factor, or indeed the records of Henry Hedges, in whose former house Hannah now lives, which include descriptive accounts of village life, lists of words in Persian, Telugu, Tamil and English, four thick volumes of observations and his household accounts.[36] Hannah notes that 'His interest in India was too acquisitive; he felt he owned it by dint of his own efforts' (p. 127). His records do not extend to the existence of his bibi, Bhagmati, with whom Hannah finally forges a close friendship. As these silences suggest, much of the story is still in the gaps and absences. Mukherjee avoids the error of being too documentary; instead she foregrounds fictionality, with various 'spaces-in-between' where we read between or beneath the lines.

One of the problems faced by the reader of *Holder* is that of distinguishing between fact and fiction in the novel. Mukherjee takes a playful delight in mock-citation of apparently impeccable sources, or in the invention of works of art, from the miniatures to the sampler, the portrait in the National Gallery of the Chief Factor (p. 180), the extracts from Edward Easton's records, a supposed volume of Hannah's letters home (*London Sketches by an Anonymous Colonial Daughter*, University Presses of New England, 1967, p. 74), a poem recited by Hannah (p. 50), a volume of letters of Puritan courtship (*Puritans Come A-Courting: Romantic Love in an Age of Severity*, University Presses of New England, 1972), racist tales of miscegenation between women and baboons, historical texts (*Neyther Myles Standish nor Solomon Pynchon Bee: Marriage Negotiations in Two New England Societies*, p. 57), tales of piracy (*Tales from the Coromandel*, p. 258), gravestone inscriptions and even a poem by an Indian fisherman's boy who reaches London, where, incensed by the Eurocentric falsity of Dryden's *Aureng-Zebe* (p. 161), he writes a play, *The World Taker*, in rhyming couplets as a counter-discursive corrective. Just as Hawthorne attributed the 'real origins' of Hester's story to a manuscript left behind by surveyor Pue, so Mukherjee describes the play as surviving in the possession of a Marwari businessman who will not permit it to be copied. 'The prohibition derives from his nationalism. He has no wish to expose the fragment to Western scholars who will note in it only a sad mimicry of lesser Dryden and Pope' (p. 204). It is a cunning avoidance of verification which also suggests that the Marwari reserves his history for himself, as data which he will not release, preferring its absence to signify. It is a reaction to the perennial problem of colonial history – that it is the plunderers who keep the records, that the neohistoricist is largely reliant upon the aggressors for the record of their aggression. Mukherjee's reconstruction is signalled as provisional and indeterminate in its mixture of the historically verifiable with the imagined, its residual mysteries left unsolved in the plot and its foregrounding – within a revisioning – of the problems of reinscription.

As events develop in India Hannah replaces the world of facts with 'a world of stories and recitations' (p. 170) told by Bhagmati and Gabriel. Readers will be unlikely to believe the latter. (The stories of baboon bibis, of a chance meeting with Peter the Great and of the cargo of three-eyed maidens, six-legged goats and a three-headed youth with seven arms are cases in point.) But on some level these rampant embroideries carry more truth than more factual letters. (Gabriel's stories, for example, all hinge on issues of emancipation from some form of captivity.) When Bhagmati tells the story of Sita, for example, Hannah questions anxiously, 'did all this happen, exactly as you're telling it?' (p. 172). In contrast Beigh Masters gives us the story of Sita in several versions, all different, and comments that 'Reciters of Sita's story indulge themselves with closures that suit the mood of their times and their regions' (p. 176). It is Bhagmati who initiates Hannah into India. Hannah's escape from the fort is a consequence of the role in Indian history played by the bibi, the passions officially denied. Mukherjee figures the event in imagery drawn (like that of her preceding novel, *Jasmine*) from chaos theory – data with dynamism. She has moved beyond finding the world 'explicable by formula and experiment' (p. 156). 'The Coromandel had started something as immense as a cyclone deep inside her body and mind ... [She] was able to let herself expand' (p. 163). When the Chief Factor attempts to blow up Gabriel and his warehouse, the plot is foiled largely because Gabriel is copulating with his bibi in a bath tank (p. 197). The explosion and the disclosures in its wake shatter Hannah's marriage. 'All around her now she saw chaos' (p. 198), as mass riots are followed by a cyclone which wrecks ships and floods the custom-house, leaving a mess of clutter and wreckage in its wake. As Venn notes *à propos* of the problems of virtual reality, life is extremely wasteful of data.

Hannah's entry into Hindu India may appear to pander in some respects to the 'rape and rajahs' stereotype of India as erotic locale. Certainly the affair with the rajah is deeply erotic, and enjoys all the props of fans, aphrodisiacs, jewels and flowers. Hannah describes it, however, only cryptically: 'An angel counseled me, a fantasy governed me; bliss descends on the derangers of reason and intellect' (p. 229). The comment suggests the values of the earlier Puritans, of a mysticism which places love above calculation. Yet it has to be said that Hannah's lover is not as deranged as she is. Obsessed with war and strategy, continually quoting apposite paragraphs from Kautilya, he is described calculating the odds in battle 'as happy as some Company factor figuring out a profit' (p. 243). Though Hannah sews him back together again, he rejects her. War, not love, is his 'business'. Aurengzebe is similarly resistant to Hannah's impassioned pleas for peace. When she speaks of the need for love (p. 268), the emperor responds in terms of imperial 'duty' and the judgment of Allah (p. 269). The innocent and dutiful need fear nothing, he argues, 'The sum of their lives will be weighed in the scales of judgment' (p. 269). Almost as much a Puritan as Cotton Mather or Wigglesworth, he speaks the language of the religious custom-house – of duty, weights and measures and calculation. 'A frail ascetic' (p. 262) dressed in coarse cloth, he too embroiders – a prayer cap, of extreme simplicity. For him, Hannah's attempt to forge connections merely makes her useful bait to lure out the rajah for the final battle. The rajah's love can be calculated upon. Above his head hangs the Emperor's Tear, 'A mobile fit for an emperor who had seized all other empires contained in the universe' (p. 263). Empire, whether British, American or Moghul, speaks the same language.

It is this diamond which provides the focus for the virtual reality experience of total immersion in history at the close of the novel, which also looks to the future. Cyberspace is also a space-in-between, a somewhere which is nowhere, with its doubtful freedoms and new forms of imperialism, a 'new world' in which we 'navigate' and 'explore', in theory a world without boundaries.[37] Implicitly Mukherjee's rewriting of *The Scarlet Letter* poses the question of this new world – as potential liberation or as a new space of global domination. Venn has been described as looking for an information formula, an Einsteinian theory that will organise facts into pattern. 'He wants to grow a crystal garden' (p. 259), using 'the data plasma that will generate a fully interactive world' (p. 279). Beigh's mind jumps to the most perfect crystal in the world, the Tear, and Venn organises her virtual time trip as a quest for the diamond. Beigh's first trip is disappointing; for some reason she intercepts a lady in a yellow jacket demonstrating faucets in Kansas City. She comments that 'data are not neutral. ... To treat all information as data and to process it in the same way is to guarantee an endless parade of faucets in Kansas City' (p. 279). Inputting literary prose turns out to be particularly difficult for the computer. When Venn's technology is perfected, however, Beigh finds herself transported back to the Coromandel, to become herself Bhagmati and to flee with Hannah across the battlefield. Hannah steals the stone and passes it to Bhagmati, mortally wounded, who thrusts it into her body. 'I feel the organs, feel the flesh, the bowels of history and with my dying breath I plunge the diamond into the deepest part of me' (p. 283). In this final scene, the emblem of totalising power is discarded, its fabulous wealth is not invested at all: Beigh is content to leave it in Bhagmati's presumed grave in Madras. Though she has found the truth of Hannah's life, it is a truth which is no longer identified with an object. In its reflective, prismatic qualities the diamond stands as an image of the ways in which history can be reflected, refracted, retrieved or revised. It is also, however, an object of monetary value and that (it is suggested) is what will really organise the data. Once Venn and his team have refined their technology MIT will prosper on the patent and maybe buy out Harvard, and the rest belongs to the heirs of the Coromandel factors, the franchisers and marketers jockeying for market share' (p. 278). Essentially Venn and his team are the heirs to the East India Company, the new imperialists of cyberspace, where, as potentially in our own canon-forming institutional practices – in Yale, Harvard, MIT – the danger looms of allowing economic pressure to efface life-giving connections. Mukherjee's novel celebrates imagination over fact, restoring a history by deconstructing neohistoricism, and warning against the transformation of transnational discursive practices into a new form of cultural authority.

The Holder of the World remains, of course, a novel which is largely concerned with historical events, and in which the return of the transnationalised heroine to America is invoked but never portrayed. India remains in some senses 'out there', rather than being localised on an American doorstep. John Updike brings the story up to date, transporting a band of Indian colonisers with a religious mission into the twentieth century, and a settlement in the heart of America. Where Mukherjee concentrates upon the risks of being swamped in data, Updike focuses much more closely upon finance, particularly the role of the transnational corporation. In *Karma Cola*, her account of the mutual self-deception of East–West cultural encounters, Gita Mehta tells the tale of an Indian boy who gave his guru his faulty watch, only for it to be returned, accurate once more, indicating the correct date, recording different time zones and with an additional meter for measuring the depth of water.

> The devotee was staggered.
> 'How did you do that?' he asked the guru.
> 'You really want to know?' said his Master.
> 'Yes, yes, Swami, I do,' exclaimed the boy.
> 'Look at the inscription on the back,' counseled the Master. The boy turned the watch over and found engraved on his changed and wonderful timepiece the following words: Guru Industries, Ltd.[38]

In its image of the technological-corporate guru, the anecdote offers an appropriate point of entry to *S.*, Updike's third rewriting of *The Scarlet Letter*, which situates its Hawthornian heroine in an American ashram, loosely based upon that of Rajneeshpuram in Oregon, demystifying and demythologising the legend of Hawthorne's heroic Hester. In *S.*, Updike makes much of Sarah Worth's Puritan ancestors, from whom she inherits a quantity of plate, a sea chest which 'accompanied Daddy's great-granddaddy back and forth to China countless times' (*S.*, p. 230), antique pepper shakers (invoking both the profits and the raw material of the trade on which Hawthorne's family fortunes were founded) and her voluptuous Oriental characteristics, glossy hair and swarthy complexion. Where Hawthorne chose to emphasise Puritan religious history, glossing over the mercantile and imperialist enterprise in the empty space between the contemporary decline of 'The Custom House' and the scene of origins of the 1640s, Updike turns the tables, displaying an Indian religious community, transplanted to America, where its leaders pursue their own 'errand into the wilderness', found their own 'city on a hill' and face considerable hostility from the inhabitants. Just as the Puritan settlement exhibited its goods as evidence of divine favour, with material goods an index of spiritual good, so Updike's ashram, dedicated to technological and capitalist triumphalism, masks global exploitation and profiteering. Updike therefore offers an instructive account of the imperialist purposes to which apparently 'alternative' religion may be put, exploring the new market in alterity, and considering the relation between American idealism and its material embodiments.

While the novel engages with issues concerning a woman setting herself free from patriarchal power, as suggestive readings by Schiff and Bower, among others, attest, it is the economic revenge of the previously exploited which occupies centre stage. Critical readings of *S.* have tended to focus upon Sarah-as-Hester, rather than on the Indian-as-Other, perhaps because the Arhat, Updike's guru, is revealed in the closing pages to be Art Steinmetz, a Jewish-Armenian-American from Watertown, Massachusetts.[39] The impersonation brings into sharp relief the major focus of the novel, the commercial uses to which the 'Other' can be put, and the advantages of exotic identity for religious marketing purposes. In his portrayal of the ashram Updike's focus is relentlessly economic, as Sarah eventually rises through the corporate hierarchy to become the Chief Accountant of what is effectively less a religious cult than a transnational corporation. Sarah writes the Arhat's begging letters, plus letters of thanks for donations; is responsible for correspondence over unpaid bills; and is also embroiled in her own financial entanglements following the end of her marriage, her mother's investments, her dentist's and psychiatrists's accounts, the bills for her hired car and her personal banking arrangements, which include accounts into which a considerable proportion of the Arhat's donations are diverted. For all the manifold connections which commentators have drawn between Puritanism and capitalism, this heroine is a far cry from *The Scarlet Letter*. Do readers ever imagine Hester Prynne walking off with the contents of the collection plate? Yet this is essentially what Sarah does. In looting, in her turn, the fortunes of the cult Sarah re-enacts her ancestors' predations and casts contemporary American materialism into sharp relief. In the epistolary form of the novel, Sarah's letters therefore offer an alternative, proliferated reading of *The Scarlet Letter*, recalling less the red letter marking calendrical holy days, religious inscriptions and moral corrections, than the red ink of old-fashioned accountancy. Sarah contributes, quite literally, to getting the ashram 'in the red'.[40] Because the ashram polices its mail, opening letters and keeping its inhabitants under a surveillance as strict as that of the Puritans, Sarah's letters fall into two categories – those for public consumption (accounts of her religious experiences, innocuous family communications, 'form' letters adapted to order at the Arhat's behest) and those (despatched secretly from a nearby motel) which bleed out the ashram's funds to Sarah's own Swiss and

Bahamian bank accounts, transfer other funds from marital to individual accounts, and (in an image evocative of a culture in which personal relationships are convertible into hard cash) convey for safe keeping (in the hands of her brother in Latin America) a tape of a sexual encounter, for purposes of future blackmail. In targeting the economic and exploitative purposes of letters, therefore, Updike's satire targets both American and Indian materialisms, and also scores a hit at contemporary cultural economics. Sarah's letters to her daughter, a student successively at Yale and Oxford, make sly sideswipes at Bloom, deconstruction and the flourishing career of that contradiction in terms, a Marxist professor in an Oxford college, along with other academics, with the result that Pearl abandons the study of letters altogether, in favour of a return to the Old World, in the arms of a Dutch count, a 'Red Letter' man in the popular sense of the phrase, a Roman Catholic.

Up to this point it may appear that Updike's portrayal is entirely satiric at the expense of Eastern religion and of American materialism. There is, however, a sting in the tale; the ashram is not quite as easily discounted as it first seems. Two intertexts are available to the reader – Hawthorne's *The Scarlet Letter*, and the Neo-Sannyas International Movement (popularly known as the Rajneeshees) led by their Bhagwan, which forms Updike's other major source. Of the two the references to Hawthorne are unlikely to be missed by any reader with a high-school education. The novel's two epigraphs are taken from *The Scarlet Letter*. Updike's Sarah, a descendant of the Prynnes (p. 21), is the wife of Charles Worth, a physician repeatedly described as of a chilly nature (Chillingworth), falls in love with her Arthur (Art/Arhat), and follows his religious leadership to the extent of decamping to his ashram in Arizona, there to indulge her own passions fairly comprehensively in a sexualised neo-Tantric theocracy. Passing through the Hawthorne area of Los Angeles, to put pursuers off her track, she drives to the ashram via the Babbling Brook Motor Lodge in Forrest, Arizona, a parodic reminder of Hawthorne's crucial 'forest scene' between Hester and Dimmesdale, and settles down in an 'A-frame' whence she writes letters to her mother, repeatedly singing the praises of vitamin A; to her 'elf-child' (p. 77) daughter Pearl; and to her brother, who stores her tape away, much as Hester's story was hidden. When Pearl announces her intention to marry, Sarah sees herself as consigned to the role of ancestor, 'a sad old story, buried amidst the rubbish in the custom-house attic' (p. 180), though pragmatically she advises her pregnant daughter to wear a concealing A-line wedding dress. The letter A unpacks and proliferates to include her decidedly non-phallic lesbian lover, Alinga ('Dearest A' in love notes), the Arhat, the ashram, accounting and Arizona. (Updike transfers events to the region of Phoenix, in homage to the personal symbol of that most perspicacious critic of Hawthorne, D.H. Lawrence.) Like her original, Sarah's hair is gleaming (p. 17), and her complexion also dark, though Updike invokes a different Indian resonance – 'like a squaw' (p. 4). Previously she had attempted to embroider a series of place mats with the letter W (for Worth) but gave up. (Hawthorne embroidered his original name, Hathorne with a W, to separate himself from his ancestors.) Since Sarah tapes some of her letters clandestinely with the recorder secreted between her breasts, the novel also recreates the spatial position of Hester's letter. Hester was imprisoned for her crimes and retained a sympathy for other outcasts; Sarah describes marriage as a gaol (p. 144) with her husband as warder, and writes sympathetically to a prisoner, her hairdresser's delinquent son. Sarah is well aware of the implications of her Puritan heritage. She describes 'earthly property as a sign of divine election' (p. 57), and laments her repressed upbringing in 'atrophied Puritan theocracy' (p. 88). Even her worries about the real estate left behind in Massachusetts are of a piece with Hawthorne's anxieties over the skyrocketing real estate values of his day, a motive force (according to Walter Benn Michaels) in his choice of the romance genre. The plot involves medical terrorism reminiscent of Chillingworth's torture of Dimmesdale (assorted poisonings with mind-altering drugs). In one respect, however, Updike breaks with his original. Sarah makes good her escape to the Bahamas. Charles is left to marry Midge Hibbens, the witchy Mistress Hibbens of Hawthorne's tale, while Sarah is free from patriarchal shaming. In Hawthorne's novel, the scarlet letter, a piece of red cloth signalling a woman's shame, has biological implications which hardly need to be spelled out, invoking Eve's female wound and her punishment. Updike translates A into S, the first letter of *The Scarlet Letter*'s title, which also means Sarah, sex, $ and serpent. Sarah is renamed Kundalini, little serpent, by the Arhat, a name which revalidates female sexual energy and its various expressive 'wiggles'. Critics, however, while generally amused by Updike's ludic play with his original, and often perceiving a general appropriateness in his adaptation of the novel, which he himself described as 'the one classic from the great day of American literature which deals with society in its actual heterosexual weave',[41] have been puzzled by the specifics of the literary reference. As one reviewer put it,

> What he has not provided is any convincing reason to consider Sarah a modern equivalent of Hester Prynne, of *The Scarlet Letter*, although he certainly wishes her to be seen in that character. Now, why should Updike cling to Hawthorne's coat-tails?[42]

The answer is to be found in the other intertext, the Indian material. In the first place the Rajneeshee sect offers almost too good an opportunity to translate Hester physically into a twentieth-century image. Like the Rajneeshees, Sarah and her fellow disciples are clad in 'sunset colours' – red, scarlet, pink, purple – the uniform of the movement. They are embodied red letters, physical representations of a religious message. Just as Sarah's own letters are irremediably concerned with the physical (bodily functions, sex, dentistry, hair dye, as Bower notes) so the sexual and physical emphasis of the cult is proclaimed in its sumptuary laws. Quite apart from the sunset colours, Bhagwan (like the Puritan elders who threaten Hester) also believed in the separation of mother and child, and one reason the local people were alienated was the Rajneeshee takeover of the local school. Importantly the Arhat leads a religion which is a reverse mirror image of Puritan self-denial – a religion of indulgence. Updike acknowledges the Rajneeshees and their Oregon settlement as his source in his 'Author's Note', though with a disclaimer underlining the novel's entire fictionality.

Readers who have yet to encounter the Rajneeshees will find an abundant secondary literature at their disposal, though the stories elaborate almost as many conflicting meanings as Hawthorne's A. In the positive version, the Rajneeshees, led by their Bhagwan, settle peacefully on poor land in a remote area of Oregon, building an ecologically friendly agricultural commune and pursuing their own ideals of love and peace. Friendly commentators emphasise the productive nature of the community, the importance of women in its governing hierarchy, a general emphasis on gender equality, a population profile of 'drop-ups' rather than dropouts, with a high proportion of middle-class, well-educated disciples, many with doctoral degrees, the interest in new irrigation and farming techniques, and the classically American Utopian mission. Although in the outcome the community collapsed, that failure is ascribed to local hostility, with the native Oregonians variously described as bigots, rednecks, right-wing fundamentalists or the pawns of the land-use lobby. The ashram fell apart largely as a result of a ruling that its main settlement, Rajneeshpuram, violated the federal Church–State separation, in short, that it was a theocracy. As liberal commentators argued, however, the Utopian religious community has a long history in America. The Shakers, Mormons, Oneida Community, Owenites, Amanas and even the Trappists were variously invoked as successful examples of American tolerance for communities at variance with the public political norm. The image of a religious group, ostensibly fleeing persecution in its original location, to find religious freedom in America, and then falling foul of the original inhabitants, struck a resonant historical chord. The question of what constitutes a religion, and what immunities are not granted to religions by secular societies, remains a delicate and still to some extent an open issue in American law. The Rajneeshees' vigorous defence of their way of life, construed by many Oregonians as over-aggressive, was also linked to the large number of Jewish disciples, a group who had continually with them the example of the dangers of not resisting sufficiently forcefully the original threat.[43] (Updike's Arhat embodies two histories of genocide, Armenian as well as Jewish.) A disturbing insight into the American psyche was provided by the many letters to local papers, often invoking the Rajneeshees' garments and the slogan 'better dead than red'. Even setting aside the usual complement of fanatics (accusations of Satanism and human sacrifice were commonplace) many US citizens clearly did not extend religious toleration beyond the various forms of Christianity. A writer to the *Madras Pioneer*, 3 March 1983, simply argued that the religious freedom of the American pioneers excluded 'the pagan religion or "isms" of the Eastern world'.[44] In realising their aim of creating an alternative model of society for mankind the Rajneeshees had a long way to go before they could earn much credit with their neighbours, to whom the red letter side of the spiritual and social ledger was a great deal more obvious. Among the accusations levelled at the sect were sexual orgies (the film *Ashram*, with its images of naked Westerners engaged in a variety of group sex acts, often violent, was widely shown in Oregon cinemas), mind control, racketeering, drug smuggling and prostitution.

Hugh Milne, a British ex-sannyassin (the term for disciple) describes the central belief system of the movement as Tantric. Members indulge themselves (in sexual or material terms) in order to transcend indulgence. All energy is understood as fundamentally sexual, finding its origin in the base of the spine, imaged as Kundalini, the little coiled serpent. When properly freed, it will travel up the spine to the brain, uniting with the mind and spiritual heart in an embrace of love and consciousness. Though the process is portrayed in sexual terms in ancient images, it is with the understanding that the Tantric energies are harnessed to a discipline of awareness.[45] Tantric followers therefore believe that it is through fulfilment rather than austerity that true enlightenment is reached. Bhagwan's beliefs come essentially from the Advaita tradition of Hinduism, a view of the universe in which there is no separation between the spiritual and the material, or between God and man. All aspects of existence are coexistent as manifestations of the universal 'one'. In India, Bhagwan had married the essentials of Tantrism with a whole shopping basket of Western 'human potential' practices – Rolfing, primal screaming, est, dynamic meditation, bio-energetics, gestalt – stirred into a potent cocktail, with an eclectic blending of Freud, Jung, Nietzsche, Maslow, Tao, Sufi and Zen to boot. As a result the movement was able to access an extensive pre-existent network of Western 'seekers'. In contrast, the reception in India cooled rapidly. Open displays of sexual behaviour did not find favour with the inhabitants of Poona. The Bhagwan's cheerful instruction to couples to 'Let the whole neighbourhood know when you are making love' was not advice likely to endear the sannyassin to their Hindu neighbours. Bhagwan became known as the 'guru of the vagina'. (He gave long lectures on the female orgasm and the function of the clitoris.) The sexual side of the movement was, however, a clear expression of a belief that enlightenment depended upon the transcendence not only of repression (and the social institutions which supposedly cripple self-realization) but also of indulgence.

As a 'mall religion', however, it was the financial aspect of the movement which was most striking. Bhagwan's first modest flat had been paid for by the A1 biscuit factory in Bombay. By the time he left India, enmeshed in complex financial disputes over tax, the movement had spread across five continents in two decades, with secondary ashrams, massage parlours, discotheques, 'Zorba the Buddha' restaurants and radical therapy centres. Milne estimates that by 1985 the movement had 28 bank accounts in five countries plus America, with 24 corporations, foundations, institutes and 'universities' worldwide and assets estimated in 1983 at $30.8 million.[46] Unlike the popular image of the ascetic guru, Bhagwan espoused capitalism with a vengeance, arguing that 'Whenever a country becomes very rich it becomes religious',[47] since it was only when basic needs for food and shelter had been met that man could occupy himself with spiritual matters rather than the daily battle for survival. Bhagwan had no time for Gandhian socialism, and saw the salvation of his fellow Indians as vested in technology. Eventually he had four websites; digitised videos of his lectures were available; and the ashram boasted extremely up-to-date bugging techniques. One of the ashram's souvenir stickers read, 'Moses Invests, Jesus Saves, Bhagwan Spends.' The prominent display of wealth included a fleet of Rolls-Royces.

As an esoteric religion, defined by practices rather than codified beliefs, and without a defined ideological system, Rajneeshism could be swiftly tailored to different markets. More literally, the ashram included its own mall, which followed the same financial principles as Disneyland: everything the visitor or resident could want was under one roof. No money could escape into the surrounding community. (Products included Bhagwan beer steins, pillowcases, videos, tapes and T-shirts.) When harassment began in Oregon, Bhagwan hired a former troubleshooter for a multinational company, whose advice was trenchant. In his view Bhagwan's mistake was to have tried to set up a non-profitmaking company with several 'front' corporations, when he was clearly making money. 'The best thing you can do is come clean. Abolish them all and form one honest, profit-making company. If you pay tax in America, no-one will bother you.'[48] This advice was disregarded, and grand juries, immigration and tax authorities and state investigators eventually closed in, with evidence presented suggesting that Bhagwan was in America under false pretences, had lied to the INS, arranged bogus marriages for immigration purposes, and contrary to US statute which enjoins the separation of Church and State, had used his religious standing to influence county elections. Bhagwan attempted to leave for Bermuda or the Bahamas, was held in custody and eventually given a 10-year suspended sentence, five years' probation, a fine of $400,000 and five days to leave the country. Supporters none the less continued to see Bhagwan as more sinned against than sinning. Control of the ashram had been taken over, in some accounts, by a group of women. Paradise had once more found its traitorous Eve. Milne paints a darker picture of bugging, wire-tapping, surveillance, poisoning, an armed security force, false AIDS tests, mind-altering drugs in the canteen food, Bhagwan's addiction to nitrous oxide (dentist's laughing gas, hence his sibilant speech) and salmonella sprinkled on the salad bars of The Dalles, to reduce the voting electorate for a crucial election – still the largest bio-terrorist attack in US history. Bhagwan's main female associate was rumoured to have a large collection of cassette tapes, secretly recording Bhagwan's instructions to her on how to run the commune, and preserved to be used in her defence. In Milne's view,

> He knew as much as the head of any large multi-national corporation knows what is going on in his organisation. He chose all his top executives, manipulated and controlled their public and private lives, and used a peculiar form of economic blackmail to keep them in harness. He allowed them to amass enormous personal fortunes, then used greed as a lever to obtain precisely what he wanted, including 43 Rolls Royces.[49]

In the event 34 Rajneeshees were charged with 12 kinds of state or federal offences – attempted murder, first- and second-degree assault, first-degree arson, burglary, racketeering, harbouring a fugitive, immigration conspiracies, lying to the US authorities and criminal conspiracy. It seemed a very far remove from the Mormons and the Trappists.

Which of the different stories does Updike espouse? The parallels between Updike's Arhat and the historical Bhagwan and his movement are very close. Updike shifts the scene to Arizona, but specific events common to Bhagwan and Arhat include the daily limousine wave-by (p. 24), the use of sunset colours (p. 27), the description of work as worship (p. 26), the construction of an enormous community hall (officially a greenhouse), A-frames, a shopping mall, the absence of children, the origins of the ashram in India (p. 27), local redneck opposition (p. 29), a central fountain surrounded by rainbow jets (p. 30), armed guards (p. 31), compulsory VD checks (p. 32), continual surveillance (p. 34), dynamic meditation involving violence and rape attempts (pp. 36–7), the combination of Tantric yoga with encounter therapy (p. 40), the educated 'yuppie' population, the guru's dental chair (p. 63), limousines and wristwatches, the suggestion of doctored food (pp. 94, 99), charges of drug smuggling and prostitution by group members (described in the same phrase as 'gathering sweets') (p. 107), problems over land-use laws (p. 123) and taxes (p. 127), immigration problems (p. 152), a flurry of lawsuits (p. 165), controversy over control of local children's education, financial decline following over-zealous centralisation policies, the evolution of a female-dominated hierarchy, blackmail tapes and the Bahamian escape. Ostensibly the closeness of the parallels inclines the reader to an unfavourable reading of the activities of the ashram, suggesting that Updike takes a satirical view of the hybrid blend of Eastern and Western beliefs. Yet in one respect at least Sarah acts upon Eastern beliefs. In *The Scarlet Letter* Hester Prynne is marked by her silence, keeping the secrets of her love affair and of Pearl's paternity, both biological and – in the person of her disguised husband – legal. The letter A keeps its meaning; Hawthorne never tells us that it stands for adultery, and Angel, America, Art, alpha, alphabet, Able, Abolition and apocalypse are only a few of the alternative meanings on offer.[50] In contrast Sarah is nothing if not voluble, babbling, disclosing, filling every last inch of recording tape, almost embarrassing her reader with an unedited flood of tapes, letters and notes to her family and friends, her hairdresser, dentist and psychoanalyst, and her husband, discussing, *inter alia*, lawn care, vitamin supplements, hair dyes and sexual encounters in minutely specific detail; in short, everything from her domestic plumbing to the state of her back teeth. Significantly, she has never worked out how to erase. The reader's experience is further complicated by the frequent use of Sanskrit words and phrases, helpfully glossed by Updike, but, as Sarah admits, susceptible to various interpretations. Every Sanskrit word contains 'a whole lotus of meanings' (p. 85).

On the one hand the very elaboration and proliferation of the letters reveals Sarah's own deceptions (of self and others). In rapid succession, for example, the reader notes a letter decrying materialism (p. 81) followed in two days' time by another depositing $18,000 in her personal account. Fulsome letters seeking a donation for the ashram from Mrs Blithedale (the name recalling the similarly naïve Utopians of Hawthorne's *The Blithedale Romance*) are followed by grateful acknowledgement of $500,000 on 1 December, and by two deposits each of $100,000 in her personal accounts on 3 December. As 'read' letters, letters which we read as the omniscient readers (as opposed to the variously deceived recipients), Sarah's outpourings betray her even more comprehensively than Hester's scarlet letter. Like the scarlet letter, however, elaboration alters the meaning, if not from adulteress to angel, at least away from straightforward condemnation. Elaboration is itself in tune with the creed of finding oneself through indulgence. At one point Sarah encloses a tape of the Arhat as a present for Midge, a recording of a long and over-detailed yarn spun by the guru in one of his public audiences, concerning the ascent of Kundalini. At the close, however, the Arhat erases the tale. 'Did you believe the story of her journey? ... All a lie. The story of her journey is a very detailed lie, like the horrible cosmology of the Jains or the Heaven and Hell of Dante' (p. 70). He closes with the moral – that immersion in such detailed accounts is none the less the way to enlightenment.

> That is why I have told you the fairy story of Kundalini, the little snake that lives at the bottom of our spine. While you were hearing it, no other garbage was in your hearts or heads or stomachs; little Kundalini burned it all away (p. 71).

The story of *S*. is also, of course, the story of Kundalini-Sarah, as told by Updike, whose witty defence of his elaborate fiction depends also upon the notion of using 'foolishness to drive out foolishness' (p. 71), fiction to gain access to truth. Sarah purifies the ashram of its 'garbage' by spiriting much of it away. Sarah's story is Kundalini's, full of deceit, foolishness, redundant details, deceptions, but her story also immerses the reader in an exaggerated version of the American mission gone wrong, of materialism, plunder and sexual indulgence, with the aim of clearing the ground for a fresh start. Where Hester's story is an untold story, undercutting its society by its secret content, Sarah's story is a 'read' story, a retelling of a story with which we are already familiar. As a 'read' letter the story reaches towards truth through over-elaboration, embroidery, over-indulgence, redundancy – exactly the *modus operandi* of the Arhat and his original, the Bhagwan. Where Hester disappeared behind the embroidered letter, her secret both advertised and kept as a secret, Sarah's wiggles (the letters which she now does 'instead of embroidery' p. 137) turn elaboration into revelation. At various points Sarah signs her letters Sarah, S. Mother, Sarah Worth, Sarah Worth (Mrs Charles), Sally Worth, Sare, Sarah P. Worth, Sis, Sara née Price, # 4723–9001–7469–8666, Ma Prem Kundalini and Arhat. Her letters are, in the serpentine imagery of Kundalini, a form of skin-shedding in the service of the emergence of a new self.

In the final analysis therefore the novel owes as much to its Indian materials as Hawthorne did to his. Its critique of materialism and deception depends for its method upon an Indian model. It also looks ahead to the future. If on one level *S*. offers the cautionary spectacle of the West depending on its formerly exploited 'Others' for self-definition, it also highlights the new imperialism of transnational corporatism. The Bhagwan's enterprise was not just a cult, but a non-located capitalist enclave with a marketable alterity. Like any giant company the Rajneeshees transferred capital, raw materials, labour and sales outlets across national boundaries, with loyalty owed to a corporate rather than a national identity. Updike commented on Hawthorne that 'It needs no Max Weber to connect Puritanism with the dark forces of material enterprise,'[51] clearly identifying the devil in Massachusetts with an emergent mercantile capitalism. In the novel, American idealism comes something of a cropper – but the economic impulses embedded within it survive and flourish. It is not for nothing that the novel ends with an alternative image of American beginnings. Sarah ends the novel in 'a little paradise' (p. 209), the spot where Columbus reputedly first landed, the alpha point for American meanings. Updike's rival tale of origins locates its newly liberated heroine, not on the shores of New England as noble spiritual pilgrims seek an immaterial good, but in the Bahamian tax haven where Columbus landed, intent on discovering the spices of the Indies, which were to become the economic foundation of New England.

2 In the missionary position

Emily Prager in China

Where Updike and Mukherjee focused on the role of Indian trade and plunder in the construction of the canonical Western work of art, exploring its imaginative genealogy through the family metaphor of intertextuality, Emily Prager is concerned with issues of modernisation and development, represented through mother–daughter relationships and focusing specifically on transnational adoption and the exploitation of the bodies of Chinese girls. China runs as a theme through Prager's work, centrally in *A Visit from the Footbinder and other stories* and *Wuhu Diary*, intermittently in *Eve's Tattoo* and *Roger Fishbite* and vestigially in her other works. Prager's biography offers a partial explanation. When her parents divorced, her mother remarried and sent Prager alone, aged seven, to her father in Taiwan. Prager spent three and a half years in the East (Taiwan and Hong Kong) and never went back to her mother. Later she adopted a Chinese daughter, LuLu, and returned to China when her own mother died, to show LuLu her native city of Wuhu. Prager repeatedly describes China as 'a very maternal place for me'[1] because, when she was a lonely seven-year-old, the Chinese people she knew were so kind to her. At the same time Prager is no sentimentalist, as her career indicates. Employed as a child as a soap opera actress, Prager became a satirical columnist, worked for *National Lampoon* in the 70s, then from 1978 for *Penthouse*. It was not then usual for a feminist to write for a man's magazine. Prager commented that 'What I found there was complete freedom to write female supremacist humour, good pay to go with it, and a thoroughly unconverted audience.'[2] Her anthology *In the Missionary Position* collects her pieces, which include pro-choice columns, the first reviews of live television, parody ('Mrs Chaucer's Canterbury Tales') and an article about the Wonderbra patent dispute which generated so much publicity that the manufacturers sent her 10 Wonderbras in different colours. Prager has offended both the puritan and the libertine. While *A Visit from the Footbinder and other stories* was banned in South Africa as a danger to public decency and morals, one of her journalistic pieces, 'How to tell if your girlfriend is dying during rough sex', was banned by the *Penthouse* editor as too sensational. Interviewed on *The David Letterman Show* in 1982, she was asked 'What's a feminist like you doing writing a column for *Penthouse?*' The implication was that she had sold out, despite the feminist content of the column. Prager's answer revealed her pragmatic concern to avoid preaching to the converted: 'I'm in the missionary position over there,' she answered.[3]

Prager's topics in 'A visit from the footbinder' and *Wuhu Diary* – footbinding and transnational adoption – raise the issue of how far she does sell out to a Western agenda in which China features as underdeveloped, timeless or backward, in need of assistance in order to participate fully in a globalised world. Both topics feature prominently in the archetypical Western vision of China as primitive and barbarous, the film *The Inn of the Sixth Happiness* (1958), in which Ingrid Bergman quite literally occupies the missionary position, in a biopic based on the life of Gladys Aylward, a missionary in China.[4] Aylward was keenly aware of the power of narrative; she ran an inn in order to convert travellers by telling Christian stories. In the film Bergman is horrified by the 'barbarity' of the Chinese (demonstrated in a particularly unpleasant public execution) but eventually adopts China as her home. In order to finance her mission, she accepts the role of 'foot inspector' following a decree against footbinding, and convinces the local villagers not to bind their daughters' feet. The reasons for her appointment are pragmatic and financial. The three previous foot inspectors, all Chinese, have been beaten up and refuse to continue; the local Mandarin will lose income if he does not enforce the decree. Bergman, of course, is effortlessly successful (cue many little Chinese girls cutely wiggling their toes) but her only real interest in the cause is the bargain she strikes with the Mandarin which allows her to evangelise in the villages she inspects, thus maximising the number of converts to Christianity. The other cause which Bergman promotes is the adoption of Chinese orphans. Again, a financial transaction generates her involvement. When she encounters a woman with a naked baby, used as a prop in begging, the rapacious mendicant dismisses the child as 'a girl child, worthless. A beggar gave it to me.' Bergman pays her to adopt the child, whom she names Sixpence, after the cost of the transaction. (The period in which Aylward operated was less sensitive in matters of nomenclature than today's audiences would be.) Eventually Bergman ends up with hundreds of orphans, and when the Japanese invade, marches them singing to safety on a heroic trek across the mountains. This is not a film with any great claims to subtlety, or presenting an accurate image of China. The main Chinese roles are not played by Chinese actors but Westerners in 'yellowface'. Curt Jürgens plays the love-interest, Lin-Nan (of mixed Chinese–Dutch extraction), Robert Donat is the Mandarin, and the film is shot mostly on the river Colwyn in Wales, with local Welsh residents of Chinese ancestry cast in supporting roles (though not in speaking parts, since they had strong Welsh accents). The 'China' displayed here is envisioned through a Cold War lens, either as greedily rapacious or as a helpless victim, needing to be rescued by Western intervention, modernisation and development. As such, the film appears to exemplify the tendency of the West to renew itself from non-Western cultures, in the imperial belief that the world is totally accessible to the Western traveller or observer, as a commodity or spectacle for Western view. In this kind of reading, the West uses the East to prove its own greater civility, using an account of horrors as a legitimation of its own domination. As Spivak has argued, 'Imperialism's image as the establisher of the good society is marked by the espousal of the woman as object of protection from her own kind.'[5] Prager is obviously open to the same critique. 'A visit from the footbinder' is a heartbreaking story, as the knowing reader follows the rapid movements of innocent Pleasure Mouse, aged six, bounding around the palace, quite unaware that after this day she will never run anywhere again but at best hobble short distances with the help of a cane. In the story Prager spares no details of the pain suffered in the process of footbinding, and is clearly open to the accusation of gratuitous horror-mongering. Nobody is footbinding today, after all.

Prager is not, however, alone in her interest in footbinding, which has become a topic for feminist theory. In *About Chinese Women* Julia Kristeva interprets the Chinese system of footbinding as having specifically feminine significance, exemplifying Chinese culture's understanding of women's equal claim to the symbolic. Kristeva notes that 'Freud saw footbinding as a symbol of the castration of women, which Chinese civilization was unique in admitting',[6] thus to a degree admitting women into the symbolic order. In the West female sexuality is denied symbolic recognition, as opposed to China, which organises sexuality differently by a frank admission of genitality. As a result of footbinding the body is marked and therefore 'counted in' to culture, rather than being excluded. Kristeva argues that because of the existence of two unequal poles of familial power, the individual has more room for manoeuvre in China than in the monotheistic patriarchal family, and that 'in ancient China a certain balance seems to be reached between the two sexes' (p. 85). In *Woman and Chinese Modernity* Rey Chow's reaction is withering.[7] Chow criticises Kristeva for the sexualisation of China as 'feminine', and Other to the West. In her view, to read with Kristeva is to envisage the Chinese practice of maiming women's bodies as if it were Chinese society's recognition of women's fundamental claim to social power. Chow argues that Kristeva fantasises the 'other' culture into some sort of timeless 'before', an originary space before the sign, so that China is constructed as the negative or repressed side of Western discourse. Kristeva, she argues, is allochronistic, situating China in an ideal time marked off from our time, a time which has much in common with the way femininity is described in her work. Woman in Kristeva is a space linked to repetition and eternity, a negative to the time of history. Her formulation is particularly Utopian in respect of the idealisation of a supposedly maternal order in China.

Prager's description of China as a mother space apparently promotes a similar vision. *Wuhu Diary* opens with her invocation to 'China, guardian of my memories, nurturer of my spirit ... China is China to me no matter who rules it. It is a matter of people, trees, birds, smells, and earth, not politics.'[8] In fact, she spent her childhood with her father as an American military dependant in Taiwan, a location which could hardly be more politically and historically resonant. Both 'A visit from the footbinder' and *Wuhu Diary* are works in which the relations of mother to child act as a figure for the discussion of development. Footbinding (at the mother's behest) holds the child static, immobilised in a traditional role, unable to develop, as is physically exemplified in the broken feet and shuffling, slow progress of the boundfoot women in Prager's story – an implicit argument for modernisation and development. Transnational adoption allows for an idealised female entity, the Chinese motherland, while a specific mother is absolutely silenced. Adoptees are encouraged to immerse themselves in their Chinese heritage; the abandoning birth mother, however, will face criminal charges if she reveals herself. To put it baldly, the moral appears to be that traditional China maims its daughters; modern China abandons them. Adopters therefore rescue the girls for a better life in a 'developed' society. In the two works considered here, the one ('A visit from the footbinder') is set in the China of 1260, the second, *Wuhu Diary*, in a China in the grip of headlong modernisation. In the one, development comes to a crashing halt, quite literally, as six-year-old Pleasure Mouse is crippled by the footbinder. In the other, the child abandoned as a result of China's one-child policy has her own individual development promoted in the West. The one-child policy is itself designed to promote modernisation and development by limiting population growth, thus regulating consumption and, in brute terms, avoiding starvation. In Prager's work, the child therefore becomes the focus for a discussion of the benefits – and costs – of development, within a form which is itself founded, as autobiography, upon notions of development.

To what extent does Prager promote a readerly politics of Western domination? And why dramatise footbinding, now a relic of the distant past? Footbinding was already associated with unmodern practices when Mao came to power and denounced those who failed to share his blueprint for revolution as old women with bound feet. In *Wuhu Diary* Prager describes footbinding as follows: 'Golden Lotus was the name men gave to the

disgusting, shrivelled up, rotten, ingrown bound foot of a grown woman …
It was comparable in size and shape to a well-chewed cat toy' (p. 169). The
story draws most of its facts from Howard S. Levy, who describes
footbinding as 'a vivid symbol of the subjection of women'.[9] First described
by Friar Odoric in 1324, with the first Chinese reference occurring shortly
thereafter, footbinding began within the aristocracy and filtered down, eventually lasting more than a thousand years. Its origin was attributed to Li Yu
(937–78), the second emperor of the Southern Tong dynasty, who supposedly forced his favourite concubine Yao Niang to dance with small, bound
feet on the golden image of a large lotus flower, and subsequently made a six-
foot gilded stage in the shape of the lotus.[10] There were opposition movements over the years. The Manchus conquered China in the seventeenth
century and tried to outlaw it, unsuccessfully (their own women adopted tiny
high-heels to simulate bound feet). Christian missionaries intensified the
challenge, and finally it was banned officially in 1902, though it still went on
until the middle of the twentieth century. Even once the practice was abandoned, women with bound feet had to keep them bound, because it was too
painful to do otherwise. Footbinding confined woman to the home, the inte-
rior, thus preserving her chastity and (in a hot climate) her facial beauty,
effectively reducing women to the operative space of the boudoir. It was
believed that it led to a teetering, swaying walk which was considered erotic
(like modern-day high-heels), and that the need to compensate for tiny feet
by clenching the upper leg led to bigger buttocks and a tighter vagina. Men
supposedly wanted to have sex with a bound-foot woman because of the
sensation of tightness on intercourse, considered akin to intercourse with a
virgin. In short, footbinding made a woman into an eternal child, to be
violated repeatedly and yet always for the first time, eternally timeless in a
rather different sense to the Kristevan. Bound-foot women spent a lot of time
and care embroidering their shoes, which are now collected as beautiful art
objects. The object stood in for the woman. A prospective bride would send
her shoes – not herself – to the prospective mother-in-law, since small and
beautiful shoes were evidence of a docile, obedient girl who accepted discipline. The physical effects were also psychological. As Fan Hong comments,

> the intense physical sufferings brought about by the process of breaking
> and binding the feet in early childhood produced a passivity, stoicism
> and fatalism that effectively 'bound' not only the feet but the mind and
> emotions.[11]

The process of footbinding was excruciating, as the small toes were bent
under and into the sole, and the big toe and heel then forced close together
till the arch broke and the foot shortened.

The flesh often became putrescent during the binding, and portions sloughed off from the sole; sometimes one or more toes dropped off. The pain continued for about a year, and then diminished, until at the end of two years the feet were practically dead and painless.[12]

It took about two years to achieve the desired three-inch model. Levy's informants describe the pain, graphically. In summer their feet swelled and smelled offensively, in winter they hurt if they approached a heat source. One describes her little toes as curled under 'like so many dead caterpillars'.[13] Unbinding restored circulation and was painful, so the feet were not often exposed to air or washed. The foot was rarely unbound, almost never seen, a more secret part of the body than the vagina. Holding a woman's foot was thus considered an act of great intimacy. The awful smell of the rotting foot was appreciated, much as that of a rare cheese is by a contemporary foodie. Although the age of binding varied, the process was usually undertaken before the age of seven, so that the bones were still cartilaginous and would be soft. The girl being bound was usually bound by female relatives, mother or grandmother, though there is a record of one town in China, Liuxia, near Hangzhou City, which specialised in expert footbinding.[14] The girl held water chestnuts in her hands so that her feet would be as small as them; her feet were soaked in a broth of monkey bones or other potions to soften them; an auspicious date was chosen, often the twenty-fourth day of the eighth lunar month, the festival of the Little-Footed Miss (usually in late September or early October, when the cooler weather began, a time when there was less risk of the feet swelling, and perhaps therefore fewer deaths from infection). Tiny shoes might be placed before the goddess's altar and incense burned. Afterwards the girl was forced to keep moving about to avoid gangrene and to speed up the process. Every week or two the feet were bound tighter and forced into smaller shoes. The result was to create a short pointed foot, always hidden beneath a beautiful embroidered shoe, which made the foot look like an extension in line of the leg.

Prager's story is faithful to almost all of the above details, and at first appears to conform to a fairly obvious feminist agenda, in which footbinding features as a classic example of the ways in which woman is subjected by patriarchy, in line with the argument that deployments of power are directly connected to the body, with membership of the community transcribed into the flesh.[15] Footbinding has also, however, been interpreted in terms of economics. Thorstein Veblen explained it in the context of the theory of conspicuous leisure – which required small hands and feet, to signify a person incapable of useful effort, and thus not a peasant.[16] Like nineteenth-century crinolines or tight corsets, the rationale is to demonstrate the pecuniary reputability of the male owner by showing that his woman is useless, expensive and has to be supported in idleness: what would today be described as a 'high-maintenance babe'. Cinderella (a story which is first recorded in ninth-century China) is a footbinding story. Small feet rescue her from kitchen drudgery and transport her into the arms of a prince. In Prager's story, Warm Milk, a peasant become a concubine, is similarly transported.

While faithful to the historical facts, Prager's story employs a fundamentally ironic perspective, privileging reader over protagonist. 'A visit from the footbinder' depends upon a series of oppositions between exaggerated movement and stasis, contrasting the rapidity of Pleasure Mouse with the slow movements of all the other women, tottering on canes or being carried. The formal effect is not unlike that of an animated cartoon, *Tom and Jerry* perhaps, or any other 'cat and mouse' screenplay. The playful, speeded-up movements of Pleasure Mouse lull the reader into a state of unwariness, as if the story were only a game in which the protagonist, however often threatened or apparently injured, will always bounce back, unscathed. In cartoons the little mouse usually wins; the reader remains distanced by the form, observing from an omniscient position, rather than anxiously involved. The fate of the other women, however, strikes a warning note. Pleasure Mouse 'danced a series of jigs', was 'leaping up and down', 'fled', 'raced', 'ran trippingly alongside', 'scampered','sped'; while her mother Lady Guo Guo 'tottered','shuffled' and 'lost her balance'; her sister 'toddled', 'wavering slightly'; and her aunt Lao Bing is carried about in a sedan chair. In a series of vignettes, the bound-foot women are portrayed as always inside, their interiority featuring as an image of a rotting, living death, from the sickening atmosphere of the smelly sedan chair to the mother's ceremonial tomb. Warm Milk, as pale and ghostlike in the moonlight 'as pure white jade' (p. 24), and heavily pregnant, complains that her feet 'stink ... like a pork butcher's hands at the end of a market day' (p. 23) and has to be carried back to her bed by her maids. When Lady Guo Guo goes out into the courtyard (p. 27) the sunlight strikes her like a crossbow bolt, because she is so unused to being outside. The static vignettes of the immobile women are connected only by mobile Pleasure Mouse, scampering between boudoirs and rooms on her last journey through a series of ominously named landmarks, the Felicitous Rebirth Fishpond, the Perfect Afterlife Garden, the Bridge of Piquant Memory, the Stream of No Regrets and the Heavenly Thicket, all of which will exist for her only in memory once her feet have been broken. They will be too far away for her to walk to them. Unlike the reader, Pleasure Mouse has no understanding of what is to come; she is eager to become grown-up. The Path of Granted Wishes reminds the reader of the fairy-tale motif of the danger of the granted wish; the Avenue of Lifelong Misconceptions is her final destination. The problem with this ironic procedure is that the story remains enclosed within the mode of omniscient narration. The narrator is entirely knowledgeable, even intervening in first-person mode to give a short account of events in the tenth century 'before our story began' (p. 16). Unlike the ignorant Pleasure Mouse, the reader is superior in knowledge, aware from the very beginning of the story what the final horror must be, and implicitly positioned within a readerly politics of Western domination. 'We' are enlightened; Pleasure Mouse is mired in ignorance. We look ahead to a final horror, secure in our own greater enlightenment.

Prager was motivated to write the story when, in Beijing in 1979, she saw in a shoe store a pair of six-inch-long slippers. When she pointed to them the patrons giggled. These were orthopaedic shoes for crippled women whose feet had been unbound when the Communists took over in 1949. Prager's reaction at that point is chilling in its insouciance: 'This was a tremendous find and the perfect gift for my collector friend Michael.'[17] Nobody would take her money, however, and finally a woman gave her the cotton coupons necessary to buy shoes, refusing to take anything in return. Prager left 'vowing to write something worthy of this gift'.[18] The anecdote, told against herself, reveals the crassness of the Westerner, buying a piece of another culture, a representation of trauma and pain, exhibited as commodified alterity. As James Clifford argues, for the Westerner 'identity is a kind of wealth of objects, knowledge, memories, experience … In the West, collecting has long been a strategy for the deployment of a possessive self, culture and authenticity.'[19] The modern period enjoys an 'aesthetics of decontextualisation'[20] in which value is enhanced or accelerated by removing objects from their contexts, as in the display of 'primitive' or 'ethnic' objects as art. In the lush colour-plates of Beverley Jackson's book on footbinding, *Splendid Slippers*, Chinese embroidered slippers are 'splendid' as art only because they have been removed from their context of smelly feet, pain and blood, and photographed against a silk background, as objects in a collection.[21] Rey Chow argues that even when looking at images of a brutal past from an 'enlightened' perspective, there remains a residual pornography of the gaze. There is therefore a risk that the woman is exploited not once but twice, in the reproduction of her as object. Western observers, and arguably readers, are 'voiced subjects' looking at 'silent objects'[22] – embroidered slippers, or in this case Pleasure Mouse, who has no voice in the story but is merely seen from outside. Narrative practice thus appears to perpetuate the opposition between Western observer and Eastern 'object'.

But the story is more complicated than this would suggest. Prager's tactic is to place the footbinding at the centre of a series of transactions, erotic and commercial, in which power is founded not on straightforward domination, but on a process of negotiation between male and female. Prager's is a risky strategy, inviting the accusation of 'blaming the victim', but it is a procedure designed to prevent the Western reader occupying a position of smug superiority. In a recent thesis Wang Ping has argued that ultimately the bound foot was the sign of division between the sexes in China – a woman with unbound feet was not really a woman.[23] By binding their feet women turned their bodies into art and culture; the raw became the cooked. In the story the tale is told of how a piece of the first footbinding became a precious stone and then a ring worn by the courtesan Honey Tongue, an image of raw material transformed into art. The footbinding process begins in art – the dancer and the poet-emperor – and it serves to reinforce and stabilise gender divisions, in a culture anxious about shifting and eroding boundaries. The practice is understood less as merely brutal subjection of women, more in terms of a transaction between the sexes in which women acquiesce to – and then exploit – their own subjection. The footbinder, a Buddhist nun, is linked to the tenth-century nun of myth, and moves across time to the present, transforming magically into Honey Tongue, a high-class courtesan, the main attraction of the Five Enjoyments Tea House, where she sells herself at so high a price as to be almost beyond Lord Guo Guo's means. As a character who moves across time zones, who exemplifies beauty as construction, and clearly has full access to the symbolic realm, she is also expert at offering sexual pleasures (implied by her name) for pay. At the moment of footbinding, Honey Tongue, with her painted face and nails, turns into the unadorned, natural-footed footbinder in the pain-affected vision of Pleasure Mouse. They are aspects of the same role, collaborators in a transaction, the natural and the constructed. One draws her power as well as her pain from the other. Honey Tongue makes this point in the story when she tells Pleasure Mouse that the pain will recede 'and then you have a weapon you never dreamed of' (p. 17). The emphasis on woman as both prey and predator continues in the imagery, and in the name of Pleasure Mouse's sister, Tiger Mouse. Her feet are described as 'no longer than newborn kittens' (p. 13). Pleasure Mouse plans to embroider cats and owls on her slippers; both feed on mice. The story plays a similar game of cat and mouse with the reader, arousing our sympathy for the child but refusing to simplify the phenomenon of footbinding into easy categories of innocent women/brutal men, symbolic East/functional West, or enlightened West/barbaric China.

In her tale Prager explicitly draws attention to the notion of a transaction, in order to alert the reader to the complexity of the issues, but she keeps the experience of pain firmly in view, taking the attack on the commodification of trauma into art as her central focus, and introducing a plot innovation. In footbinding practice it is usual for the mother to bind and break the daughter's feet. Here, however, she invents a professional footbinder who is employed for pay. The process is not so much traditional as partly modernised. Lady Guo Guo justifies the departure from custom in terms of modern progress, and a better aesthetic result. 'It is an aesthetic act to her, objective, don't you see? For us it is so much more clouded. Our sympathy overcomes our good judgement' (p. 32). Importantly the footbinder sends away the large audience gathered to enjoy the footbinding, and its attendant zither players, tellers of obscene tales, skilled kiteflyers and owners of performing fish. She gets rid of the 'traditional' elements of the event, in favour of the modern approach. As readers we are therefore invited to register our distance from the audience on the page and to question our own role. Is Prager's also an obscene, gratuitously horrific story? How are we different from those who are waiting to hear obscene tales as Pleasure Mouse screams? Are we merely, as readers, voyeurs to a staged ethnic spectacle? The third-person narration makes us into spectators, an audience watching a series of scenes, only to make us recoil in horror from the actual spectators. The technique plays with our distance from events by placing a second audience inside the story.

Above all, the story condemns the commodification of trauma. The woman's flesh is treated by the footbinder as the raw material of art. Pleasure Mouse's artist friend Fen Wen, the master painter, weeps when he realises that Pleasure Mouse will never be able to visit him again in the Meadow of One Hundred Orchids. The symbolism of the orchid is significant here. In Chinese culture the 'four gentlemen' (plum blossom, orchids, bamboo, chrysanthemum) are popular subjects for paintings, signifying the four seasons. The orchid (spring) represents purity, an appropriate association for a six-year-old child, whose carefree spring is about to end abruptly. Yet Fen Wen buys into the cultural for his living; he sees Pleasure Mouse as an art object, constructed rather than natural, who has 'grown from a single brush stroke to an intricate design' (p. 14). In the story, Pleasure Mouse runs through a landscape of signs, of carefully constructed gardens and enclosures. Fen Wen's meadow encloses lines of trees, on each of which grows one orchid; the scene is explicitly cultural rather than natural. He is employed by Lady Guo Guo, painting scrolls for her enormous ceremonial tomb. The tomb is employing hundreds of artists, making screens, scrolls, hangings, paintings and sculpture, plus silk weavers, poetry chanters, trainers of performing insects and literary men, 'throngs of humanity of every occupation crammed into the burial chamber and its anteroom hoping to be hired for a day's labour' (p. 19). Some artists live off death, some off the child's mutilation. The chamber's interiority is a monument to a life which is a living death. Lady Guo Guo is entombed, confined by footbinding to immobility.

In the story we see 'beauty' paid for – but we also see it paying off. The footbinding is at the centre of a series of transactions. While ostensibly preoccupied with immortality and the eternal, Lady Guo Guo is entirely focused on economic negotiation. She has spent the preceding 16 years seeing to the construction of her tomb and is now decorating it, haggling briskly over the soft furnishings from a bargaining table set up in the tomb itself. The death mask and ancestral portrait are next on the list to be commissioned. When her husband appears there is a rapid exchange of hostilities concerning her extravagance, which he argues will bring down the aristocracy by enriching the merchant class. She counters that he has been trading as a merchant himself under a false name, while imposing excessive taxes and price-ceilings. Lord Guo Guo, infuriated at the discovery that she has been buying marble expensively imported from the West (Egypt), cuts off her funds. To obtain extended credit from her husband for the tomb, Lady Guo Guo successfully deploys the threat to leave Pleasure Mouse with natural feet – unbound, and therefore unmarriageable. She uses a non-Western concept of time to pressurise him into an immediate decision, citing the geomancer's insistence that the 'propitious hour' (p. 29) for footbinding is upon them and will not recur for 12 seasons of growth. Time is money for Lady Guo Guo. Their conversation exposes the collaboration between the male and the female in maintaining footbinding. Although he argues that 'No man could do a thing like that' (p. 29), and that it is women who carry out the practice, she counters that 'No man would marry a natural-footed woman' (p. 29). Faced with the threat of Pleasure Mouse's social ostracism, the husband capitulates – and in his turn presents an imported Western object, an expensive ebony cane from Africa, for Pleasure Mouse to lean on. The story exposes the fact that a bargain has been struck between the different camps (aristocrats and merchants, East and West, male and female) in a mutually beneficial transaction over the child's body. Essentially therefore Lady Guo Guo has traded her child's body for her own profit, enforcing the 'correct' sexual definitions in a transaction with her husband in which she uses her own subjection to her advantage. Pleasure Mouse's pain pays for both the expensive raw materials and the artistic realisation of the monument. Just as beautifully embroidered silken slippers conceal beneath them the deformed and rotten feet of the women, so an entire artistic economy is built upon the mutilation of the female body. Kristeva says of the Chinese woman that she will suffer, 'But in the long run she will have the symbolic premium as well: a sort of superior knowledge, a superior maturity' (p. 84). Lady Guo Guo, manoeuvring and striking a balance with her husband, gets a premium which is far from symbolic. Pleasure Mouse's entry into the symbolic as an 'intricate design' is accompanied in Prager's story by heartrending screams.

> Waves of agony as sharp as stiletto blades traversed the six-year-old's legs and thighs, her spine and head. She bent over like an aged crone, not fully comprehending why she was being forced to crush her own toes with her own body weight (p. 36).

Honey Tongue offers her the choice of life or death, and for a moment 'Time was suspended in the temple' (p. 36), until Pleasure Mouse opts for life, bellowing with pain, and 'Time, its feet unbound, bounded on' (p. 36). What Kristeva leaves out of her account – and what Prager leaves in – is the pain of a very small child.

Importantly in *Roger Fishbite*, her rewriting of Nabokov's *Lolita* (also a novel centred upon female child abuse), Prager restores the voice to her abused child, now a first-person narrator, and puts the blood back on the shoes. Unlike Nabokov's victimised heroine, Lucky Linderhof shoots dead her abuser (in Disneyworld), and founds a charity and a TV chat show dedicated to combating abuse. Lucky's mother collects chinoiserie, including bound-foot shoes. 'She had the tiny pairs of shoes in little glass boxes all over the house.'[24] Obsessed with her 'retro Chinese life theme' (p. 71) she is murdered by her new husband, the predatory Roger Fishbite, in a staged hit-and-run accident outside a shop, Boxer Rebellion Antiques, where she has just purchased lots of pairs of tiny shoes, now scattered all over Madison Avenue. The Boxer Rebellion, in 1900, was of course the pretext on which the United States gained a trading foothold in Chinese markets, and involved wide-spread looting of the Forbidden City by the International Relief Force. The shop might as well be called 'Eastern Loot' or 'The Spoils of the Orient'. Afterwards Lucky finds the shoes stained with blood – her mother's (p. 149). As the rest of the novel demonstrates, the Chinese retro lifestyle is not as 'retro' as it appeared, as the Chinese shoes turn into the sneakers made by bonded child labour (against which Lucky demonstrates) and the small shoes of sexually exploited American child models, actresses and child beauty queens. Tellingly, however, Lucky's fellow demonstrators in the piece of anti-globalisation street theatre which she devises are rich Asian consumers, the daughters of a deposed Cambodian war criminal (Keema Thep), a Hong Kong multimillionaire importer (Inharmonia Chen) and a social-climbing software billionaire (Sondra Kowtower). Where 'A visit from the footbinder' incriminates the past and the Chinese abuser, *Roger Fishbite* turns the tables to direct the spotlight onto abuse going on in the developed world. It is rather as if Cinderella's slipper had transformed into Naomi Klein's trainers. Lucky's mother's fate demonstrates the risks of museumising cultural otherness. But Lucky's Naomi Klein-inspired protests are examples of limousine liberalism, still part of a consumerist world, in which shopping is envisaged as a weapon and a moral statement.[25] Katharine Viner reports Klein as suggesting that the careful use of enlightened consumer power (supermarket activism) could counter the reach of globalisation. Her own sweatshop-free wardrobe depended upon the fact that 'I happen to live a few blocks from some great independent designers, so I can actually shop in stores where I know where stuff is produced.'[26] When the newspapers describe her fellow protesters as wearing 'Ninja outfits' (p. 180), Lucky is shocked to her uptown core: 'We're in a time when salesgirls on Madison Avenue can't tell Armani when they see it' (p. 180). Despite her resistance, Lucky is still part of the commercial mechanisms which she seeks to oppose by buying 'No Logo' goods.

Nobody is footbinding today, but they are buying trainers made in Asian sweatshops and envisaging the East as a global market. They are also still adopting abandoned Chinese girls. 'A visit from the footbinder' shifts from an understanding of footbinding as either patriarchal horror story or feminist symbolic capital, to envisaging it as part of an economic transaction. *Wuhu Diary* moves to the present and a sharpened sense of Western complicity in relation to transactions involving children. Transnational adoption is a new phenomenon and transnational adoption narrative a new genre, with its own conventions and recurrent motifs. While what is interesting about *Wuhu Diary* is the fashion in which Prager exploits and reconfigures these motifs, the aesthetic decisions are taken against a complicated historical and political background. Transnational adoption has been understood as dealing in human beings as commodities, in a trade regulated by laws of supply and demand. In the West, the sensational media exposure of conditions in China's orphanages propagated a horror story to which the overwhelming response was a belief in adoption from China as entirely humanitarian. The British documentary *The Dying Rooms* (aired in the United States on 24 January 1996 on Cinemax and afterwards on CBS) showed conditions of squalor and misery in Chinese orphanages, with some children apparently emaciated and left to die. The *New York Times Magazine* headlined a story about the adoptions of baby girls in Wuhan, 'China's Market in Orphan Girls', with the subtitle 'Unwanted and Abandoned Baby Girls Have Become the Newest Chinese Export'.[27] Holly Burkhalter reported in the *New York Times* that Human Rights Watch had claimed that thousands of children in Chinese orphanages had died of starvation, abuse or neglect, in an article headed 'China's Horrific Adoption Mills'.[28] Although the Chinese government disputed the charges of neglect (and there was counter-evidence of good orphanages) there seemed little reason to most Westerners to envisage adoption as anything other than a rescue mission. A further trigger to American women is the awareness of the gender imbalance of the adoptees. As a result of China's one-child policy, the overwhelming majority of the children are girls, abandoned by parents who prefer to have a chance to have a son, a decision informed by years of cultural experience in which a boy was more valuable for production (in labour) and more likely to remain at home than a daughter, who would be traded off in marriage.

Though figures vary, in China it was estimated in 1992 that, given the usual ratio of male to female birth of 105 to 100, some 1.7 million baby girls go missing each year.[29] More ambiguously, however, for feminists, transnational adoption none the less transfers babies from disadvantaged to privileged women. For some commentators *The Dying Rooms* wrongly demonised China, when the real problem was the context of extreme poverty.[30] More sceptical observers noted that the Chinese authorities kept adopters out of the orphanages, often delivering the babies to them in hotels, even hotels in different cities. Of the thousands of state-run institutions, foreign adoption agencies have contact with only about 50. Most are quite inaccessible to outside observers. (Prager received her daughter in the Anhui hotel in Hefei. When she returns to China to visit Wuhu, LuLu's birthplace, she is faced with every possible obstacle and never succeeds in visiting the orphanage where LuLu spent her earliest years, or gaining access to her records, though she is allowed to see a very pleasant orphanage elsewhere.) It was also argued that some institutions offered better care to infants who were 'marketable' to foreign adopters. Harry Wu, the survivor of a Chinese labour camp, points out that adopting Americans bring millions of dollars into China each year, and make large compulsory 'donations' to Chinese orphanages. The money, however, does not necessarily stay in the orphanages.

> The government is selling the babies and making money for the purpose of controlling the population. It's political. You have to realize that the people in the orphanages are government employees.[31]

Difficult as it is not to respond in purely humanitarian terms, transnational adoption poses particular problems in the context of any discussion of development. As Karin Evans notes, the Chinese people broadly accepted the one-child policy, despite the draconian measures which were taken to enforce it – from the public monitoring of women's menstrual cycles to the fining or eviction of offending families, coercive abortion and sterilisation. Even in the student unrest of 1989, reproductive rights were not an issue. The policy was accepted as a prerequisite for the country's economic development and individuals' upward mobility.[32] For Westerners it is often axiomatic that a Chinese child will stand a better chance of individual development – indeed, of survival – in the developed West. Others take a less positive view, emphasising the exploitation of poorer countries, the commodification of children, the implication that Chinese girls are an expendable surplus, available for a price, and the continuity with previous history: 'the practice is a new form of colonialism, with wealthy Westerners robbing poor countries of their children and thus their resources.'[33]

Rescue – or theft? American responses are divided. It is, however, indisputable that the adoption of Chinese girls is a large-scale phenomenon with significant consequences for American society. Evans, writing in 2000, estimates that some 18,000 Chinese children had already come to America, with some 350 girls arriving each month, forming a nationwide sisterhood.[34] Adopters tend to be middle class and professional. The organisation Families with Children from China (started in New York in 1993) has chapters in every major US city. Both FCFC and Our Chinese Daughters Foundation are grassroots organisations, linking local chapters to global issues. 'This East-West group of parents and children has become a global village.'[35] There are now thousands of websites describing personal adoption journeys, offering up-to-date information on the process, giving advice on what to pack for China and directing parents to local playgroups.[36] Most adoption agencies advise parents to affirm their children's Chinese heritage, and offer assistance in bicultural socialisation through reunions, pre- or post-adoption workshops, summer culture camps, Mandarin classes and various other events which are designed to foster the adoptees' sense of their Chinese identity. As Evans notes, some of the adoptees may know more about traditional China than their unknown siblings, back in a Westernising China, watching Disney and eating pizza. For some commentators this is a potentially positive social movement. In *Adoption Nation* Adam Pertman sees transnational adoption as a redefinition of America, linking Americans permanently to other countries and establishing a global sense of connectedness.[37] American parents 'adopt in' not 'from' China, and the impact of going there and adopting a child in the cultural context cannot be underestimated. Because transnational adoptions are often also transracial, the image of adoption as in some ways promoting racial diversity and acceptance of others is tempting.

Claudia Castañeda is one of the few writers to consider transnational adoption in the context of wider theoretical debates. Castañeda argues that the notion of development is implicitly inscribed in the child. What is unique to the child is its capacity for transformation. In debates about transracial or transnational adoption (and Chinese adoptions are both) what is at stake is the power to define the kind of person a child will become. In the context of Prager's 'return' to her childhood in China, two aspects of this analysis are suggestive. Castañeda notes that childhood can be a highly valued feature of adulthood. To turn back to one's childhood to repair 'the child within', to use the past as a resource to establish a more stable self, is almost a cliché of self-development programmes. 'Hence, the child is primarily valuable insofar as the condition of childhood can be revisited in order to be left behind again.'[38] Prager returns to China on her mother's death in order to re-experience the 'mothering' of China. At the same time *Wuhu Diary* is a record not only of Prager's own development in China, but also of LuLu's. It is in some senses a 'baby biography' in Castañeda's terms, a record of development. The visit to Wuhu is a 'roots' trip expressly designed to foster a stronger sense of her identity in LuLu, to ensure psychic health, in the belief that the separation of the child from the birth culture may result in long-term difficulties with identity development, genealogical confusion and loss of heritage.[39] In *Wuhu Diary* Prager carefully charts LuLu's reactions as she processes the experience of China. For the adoptive child what is being produced is ethnicity, connection to heritage, the sense of a stable self which is 'grounded' in origins. Castañeda notes that Article 16 of the 1993 Hague Convention on the Protection of Children and Cooperation in Respect of Intercountry Adoption (signed by the United States in 1998) links the child's best interests to issues of identity, enjoining that the 'central Authority' regulating adoptions should 'give due consideration to the child's upbringing and to his or her ethnic, religious and cultural background'.[40] In the past the foreign adoptee was transformed into a familiar family member; now the movement is towards a multiculturalist valorisation of racial diversity. Adoption is a threat to nationalised racial, ethnic or natural belonging, and instigates social change. It even deconstructs compulsory reproductive heterosexuality. (Single and gay parents can adopt Chinese children.) Adoption is understood not just as family-making but also as a site of racial and global harmony. This may well be seen as eminently desirable. Elisabeth Bartholet has argued powerfully for the abolition of race-matching of adoptive children and parents, to avoid propagating separatism and to regard the elimination of racial hostility as a primary aim, ensuring that the child is free not to reproduce the group-of-origin, and not to be envisaged as a form of natural resource belonging to a particular community.[41] Race is thus relocated in a discourse of freedom, choice and mobility, with the child embodying harmonious global relationships without any history of racial or cultural oppression (or resistance). Castañeda, however, argues that what is really being offered is greater freedom of choice for adoptive parents, as consumers in the adoption market. Laws of supply and demand link poorer 'sending' countries and richer 'receiving' countries. Castañeda therefore identifies adoption as a reproductive technology (comparable to surrogacy, *in vitro* fertilisation or artificial insemination), in that it lies somewhere between cultural phenomenon and natural fact. This particular technology is firmly in the service of modernising and developmental agendas common to China and the West.

From a consumerist point of view, Chinese children have many advantages over adoptees from other cultures. The process of adoption is swifter than from most other countries,[42] there is more acceptance of older or single parents than in Latin America, the process is not tainted by rumours of stolen children and 'babies for sale', the health of Chinese babies is perceived as good (with little evidence of HIV infection or of foetal alcohol syndrome, unlike some Eastern European and Native American adoptions), and the babies are young, usually under a year old. In addition the children are not 'available' as a result of US military action (unlike Korean or Vietnamese orphans) and there is therefore no ambivalence on the part of members of the extended family, who might have experience of combat in Asia. Chinese-Americans are also often seen as a 'model minority'. Although some racial discrimination may be encountered by the children, the prejudice against foundlings in China is also severe (a point noted by Prager at several reprises), so that the risks are evenly balanced. In America private adoption fees are as high as $30,000, whereas a Chinese adoption will cost between $10,000 and $20,000. In America, for every person who succeeds in a domestic adoption, at least five or six will fail. Chinese adoption is also unchallengeable, whereas in America various well-publicised cases where the birth mother reclaimed the child (popularised in several television 'trauma dramas' in the 1980s[43]) have increased worries about the security of the legal adoption bond. In China, since the abandonment of babies is illegal, the birth parents are highly unlikely to appear to reclaim their child, quite apart from the difficulties posed by distance and impoverishment. Nor can the child easily trace the mother. Very little is known for certain of the origins of the children. Unless found with a note, or delivered in a hospital by a mother who subsequently flees, the child merely has a name and birth date assigned to it. Paperwork may have transferred between children; if a child's age and birth date don't match up, the American parent can change the birth date as well as the name. As Prager herself discovers in Wuhu, China is developing rapidly, tearing down older neighbourhoods and transforming its geography. Even the place where the child is abandoned may disappear overnight. In short, the 'property rights' of the adoptive parent in the child are absolute. The Chinese child is visibly different from her parents, and to that extent the adoption is 'open'; but in the sense that access to the birth parents is impossible, the adoption is effectively 'closed'. Adoptive parents are themselves well aware of the potential commodification involved in transnational adoption. Karin Evans, who adopted her baby during the Chinese Export Commodities fair, with a whole city decked out for wheeling and dealing, noted that when she shopped for baby clothes in America, and for the recommended 'transitional comfort object'[44] (a Winnie the Pooh toy), everything she bought had been made in China. 'But it seemed a bit hypocritical to be politically correct in the discount store when I was about to be involved in a far larger transaction.'[45] When she undressed her daughter in China she found that she was wearing a T-shirt printed with 'Trump's Castle Casino resort'. Ironically, in China, to ensure that the child is found swiftly, babies are usually abandoned in places of lively commercial activity, even in markets. The American press has also satirised the consumerist nature of the process as an upper-class fad. *Vanity Fair* listed as a necessary 'accessory' for fashionable summer vacationers in the Hamptons a 'Chinese baby'.[46] A *New Yorker* cartoon shows two American couples, loading their plates at a buffet, with the caption, 'We're so excited. I'm hoping for a Chinese girl, but Pete's heart is set on a Native-American boy.'[47]

In view of the potentially consumerist nature of the process it is useful to adopt Rey Chow's terminology of 'biopolitical transactions'. Chow draws upon Foucault's argument that the various institutional practices devised by society to handle human sexuality are part of a biopolitics, a systematic management of biological life and its reproduction. Although the point of biopolitics is to generate life, manage and optimise it, in order to make it better for the human species, racial discrimination and genocide are also the logical manifestations of biopower, 'because power is situated and exercised at the level of life, the species, the race, and the large-scale phenomena of population'.[48] Although Chow's major focus is upon ethnicity, in the course of her discussion she raises the image of China and the West as collaborative partners in an ongoing series of biopolitical transactions, where human beings are the commodity par excellence. In her example, political dissidents are exiled one by one, as others are arrested, so that the Chinese government is setting itself up as a business enterprise dealing in politicised human beings as precious commodities, as if China has to maintain a supply of the 'goods' demanded by the West. If some are traded off, others will be caught:

> human rights can no longer be understood purely on humanitarian grounds but rather must also be seen as an inherent part – entirely brutal yet also entirely logical – of transnational corporatism, under which anything, including human beings or parts of human beings, can become exchangeable for its negotiated equivalent value.[49]

The West is not innocent in the transaction. The humane release of famous dissidents is also a means of palliating the embarrassment of Western companies doing business with the Chinese regime. Chow uses the example of dissidents, but the argument can be extended to abandoned girls, also a subject for Human Rights Watch. Indeed, Chow's analysis would fit many similar forms of global exchange. In Britain, on 6 February 2004, 23 Chinese workers (mostly illegal immigrants) were drowned while gathering cockles in Morecambe Bay. Sensational press coverage loaded blame onto the Chinese 'snakehead' gangs, which smuggled them into Britain.[50] But was this not also the fault of British immigration laws which ensure a constant supply of cheap labour, since illegal immigrants are in no position to protest against their wages or conditions? Is it not, in short, a two-way traffic or exchange, a biopolitical transaction? And is not the same true of the process of transnational adoption?

How then to adopt a literary strategy adequate to the complexities of the topic? And how to create a narrative for an adopted daughter? *Wuhu Diary* is both a deeply personal account of LuLu's return to China and a narrative which challenges the model of the West-as-parent developing the underdeveloped East. Prager uses a deliberate technique of reversals – reversing the usual conventions of the adoption narrative and creating alongside the account of child development a recessive subtext concerning Prager's own development. This is not a naïve account of healthy national development as China modernises, in tandem with healthy child development. The easy polarities of the Western parent/Chinese child are reversed, as the Western parent becomes the child, the Chinese child becomes the protector of the parent. The possibility of China as human rights violator is both acknowledged (imagistically in a subtext of brutality and danger) and countered with examples of American abuse. Prager's trip to China coincided with the bombing by US planes, under NATO control, of the Chinese embassy in Belgrade, an incident (apparently the result of a mistake) which led to widespread (and orchestrated) anti-American unrest in China. The embassy district was invaded by 100,000 people, the ambassador trapped in the embassy, the residence of the US consul general in Chengdu was stoned and partially burned, and American products (Kentucky Fried Chicken and Coke) boycotted. Showings of US movies (*Saving Private Ryan*) were cancelled in favour of movies about the Chinese fighting the Americans in Korea. The incident was probably the greatest test of friendly US–China relations in the decade. As a result global politics erupt into the personal story. Prager thus positions the main story – LuLu's development in China – between recessive subtexts – her own return to childhood (underdevelopment) and Chinese Westernisation and modernisation (development). China may appear to be a dangerous environment for LuLu but neither East nor West emerges as providing the best 'growth medium' for development. LuLu's bicultural socialisation involves her mother yielding her control to others and acknowledging both Chinese values and deficiencies.

Adoption and fictionalisation go hand in hand. Prager has to decide what story to tell LuLu in the knowledge that the story she tells will condition LuLu's development. The term 'adoption narrative' is a slippery one, referring both to the narrative by a parent of an adoption, and the story told to a child to explain her adoptive status. Because transnational adoption is a relatively recent phenomenon, there are few narratives for its practitioners to use. If culture is seen as the resources through which people generate narratives of individual and social meaning[51] then in this case the resources on offer are relatively limited. Oedipus may be the first transnational adoptee[52] but his story is not conspicuously helpful to a small Chinese girl in New York. Happy adoption stories (*The Winter's Tale* or *Mansfield Park*) suit an older age group.[53] Adoptive parents therefore invent narratives for their children almost from scratch, creating one of the first new genres to emerge in response to transnational activity. Enormous responsibility hangs upon the imaginative flexibility of the parents. The child will read the narrative, and draw individual conclusions about her own worth, while the general readership is forming a view of China. Throughout, Prager therefore emphasises the imagination as power, and credits LuLu with considerable individual agency. The transnational adoptee is taken away from any traditional narrative of origins, and a new narrative of cultural meaning is created both for her – and by her. She is not merely the passive recipient of a narrative rescue mission. Narratives of adoption thus offer a particularly good example of the imagination as defined by Appadurai, as a social resource, not as fantasy, elite pastime or contemplation, but as an organised field of social practices, a form of negotiation between sites of individual agency and globally defined fields of possibility.[54]

Wuhu Diary is a combined autobiography and baby biography cast in the shape of a journal. The apparent spontaneity of the diary form ('27 May Sunny', p. 162) and the apparently contingent details of stomach upsets, laundry costs, menus and weather, create a sense of the improvised, the less than fully shaped, the still-developing. The form is quite the reverse of Lady Guo Guo's 'dead perfect' tomb. Even the lengthy subtitle 'On Taking My Adopted Daughter Back to Her Hometown in China' suggests a series of occasional notations or contingent, essayistic observations. The diary form (running from 30 April to 18 June 1999) means that the visit is very precisely timed, firmly set in a specific historical and political context. In addition, the everyday nature of the narrative implies a rejection of 'culture' in terms of 'heritage' (art, history, grand monuments) in favour of culture as learned through the daily living of values and attitudes. The Belgrade bombing prevents the Pragers making tourist trips and keeps them tied to Wuhu, allowing for a deeper engagement with local culture. Throughout the narrative, the details – sensuous, trivial and sometimes apparently superfluous textual presences – carry a freight of meanings related to the larger themes.[55] Not all local details are innocent or 'exotic'; many carry a counter-message to the global, developmental narrative.

Most parental adoption narratives are carefully apolitical accounts of 'how I got my baby', and how wonderful it was, culminating in the 'Gotcha moment' when parent and child first meet, with very little emphasis on the fact that every adoption is also a tragedy, involving a woman who has lost a child. Stories are controlled by adoptive parents, not the birth mothers, whose stories go untold.[56] Accounts tend to involve the motif of the rescue mission and the triumph over adversity (bad orphanages, hostile bureaucrats, false starts), the notion that fate or God brought parents and child together, that the child is just the right one (the 'chosen child'), or a lucky survivor, plus some emphasis (once the family are back in the United States) on the 'positive' aspects of Chinese heritage.[57] The pitfalls are multiple. A child may find it hard to live up to the ideal of the perfect chosen child, may feel the guilt of the survivor, and may experience Chinese culture only in museumised form. The common explanation of abandonment (that the mother bravely risked discovery to assure the child's safety, by leaving the child close to an official place, or by hiding nearby) still implies that those who love you can also abandon you. Prager's narrative operates almost in reverse order. Rather than writing an account which culminates in the return to America with the baby, the story begins with a return to China, culminates in the cataclysmic grief of LuLu as she recognises that she was abandoned alone on the street, and closes with a letter to the birth mother, acknowledging her importance.[58] The story may begin apolitically, with a reprise (in memory) of the 'Gotcha moment' but develops a political subtext, and shows the mother letting go of LuLu, in some respects. As LuLu becomes more involved with Chinese children and young adults, Prager sees her moving away from her.

> It is scary, but I'm not pulling her back to me. I am going with my deepest instinct that she and we will benefit so much if I let her go free. So I'm releasing her to have her experiences without my hovering over her (p. 219).

Above all, Prager reverses the terms of the rescue mission. Prager maintains some elements of the genre, considering LuLu's survival as miraculous (p. 87), and telling her that her mother was brave to hide her near a police station. But she is forced to confront different realities in the course of the story. The Belgrade bombing creates real hostility to Prager and lets politics into the story. The bombing itself occurs in the context of a Western mission designed to protect human rights in the countries of the former Yugoslavia. As well as undermining the image of the US as rescuing others from the wicked abusers of their rights, it also reverses the mother–daughter relation. Prager is tolerated only because of LuLu.

> LuLu is in no danger here at all … On the contrary, out on the streets of town, LuLu is my protection, not the other way around. By virtue of being the mother of someone Chinese, I am allowed to pass almost unnoticed (pp. 128–9).

Even more tellingly, Prager confronts her own experience of abandonment. Her own first experience of the East was when she left her mother 'and her new family' (p. 11) behind, and joined her father. When she returned to America, she never lived again with her mother. When she goes to China with LuLu it is 'again without my mother' (p. 13), two months after her mother's death. She remembers her mother as 'out of reach to me' and after the age of seven 'never mine again' (p. 13). In addition, she several times describes China as it emerges from the Communist period as 'like the 1950s' (p. 30), the period when Prager was in the East as a child. The trip to China is therefore explicitly positioned as a repetition of Prager's own experience of abandonment, returning her to the status of child, and confusing generational patterns. Because of her mother's death, Prager retraces her mother's own history. Her mother was a child actress who supported her mother (Prager's grandmother) from the age of eight, reversing the usual economic roles. Prager's was a stage family and her mother only discovered her father's real name (O'Keefe) late in life. He had *adopted* the name of Romano as a stage name. The memory reveals Prager's awareness that roles can come unfixed, names change, family structures alter, even without the adoption process. At one point she wonders if LuLu (highly musical) also came from a theatrical family (p. 50), an unsurprising observation given that it follows on from a series of scenes of role-play, in which the roles of mother, daughter, grandmother criss-cross, as Emily relinquishes the role of mother (as far as circumstances allow) in favour of constituting LuLu as a daughter of China, and allowing herself therefore to become a daughter, remothered in her own turn. When LuLu dreams that 'they shot my mother. Now you're my sister' (p. 45), Prager takes this to mean that 'her surety of me in the role of mother has gotten rocky now that we are in China' (p. 45). LuLu acts out various family roles, acting out her own birth by sliding through Emily's knees, and staging a game with toy pandas in which she sometimes acts the birth mother, sometimes the baby. 'We both gave her away and adopted her many times' (p. 29). LuLu's agonised cry when she realises that she was abandoned, 'Why did they leave me alone?' (p. 227), is also Emily's own cry of outrage ('being left alone is just a metaphor for being left', p. 227). Emily accompanies her daughter to China, unlike her own mother, who left her to go alone. The 'roots' trip to develop LuLu is also therefore a reparative journey for Prager. Watching Chinese mothers and daughters she notes that 'Girls don't seem to hate their mothers at puberty in China' (p. 75), unlike (by implication) certain American girls. LuLu also gains comfort by role reversal when her grandmother is dying, drawing on notions of reincarnation to imagine that her grandmother will be reborn as a baby. But when she sees her grandmother, very ill, she states quite firmly that 'Grandma is going to die, Grandpa. Very soon' (p. 89). LuLu remembers a baby dying in the orphanage where she had spent her first months and correctly reads the signs of impending death, despite the assurances of the medical staff. Her knowledge is superior to her mother's, just as she is now 'older' at four than her 'baby' grandmother. In generational terms LuLu now seems to be further advanced than her mother (the child) and her grandmother (the baby). LuLu also creates her own Chinese family from the friends she makes in Wuhu, with TohToh as father, JiaJia as mother, plus assorted siblings, until

> as the days go by, the frantic, always-moving quality about her relaxes and calms, and the emptiness she has tried to fill with perpetual motion slowly swells with being. And slowly, slowly, this little girl, the one who was abandoned far away, is no longer that in her own mind ... She is now a proud citizen of Wuhu (p. 157).

The 'abandoned' child is also Prager, regressing to a child again, growing back through the roles of sister and mother, and then overtaking her own mother (now a baby). LuLu has become her mother's mother – as was suggested in the adoption photo in which 'she looked exactly like my mother when she was young' (p. 134). Nancy Chodorow has argued that women choose to have children in order to re-experience mothering, to recapture that blissful primary attachment of mother and child by recreating the exclusive symbiotic relation of their own infancy.[59] Mothering therefore involves a double identification for women in which they take both parts of the pre-Oedipal role, as mother and child. Where a child has not been sufficiently mothered she may be more disposed to become a mother herself, to recreate the mother–child bond. This is not the place to indulge in amateur psychoanalysis, or to expand upon Chodorow's essentially neo-Freudian analysis of the dynamics of the mother–daughter bond. Here, the narrative interest is less psychoanalytical than political, as the story demonstrates that Prager develops by going back to a less developed state, guaranteed by her supposedly underdeveloped Chinese daughter.

A second subtext is carried by the detailed travelogue describing the scene around them. On the surface, the description of Wuhu as a place of danger creates an implicit argument for adoption. China is like LuLu, half-finished, still developing. In Shanghai, Prager's hotel is surrounded by half-built skyscrapers and cranes, with a constant booming of construction noise. Construction work places many obstacles in their path; scaffolding obstructs the route to the waterfront in Shanghai. Reaching Renmin Park involves using a road with nothing on either side but enormous pits and stacked girders. The stores are so packed with people that it is impossible to move inside them. Prager's childhood memories were of a pastoral, unchanging beauty, rice paddies and the water buffalo, 'the yoke eternally around his dutiful neck' (p. 52). But in fact when she reaches Wuhu (formerly a treaty port) the first thing she sees is a miniature Eiffel Tower. Wuhu too is under construction, with rubble nine-feet high on either side of the road. Carpets are not tacked down, work is unfinished, lights are dim or nonexistent, electric wires are exposed and the air is full of rubble dust. (LuLu gets bronchitis.) For Prager, 'the real human rights story in this country, right now, is the dangerous living conditions of the average person' (p. 225). The dangers of the streets are a constant theme, with the subliminal message that these are the streets on which LuLu was abandoned, that she was fortunate to be rescued.

When the Chinese embassy is bombed (7 May 1999) the event coincides in Prager's narrative with the visit to LuLu's place of discovery. Her documents note, 'Found near the Qing Yi Jiang Police Sub-Station'. To Prager's surprise the bridge where she was supposedly found is industrial and modern.

> I find it totally surreal. I hadn't expected the place to look so ... what? So urban, so twentieth century. I don't know what I thought: that it would be more ancient-looking somehow? Just as I thought that Wuhu would be more like a village, with a dusty main street (p. 82).

Prager associates Chinese child abandonment with a 'traditional' rural environment, not with the developing world. But the side of the bridge where she stands is close to the new department store Xin Bei, overflowing with consumer goods, and to piles of construction rubble; the other side is the older, unreconstructed Wuhu. LuLu was found lying right in the middle of the city, near a bridge which half of Wuhu crosses each day to get to the main shopping area. It is the modernity of the scene of abandonment which is shocking. Prager had decided that there was 'no need' for LuLu to know about the bombing (p. 99), just as she had also decided not to tell her that she was abandoned in the street, but to say that her parents took her right to the orphanage to give her a better life. The most commonly accepted explanation of the bombing is that the pilots had the wrong map. Now it transpires that Prager also had 'the wrong map'. The place where she thought LuLu was abandoned was the wrong one. A Chinese journalist, Stephen, offers to take her to the right place and also to check the files of the inaccessible orphanage. Prager comments, 'Just when you think China has abandoned you, she turns around and picks you up again' (p. 220). In fact, however, this new turn in the story reveals the reverse, confronting LuLu with her abandonment and Prager with Chinese economic realities. When the place is discovered (another bridge on the same canal) the location has changed completely in the four years since LuLu was found. Formerly a poor area of shanties, it has been cleared and transformed into 'a new but nondescript business neighbourhood' (p. 220). The price of development is abandonment. Far from being the result of traditional attitudes, abandonment is the product of modernisation. While the Western press tends to describe it as the result of a traditional desire for sons, the abandonment of daughters is not equally prevalent across China, but much more common in the provinces contiguous to, or south of, the Yangtze River, an area of unprecedented economic development, rural to urban immigration, privatisation of state-owned enterprises and accelerated social change. LuLu was abandoned in the province of Anhui in southern China in June (Western calendar) 1994. There had been an intensification of birth-planning efforts in Anhui in the early 1990s.[60] So what is more dangerous? The traditional gender bias? Or modernisation? Prager visits the 'new urban area' (designed to save Wuhu from its immemorial poverty) immediately after she has been to the place where LuLu's fellow adoptee Francesca (Lao Li) was abandoned. It is as if Prager is aware that transactions are being struck, that the price of business development was the one-child policy and the adoption of girls.

The bombing also brings to the fore the financial transactions underlying the China–America relation. The reversal of generational patterns no longer appears as benign role-play. The bombing killed two young people, and the mother of the young woman who was killed is quoted as saying, 'Should a mother have to decorate the mourning hall for a daughter?' (p. 115). It is not just the Chinese who are a danger to the young. When Caroline, Prager's guide, denounces her furiously, refusing to believe that the bombing was a mistake, Prager's reply is telling: 'Why would we? Why, when we have all this business with you?' (p. 111). The relationship between America and China is no longer personal, maternal, but political, economic. The economic transaction is exposed as the real guarantor of continued ties of friendship. What returns relations to normal and calms down the unrest is the involvement of the business community. Because of the bombing nobody is eating at Kentucky Gi (KFC); production has slowed in factories. The anti-American television news bulletins soften. By 13 May the news, aimed at the American business community, assures them that it is safe do business again. A day later the top story is no longer the evil Americans, but the post-bombing woes of American companies, which are losing money. 'Clearly the business community has weighed in' (p. 126). Prager realises that 'no one here wants bad relations with the United States or the West in general right now. Prosperity is just ahead, and everyone here can see its tail feathers' (p. 120). Business has restored normal relations and the bombing has receded. In creating the parallel narratives of personal and political development (LuLu's and China's) Prager faces up to her own illusions. Adoption and fiction go together. But by not telling LuLu the truth of her abandonment, she makes a potentially damaging mistake. The truth is revealed as a direct result of the bombing, which she also concealed from her. Because 'senti-ment is not with you right now because of the bombing' (p. 172), Prager is not permitted to visit the Wuhu orphanage or consult their files for informa-tion. This is why Stephen makes the offer to check the files for her, and there-fore also offers to show her the correct bridge – where LuLu hears their conversation and realises, to her anguish, that her birth parents had not taken her to an orphanage as part of an adoption plan, but had simply aban-doned her. Stephen also reports that there is nothing in the files about LuLu. But his promised story about LuLu is never written and Prager wonders uncomfortably if he was actually working for the city government, which has killed the story. The story, in short, has never really been purely personal, but has always depended on politics.

Prager is, however, permitted to visit a different orphanage. Just before the visit she relates a memory of her own. Aged nine, in Hong Kong, she had visited a Chinese orphanage (in the New Territories) with her schoolmates, in order to present the orphans with embroidered bibs. In the ward, her eyes locked with those of a two-year-old orphan who glared at her with

a gaze of such hatred and fury that I began to burn with shame. I felt what it was to be her and to be in that crib and to see me, a privileged little girl all dressed up and wandering by, as if at a zoo (p. 185).

This is a deeply disturbing moment. Emily, although a child, is not portrayed as innocent. The little vignette demonstrates that Prager, far from being an innocent rescuer, is really immensely privileged. The child in the orphanage stares at her with hatred, not gratitude for her gifts. The memory is recalled after the bombing, when Prager has experienced Chinese hostility, and can no longer gloss over the facts of LuLu's abandonment. It is also highly suggestive, in that it clearly signals the existence of suffering in an orphanage and is described by Prager as a 'guilty secret' (p. 185). The memory occurs immediately before Prager visits two locations: a 'show orphanage' (p. 185) in Hefei and a zoo, the Hefei Wild Animal Park; the little girl, compared to a creature in a zoo, links the two. Throughout the story, Prager's text is highly attentive to creatures commodified in zoos. Any parent taking a child on a trip will be likely to visit similar attractions. But Prager's eye lingers on details which are not at all random. The descriptions of the zoos, often with poor conditions and suffering animals, are often situated at points where they undermine the 'controlled exhibit' offered by Chinese officialdom, with suggestions of brutality. Stuffed animals are a motif linking zoos and orphan-ages in an apparently benevolent series of exchanges. Prager presents Wuhu orphanage with 20 stuffed animals (p. 103); LuLu is given a stuffed duck (p. 165). Prager prefaces the visit to the zoo in Shanghai with the comment 'The orphanages are closed to foreigners now' (p. 40). In the Shanghai zoo Prager sees a life-size stuffed lion on display (rather badly stuffed and not nearly as cuddly as the toys) and takes a photo, only to discover from an angry man that the animal is a prop for photographs. She has to pay him to take a photo of this exhibit. It is only there to extort money from her. The theme of 'brutality on display', suggested by the animals exhibited in the various zoos, surfaces even more emphatically in Pets World, part of the Shanghai zoo. Here the Chinese have put domestic pets in cages, where they are sad-looking, lonely and dirty. The display is aimed at emulating the West and thus extracting money from Western visitors. Misunderstanding the term 'petting zoo' (where children are able to safely handle small domestic animals) the Chinese have put pets in cages. One message is that children are not well protected in China. The zoos are actually quite dangerous for children. At one point a camel tries to eat LuLu's hair. In Pets World there are dangerous uncontrolled pony rides and children can hug the giraffe (p. 44). A child beggar operates at the gate. The pets are also for sale – hamsters and guinea-pigs in cages. It is not difficult to see the subliminal analogy here as the nexus of imagery links cute, well-stuffed animals in orphanages, to less well-stuffed animals in zoos, places of danger and suffering, where small creatures can be bought. A sense of danger pervades all the exhibited animals and the juxtapositions – a memory of a miserable orphan stared at like an animal in a zoo, a visit to a show orphanage, then to the Hefei Wild Animal Park – are startling. In the Tie Shan zoo LuLu clambered dangerously onto the wall of the baboon enclosure (p. 148). In the Hefei Wild Animal Park LuLu actually enters a baboon enclosure (to her mother's terror), where a brutal looking man with a club controls the animals. This is a society which controls what it exhibits, and the brutal elements are never far from the surface.

Prager is not merely a naïve observer, offering a travelogue of exotic notations to her readers, but also provides coded or subliminal messages. As a former TV critic, for example, she is keenly attentive to what is shown on Chinese television. While some programming is nakedly propagandistic (a programme on the history of American aggression, for example), modernisation does not appear to have produced cultural homogenisation and she notes approvingly the abundance of special effects and colour, the variety of programmes and the stark reality of some of them. Again, however, the devil is in the detail. Commentators have argued that the gender imbalance resulting from the one-child policy will create a generation of aggressive young males, competing for women. Increased trafficking and abduction of women have been reported.[61] Prager's eye lingers on two children's programmes. In one, a dog cartoon called *Danny Danyao*, set in the period of the Spanish Inquisition, 'a bunch of mean dogs in ruffs abduct a female dog' (p. 125). In a children's sitcom set in modern Shanghai, the storyline involves a girl who dies, killed in a war game with boys.

So does the foreign adopter save the adoptee from dangerous 'brutal' China? Or from a China where modernisation on the Western model (like Pets World) was the real source of danger? In short, was there in some ways a bargain between East and West? LuLu is to be allowed to move freely between the two cultures, making her own choices. Prager, like many adoptive parents, is more constrained. Bad publicity has previously cut off the supply of orphans in other nations. But the story does not end in unalloyed affirmation. Prager concludes with the letter which she was encouraged to write to LuLu's birth mother, in which she recognises that her own happiness is the result of the birth mother's greatest tragedy.

> That you should have your daughter forced from your arms by a government who I then must pay to envelop her in mine is the stuff of which I have fought against my entire career. That I should end up tacitly supporting this policy is my shame and, yet, my fate (p. 257).

Happier times may be in prospect, given recent reports of premiums paid to Chinese parents to have girls.[62] *Wuhu Diary* represents a real effort to avoid dealing in platitudes and to construct a subtle narrative which raises the full complexities of the relation of East to West, tradition and development. How successfully the message can be communicated to global readers remains a moot point. Ironically the British paperback edition of the book, published by Vintage, sells a different image through its paratextual apparatus. The letter to the birth mother is printed inside the front cover, almost like a blurb, essentially exonerating and absolving Prager before the reader encounters her. In contrast the hardback moves towards a recognition of the silenced mother and of Prager's guilt. In the hardback, the back flap merely mentions tensions in China. The paperback informs the reader that 'mother, daughter and townspeople became involved in a relation of warmth and complexity that stands politics and prejudice on its head. It is LuLu's joy and pride in having found them that people cannot get over. After all, this is the same town that threw her away.'[63] LuLu, in short, is a little charmer; the story is not about politics at all; but the Chinese are guilty none the less because they abandoned her. The paperback also loses the original subtitle in favour of 'The Mystery of My Daughter LuLu'. The mysterious East appears also on the cover. Where the hardback featured one of Prager's everyday photographs of LuLu and her Chinese classmates, a happy group of modern boys and girls staring right at the reader, the paperback substitutes a professional image of a small Chinese girl in traditional costume, with flowers in her hair. She looks bashfully and submissively to one side, against a background of traditional Chinese houses, very much the 'China Doll'. She could almost be Pleasure Mouse, commodified anew.

3 Black Atlantic or Black Athena?

Globalising the African-American story

Globalisation is usually taken to refer, narrowly, to the deregulation of capitalist markets in the last decades of the twentieth century, or (more broadly) the result of new technologies of communication and transportation in the twentieth century, leading to people becoming increasingly interconnected across national borders. As Ulf Hannerz points out, however, the process may go through different phases, or even move backwards, involving different areas of the world in different ways. Preglobalisation and deglobalisation bring their own issues to bear on culture. Among those who found themselves forcibly globalised were the first black Americans. 'The centuries of the transatlantic slave trade had been a long period of very traumatic globalization.'[1]

The idea of slavery as the engine of the Industrial Revolution has been hotly debated since 1944, when Eric Williams first advanced the hypothesis that it was slavery which propelled Europe's rise to global economic dominance.[2] Williams argued that Europeans' settlement of the New World depended on the enslavement of millions of black slaves, who helped amass the capital that financed the Industrial Revolution. In short, slave labour built the foundations of modern capitalism. In this sense biopolitical transactions are at the roots of the modern world; in the example of slavery, human beings are treated as commodities in a process of forcible globalisation. Economic arguments, however, do not easily translate into engaging – or engaged – fiction.[3] Indeed, the mass marketing of the story of slavery and its aftermath risks appropriating and selling the slave experience all over again, as if to confirm the assumption that in the globalised marketplace all consumers are equal and all cultures available for consumption. A case in point concerns the explosive growth in number in the last decades of the twentieth century of novels which are generally termed 'neo-slave narratives': fictions which dramatise the slave experience, modelling themselves, often very loosely, on the classic slave narratives of the nineteenth century. Arguably the sudden resurgence of this particular literary form is as much a phenomenon of a globalised world as it is a response to a preglobal past.

Why this sudden resurgence? At first glance it might seem obvious that neo-slave narratives trace their origins back to nineteenth-century slave narratives. Yet historically this is a genre with a discontinuous history, disappearing from view for almost a century to resurface in a generic renaissance in the works of Sherley Anne Williams, David Bradley, Ishmael Reed, Paule Marshall, Octavia Butler, Caryl Phillips, Charles Johnson, Toni Morrison and a host of others. Arguably, the *Roots* phenomenon suggests a direct connection between the resurgence of the neo-slave narrative and a concern with tracing familial and racial roots, a recursus to essentialism in an age only theoretically convinced of the constructed nature of race, reflecting the *Black Athena* model of returning to origins. In *Black Athena. The Afroasiatic Roots of Classical Civilization* Martin Bernal argued powerfully that the birthplace of European civilisation – usually thought of as Ancient Greece – should be relocated to Africa, specifically to Egyptian civilisation.[4] Bernal's thesis, which aroused a storm of controversy, was welcomed by Afrocentric scholars, impatient with the notion that all civilisation comes from Europe, and that Africans are merely objects studied within a Eurocentric frame of reference. Afrocentrists point out that such entities as, say, a School of Modern Languages which includes only European languages, or the notion of classical music as merely European reinforce the view that nothing interesting or significant in culture comes out of Africa. Revalidating the importance of Egypt as an African cultural centre goes hand in hand with a re-emphasis on familial origins, and the notion of finding oneself – or recentring oneself – by tracing one's personal origins.

Roots is the classic example.[5] *Roots* was first a serial publication in *Reader's Digest* in 1974, then a novel in 1976, then a made-for-TV miniseries in January 1977. *Roots* devotes a huge amount of space to the story of Kunte Kinte, the African boy who was captured outside his village in the Gambia, and taken off on a slave ship to America. The reader meets him as a boy and follows him through to the sale of his daughter Kizzy, 453 pages into a 729-page novel. Less than half of the novel then covers the six generations that supposedly led to Alex Haley. In the miniseries the proportions were similar – four and a half hours were on Kunte Kinte's story. The structure reflects the desire to attach oneself to a past which is close to Africa, and thus to a slave past, rather than to engage with the nearer past. Haley described the experience of writing the book as forging the tie that links the child to its origin. 'I spent half of my life dragging manuscripts around. It was umbilical, like Linus's blanket.'[6] Haley's book encouraged a widespread interest in black genealogies, and has been described as responsible for the phenomenon of the hyphenated American, initiating the movement which led to people of colour changing their self-understanding from black to African-American. According to Manthia Diawara, 'Africentricity could not have existed without *Roots*.'[7] If the *Roots/Black Athena* model is one way of accounting for the popularity of neo-slave narrative, an alternative approach is the 'Black Atlantic' model. In his work of that title Paul Gilroy argues that 'black survival depends upon forging a new means to build alliances above and beyond petty issues like language, religion, skin colour.'[8] Gilroy insists on the hybrid character of African diasporic cultures, highlighting 'routes' (of trade and transportation) rather than roots and origins, and understanding space less in terms of notions of fixity than of flows. Similarly, in Julie Dash's film *Daughters of the Dust* (1991), the matriarch, Nana Peazant, insists that there will always be a hybrid, mixed, divided quality to her family's existence, because of slavery. The film depicts the women's hands, even the hands of the children who were never slaves, as blue from the indigo dye with which they worked. The blue hands do not testify to a racial or biological heritage but to one of work, trade, hybridity, borderzones, migrancy. In Charles Johnson's *Middle Passage*, Rutherford Calhoun, a free black, unwittingly stows away on a slave ship. When the Allmuseri people revolt and take over the ship, enslaving the white crew, Rutherford goes through a middle passage of his own. The mutiny therefore denaturalises and deracialises slavery – revealing slavery to be less about race than about power. The novel repeatedly undermines any idea of biological kinship, even among the black slaves. Calhoun notes that the Allmuseri (an invented people) seem less a biological tribe, than a clan held together by values and by a certain vision. Similarly in Toni Morrison's *Song of Solomon*, when Milkman does unearth a family genealogy it seems less important that he has actually found who his great-grandfather really was, than that he believes that he has done so. As one character points out, almost everyone in the area around the town of Shalimar claims kinship with Solomon: 'he had a slew of children all over the place.'[9] It is like claiming descent from Adam and Eve. There is nothing so very special about Milkman's family. Laying claim to a past, therefore, may be quite different from claiming biological ancestry.

One recentring tactic exploited by writers and theorists has been the invention of 'race' as family, so that notions of Africanness, conveniently dissociated from the politics of contemporary Africa, operate transnationally through the symbolic projection of race on kinship. As Paul Gilroy argues, this is a strategy which constructs black cultures outside any sense of nation, figuring sameness across national boundaries and between nation states. It is in many ways less a means of engaging with public politics, than a form of therapy.[10] In *Crossing the River* Caryl Phillips offers, as a counter-example to *Roots*, a diasporic fiction focused on family. As opposed to *Roots*, *Crossing the River* is a long way from any easy nostalgia for African origins, as its first sentence indicates: 'The crops failed. I sold my children.'[11] The three children, sold to a slave trader in 1753, become a nineteenth-century missionary in Liberia, a pioneer on a wagon train in the West, and an American GI posted to a Yorkshire village in forties Britain. Nobody finds their missing children or unravels their ancestry here. As Bénédicte Ledent has argued, the characters acquire adoptive parents and surrogate family ties, woven to replace original ones, imperfect consolations but none the less existent, and representative of the love–hate dimensions of the colonial experience. The family trope is used less to support ethnocentric perspectives, than as a loose, puzzle-like image, a metaphor for the Black Atlantic culture which Gilroy describes as having a transcultural, international formation.[12] By including the journal entries of the slaver's captain and his letters, plus material from John Newton's *Journal of a Slave Trader*, together with nineteenth-century American and twentieth-century British history, the diasporic experience spans 250 years, juxtaposing four inconsistent stories about the past, scrambling the chronological and presenting its protagonists obliquely through letters or interposed narrators. It is a subtle and complex novel, which translates the slave narrative into a transnational context. If *Roots* is local, *Crossing the River* is emphatically global.

Three critics have produced major studies of the neo-slave narrative, all to some extent focusing upon its origins. Ashraf Rushdy (in the first, deservedly acclaimed study) looks to history, and locates the 'moment of their formal origins'[13] in relation to the 1960s, first as 'writing back' against Styron's *Confessions of Nat Turner*, and second in the vexed relation of his chosen writers (Williams, Reed, Johnson) to the Black Power advocates of the sixties. Rushdy's focus is political and historical. In the 1960s, he argues, there was a shift in American history as the rise of Black Power and the New Left social history made it clear that history was not just made by the imperial powers of a nation but by those without any discernible power. 'History from the bottom up' made its appearance, in labour and working-class history, women's and ethnic studies, and a revised respect for oral history and testimony. The nineteenth-century slave narratives were suddenly back in favour; and as a newly emergent black political subjectivity emerged in the sixties the parallels between the two periods were obvious, with a renewed interest in questions of race and power. Rushdy argues that contemporary novels concentrate particularly on issues of power relations in the field of cultural production – what the forces are behind the creation of a literary tradition, how national narratives emerge, which groups get to tell their story as THE story, which stories are 'minority' or marginalised, controlled by media institutions. Concentrating on origins in a broader, gendered sense (the mother as origin), Elizabeth Beaulieu's study confines itself to women writers.[14] For Beaulieu, neo-slave narratives place the enslaved mother at the heart of the tale, reacting against the overemphasis in the nineteenth century on the male paradigm (literacy–identity–freedom) and the underestimation of the female paradigm (family–identity–freedom). Beaulieu also takes *Roots* into account, but points out that Haley's tale is very much a male story, with Kunte Kinte as a loner, and his daughter Kizzy a stock character of the suffering slave woman. Kizzy is really 'George's mother' in the story; George is prioritised. Similarly Binta, Kunte Kinte's mother, is valued only as a breeder of sons – an ironic role in a story about slavery, a system which also valued women as breeders. The opening chapter of *Roots*, for example, begins with the birth of a 'manchild' and outlines the rituals and naming ceremonies associated with the birth of a son in a tone of considerable pride. (It would have been very different if the child had been a daughter.) In contrast, the stories of the women in the novels of Morrison, Butler or Williams put gender back on the agenda, and especially maternity. *Dessa Rose*, for example, prioritises motherhood. Dessa's pregnancy is what saves her life; motherhood is the source of her strength. Motherhood is absolutely central to *Beloved*, in the infanticide plot, the milk-stealing and the connections between foremothers, mothers and daughters. Beaulieu's account of *Kindred*, however, may give us pause and suggest some reservations concerning the issue of empowering women. In *Kindred*, Dana goes back to the past to facilitate the rape of her great-great-great-grandmother, the acknowledged starting point for her own family line.[15] (Dana has to keep Rufus, the white slaveholder's son, alive long enough for procreation to occur.) In other words Dana is in some senses a surrogate mother, birthing her ancestor as well as herself, and protecting and nurturing Rufus, whose own white mother is ineffectual. It is a completely new take on the 'Black Mammy' model, with Mammy as the rapist's accomplice, and offers a somewhat ambiguous testimony to women's power.

In contrast to both Rushdy and Beaulieu, Alison Landsberg's study is implicitly antioriginary, placing neo-slave narratives within a much broader non-racial paradigm as examples of the late-twentieth-century tendency towards 'prosthetic memory' – produced in response to new electronic and visual media. Her interest is in how individuals come to own and inhabit memories of events, the experience of which they never lived through – with memories rather like artificial limbs, worn by the body, or like clothes which we change at will in order to retailor our identities. Because under slavery the bond between children and parents is broken, history cannot be easily passed on, and children have to produce 'memories' which have never been really lived, to produce a feeling of belonging. In Paul Gilroy's words, the door to tradition remains wedged open not by the memory of modern racial slavery but in spite of it … It seems as if the complexity of slavery and of its location within modernity has to be actively forgotten if a clear orientation to tradition and thus to the present circumstances of blacks is to be acquired.[16]

Landsberg is not interested in authenticity or origins at all but in the constructedness of memory, and the popular longing to experience history in a personal, even a bodily way. Landsberg argues that novels such as *Roots* can unite white and black readerships by exploiting an emotional interpretation of history. If a miniseries can create affective bonds which transcend race, affect is not merely emotionalism but might be understood as producing the first occasion when many whites had been able to identify with blacks, thus offering a political strategy. For Landsberg, for example, the *Roots* phenomenon is a story transferable across cultures (as its bestseller status in hundreds of languages suggests) and is more about the interpellative power of the past than about African-American history. Those readers who are more concerned with historical accuracy, or who remember the slogan of *Nineteen Eighty-Four*, 'who controls the past controls the future', may well think that Landsberg neglects the Orwellian overtones of her thesis, in order to applaud a future of hybrid imaginative and political alliances. Economic and political specificities have been left some way behind.

In the context of these conflicting approaches to the neo-slave narrative, one specific neo-slave narrative offers a symptomatic case study, a 1993 novel that corresponds very exactly with the formal features of the nineteenth-century genre. The hero is sold at the age of four, and permanently separated from his family, unsure of his name and ignorant of his birthdate (which he invents). As he says, 'My family tree stops dead at this deed of purchase.'[17] He struggles to gain literacy, reading over a white child's shoulder; he is highly intelligent in the Frederick Douglass mode and makes ingenious machines; is starved and beaten, treated as an animal, has his language taken from him (all his teeth are forcibly removed, reducing him to sign language), and makes repeated, failed escape attempts. He undergoes religious conversion and invokes the example of the Israelites in bondage, successfully calling down a plague of locusts on his master's crops. He then escapes by means of a violent fistfight, and becomes first a skilled railroad worker, then a preacher. The contemporary narrator, his granddaughter, pieces the story together from oral (tape-recorded) sources (her uncle) and from her grandfather's diaries, written in code after his escape. In a note to the novel, just like the nineteenth-century abolitionists, she assures the reader of the authentic factual basis of the tale. In short, in its generic features the novel corresponds point for point with the conventions of the nineteenth-century slave narrative. In all but one respect. The 'Author's Note' reads

> My grandfather was a slave. This isn't an uncommon claim for an American to make if the American is black. But I am not black, I'm white. My grandfather was white, too. And he was sold into slavery (n.p.).

Joan Brady's grandfather was sold for $15 to a mid-Western tobacco farmer (such sales were common just after the Civil War) and her novel *Theory of War* is the result.

I invoke this example – contentious though it is – to raise a vital question. While the reader may be impatient with the claims for the primacy of African origins made by *Black Athena* and *Roots*, can the African-American story be cut loose quite so easily from its historical specificity? Does the Black Atlantic model, with its broadening out of the history of African-American slavery to include a wider time frame and a geographical extension, itself amount to a form of globalisation of African-American stories? As the specific becomes the generic, so the literary genre becomes transferable. As Laura Chrisman argues, Gilroy's thesis 'has made it difficult to consider how Black Atlanticism articulates specific intellectual and cultural relationships with imperialism and capitalism'.[18] As a 'bounden boy' Joan Brady's grandfather certainly suffered brutal misery. But in casting his story within the norms of an African-American form is Brady practising an annexation of a specific history to her own distinct purposes? It is noteworthy that in the novel Jonathan Carrick, the hero, shows his whipping scars to a freed slave, Nero, who becomes his only friend. Brady quite intentionally invites the reader to see the two men's histories as equivalent. Like the Black Atlantic model, the emphasis throughout is less on slavery and more on economic and national power, with the novel's structural backbone a series of allusions to von Clausewitz on the subject of war. There is a distinct danger here (to use Geoffrey Hartman's terminology) of revision through 'equalising comparisons'. Following the 'historians' controversy' in Germany in 1986 over the use of history for political purposes, scholars have become familiar with the dangers of making historical arguments that tend either to 'relativise' or to 'normalise' the Nazi state's killings of Jews. Discussing Ronald Reagan's respectful tribute at the graves of SS soldiers at Bitburg in 1985, Geoffrey Hartman warned of 'a more subtle revisionism ... all around us that mitigates the horrors of the camps, not by denying it but by using equalizing comparisons'.[19] In this way Vietnam becomes a Holocaust, or slavery a psychological equivalent of the camps; or slavery is equated with the oppression of women, or (as here) with bonded servitude. It is a problem that besets any comparative study, offering a fatal temptation to writers to indulge the rhetoric of blame with rival calculators totting up the mortality rates. Brady's novel had a modest success, but the commodification of the form is not limited to Brady. As other commentators have noted, in *The Handmaid's Tale* Margaret Atwood simply substitutes gender for race within the same frame of conventions – forced reproduction, naming for white owners ('Offred'), family separation, public lynching, struggles for access to writing and a final escape attempt by the heroine (aided by the 'Underground Femaleroad') to Canada.[20] Although Atwood explicitly excludes African-Americans from the tale (the narrator learns that 're-settlement of the Children of Ham is continuing on schedule' in North Dakota[21]), the form is that of the first-person slave narrative, adapted to portray women as slaves, and complicit slaves at that. It might well seem that – in a hideous literary irony – the neo-slave narrative has become a commodity, sold in the literary marketplace, its links to its origins fractured.

Like any nineteenth-century white abolitionist, constructing an authenticating frame for the slave's story, Atwood adds 'Historical Notes' from Professor Pieixoto who (in 2195) edits the oral testimony, transcribing the 30 cassette tapes, to reconstruct and probably deform the story. At the close of *The Handmaid's Tale*, Pieixoto's 'Notes', the partial transcript of his lecture, provide a wicked satire on academic commodification. Professor Pieixoto, a major scholar from Cambridge who is slumming it at the University of Denay, Nunavit, is introduced obsequiously by the fawning Professor Maryann Crescent Moon, and proceeds to patronise his chairperson, his audience and his eponymous subject, demonstrating that patriarchal prejudice remains almost unchanged over the centuries. Pieixoto considers the possibility of forgery, analyses the technology of the tapes on which the story was recorded, earnestly discusses the possibility of using musical traces as dating devices, attempts to trace the history of the house where the tapes were found, offers a great deal of information about each of the two men who might have been the handmaid's master, but discovers absolutely nothing about the handmaid herself: not her name, not her origins, not even whether she escaped from bondage. Pieixoto is sharing the conference podium with Professor Sieglinda Van Buren from the Department of Military History at the University of San Antonio, Republic of Texas. As Michael Foley has argued, despite the presence at the conference of women professors and ethnic minority speakers (Professor Johnny Running Dog, for example) not much has changed, and the supposed admission of women and minorities to the academic mainstream is merely a smokescreen for their continued domination.[22] The handmaid is Pieixoto's cultural capital, a source of prestige, and an opportunity to participate in an academic beanfeast. Marginality (in this case, female) can be a very valuable commodity, especially to a celebrity academic like Pieixoto, a cultural broker, mediating a global trade in cultural commodities, while denying himself none of the local attractions (Arctic char and a charming Arctic Chair) in Denay, Nunavit.

Today Atwood's tongue-in-cheek parody appears positively old-fashioned in its image of the scholarly edition published by Pieixoto. When Henry Louis Gates discovered the manuscript of *The Bondwoman's Narrative*, supposedly a novel by Hannah Crafts, an African-American woman, in an auction of Africana in February 2001, it was published not by a scholarly press, but by AOL Time Warner.[23] As Paul Grainge comments, the buyout of Warner Communications by Time Inc., in June 1989, and the merger of Time Warner with internet giant America Online in January 2000, created a media conglomerate of enormous size in which publishing was merely a small part of 'a decentralized corporate monolith trying to maximise the synergistic potential of its investments in cable, programming, film studios, music and online services'.[24] According to the *Chicago Sun Times* 'Gates has sold the movie rights for a possible HBO production.'[25] *The Bondwoman's Narrative* had its own website (http://www.bondwomansnarrative.com) listing events, discussions and signings. The marketing operation was intensive. Hannah might be unknown but Gates was not. As Jeff Zaleski commented in *Publishers Weekly*, 'With Warner's publicity push (editor tour, TV appearances, national advertising), Gates's first-rate reputation, the prospect of this being the first novel by a former slave woman and the manuscript's own merit, count on this title to be a very big seller.'[26] David Shumway has argued that the emergence of a star system in literary studies is a function of consumer culture, with celebrities presented as images, surrendering to a mediatised view of personal intellectual performance which inhibits the production of collectively held knowledge and weakens public confidence in the profession.[27] The way in which the press approached *The Bondwoman's Narrative* exemplifies the process.[28] Gates embarked on a signing tour. The *Commercial Appeal*, Memphis, described him as scheduled 'to read from and sign his new book'; the *Seattle Times* managed to run a photo of Gates without mentioning the name of Hannah Crafts. Gates was big news in *The Rocky Mountain News*, the *Guardian* (a two-page spread), the *Scotsman*, the *Greensboro News and Record*, and the *Sunday Gazette-Mail* of Charleston, which juxtaposed the review with a piece speculating on the possibility of Gates leaving Harvard for Yale. Ironically this speculation was apparently prompted by an academic row in which Cornel West had been accused in the *New Republic* of turning himself into a celebrity.

Fairly obviously, as far as the market was concerned, the story was only of interest if Hannah was identified as a black ex-slave, and this is how the book was sold to readers. Its appeal depends absolutely on the 'fact' of its being authored by a black woman, and its readers are expected to value it according to the marginal and oppressed status of the author, her racial definition and the particularities of her life. The dominant question is 'Who was Hannah Crafts?' not 'What can this manuscript tell us about slavery?' or 'What literary value does this book have?' Paratextual traces – the blurb, back cover, inside cover, notes and title – are part of the marketing process. Gérard Genette has distinguished between paratexts according to the degree of control which the author exercises over these threshold textual phenomena: a title would be considered a *péritexte*, a back cover blurb would be an *épitexte*. In this case, of course, the author has no control over any of these features. If, as Wendy Waring argues,[29] the function of the back cover blurb is usually economic interpellation, its goal to induce readers to buy the book, to persuade them that the book speaks to them, this book is well served by its contributors: Maya Angelou ('we get the story from the woman's mouth itself') and five professors, all major authorities on slavery and its literature, three of them women, who compare the narrative to Morrison's *Paradise*, and invoke nineteenth-century women's literature and black culture. Just in case the reader were in any doubt that this was a book written by a black woman, the front flap of the hardback jacket describes the book as 'a genuine autobiographical novel by a female slave', highlighting Gates's exhaustive research and the fact that the work is 'unaltered and under its author's original title'.

Actually, on the front cover, the title is *The Bondwoman's Narrative. A Novel*, with the lettering in cursive script on the image of what appears to be a slightly ragged manuscript tied with coarse brown twine which continues over onto the back. Cut the string, however, open the book and release Hannah from her symbolic bondage, and the words '*A Novel*' disappear from the printed internal title page. Nor are they present in the reproduced image of the manuscript title page. The front of the hardback jacket features Hannah's name in smaller type than Gates's, though on the spine Hannah gets larger letters (though vertically) and Gates is in smaller type (though horizontally, and therefore readable by the browser). Take off the jacket (once you have bought the book) and Gates gets equal space on the spine. Those intent on getting the story from the woman's mouth will find that it begins only after 65 pages of scholarly introduction and is followed by almost a hundred pages of annotations, appendices and bibliography. As Benjamin Soskis commented 'Gates has, in a way, inherited the role of the white abolitionists whose introductory remarks assured the reading public as to the authenticity of slave testimony.'[30] The 'market reader' is contradictorily seduced, by a text which is offering very different things: a black woman's true story or a novel; a raw, unmediated narrative, or a work guaranteed by a reputed editor and authority. Cover designs set up an initial horizon of readerly expectations, mobilising a certain type of consumer. The 'market reader' will pick up the dominant message, that the work is written by a black woman; the academic reader is liable to be equally seduced by the various legitimating agents deployed.

Paratextual traces extend in this case into the virtual dimension. As well as the book, the website advertised an audio version (read by Anna Deavere Smith, with introduction by Gates) and a *Companion* available through XanEdu, an e-learning company. The website described the book as 'the oldest known work of fiction by a female slave'. No negative arguments were presented, with the exception of a comment by William L. Andrews that 'If, on the other hand, Hannah Crafts was white, *The Bondwoman's Narrative*, though an intriguing act of literary ventriloquism, does not compel attention and analysis except for specialists in nineteenth century American literature and history.'[31] The *Companion* website included critical essays, an interview with Gates, historical and legal material, a facsimile of the manuscript, photographs of manuscript features, maps of the Underground Railroad, multimedia and sound presentations, and period images of portraits, landscapes and sculpture. There were selections from slave narratives, plot summaries of each chapter of the novel, digitised versions of novels which probably influenced Hannah, information on the Wheeler family who are alluded to in the text (and the catalogue of Wheeler's library, to which Hannah may have had access). Rarely has an 'unedited' work been so swiftly processed and commodified. Hannah becomes the centrepiece of a huge collection of variously relevant documents and images, swamped in ancillary material, merely one more exhibit in a museum which is almost a minicurriculum for courses on slavery. The website added high-resolution photographs of Gates, instructions on how to schedule an interview and interviews with and photographs of Joe Nickell and Kenneth Rendell (the experts who established the probable date of the manuscript from analysis of the paper, handwriting style and ink). As a final bait to the academic: 'College instructors who adopt and use the *Educational Companion* for classes taught during the Fall 2002 semester can submit student essays from each class for consideration for the H.L. Gates, Jr. Scholarship for Research Excellence.' A committee selected by XanEdu was to judge the essays and award $2,000 towards the lucky winner's college education. As the site put it 'The Momentum Continues to Build', and those who registered would be emailed with details of further events. And there was the catch: to access this wealth of information and to keep your students' eyes on the prize, it was necessary to buy the *Educational Companion*, and adopt it for your course. Each copy of the book contains a numerical key, unique to that copy, which allows the purchaser of the slim volume (118 pages, consisting of five essays on the *Narrative* and a general overview of slave narratives) to register and gain access to online resources. At $15.00 (plus shipping) it was not beyond a salaried academic's budget, but most students would expect to use it in a library. Nor can the individual pass on the unique numerical key, as the website cautions that it is for individual use only. Every student who wants to access the site needs a number. This is very different from the *Archives of Slave Narratives* site at http://docsouth.unc.edu/neh/ which offers free access to any number of slave narratives, and will eventually have digitised some 200 texts, with commentary. Could the British inter-library loan service outwit the conglomerate? Yes; after a delay of three months and a fee of £8.00, it supplied access to both the *Companion* and the website. In essence, the prize may look like a well-meaning effort to concentrate students' minds on the various mysteries of the text, but it also functions to euphemise the more commercial aspects of this particular publishing operation. Hannah is sold to her readers as an American ex-slave, and as an opportunity to exercise benevolence towards one's students. Far from allowing a Utopian view of the internet (of peer-to-peer interactivity) there is no free exchange of data. You pay – or perhaps if you are a college instructor rather than a member of the general public, you invest in some cultural capital. Far from being a good companion, this volume is closer to those friends your parents and teachers warned you against.

But perhaps content is all. Whoever wrote the novel, it remains an interesting artefact. Authors and academics are not responsible for the publishing industry's marketing devices.[32] But why did nobody suggest that the author might be white? It is as if, in contemporary America, sensitised to any form of racial slur, this was literally unthinkable, comparable to the doubts poured upon nineteenth-century slave narratives by Southern pro-slavers. Surely the best compliment one can pay to Hannah Crafts is to treat her work with full intellectual rigour? And the case for her as a black writer remains unproven. Several factors made Gates conclude that this was an unedited manuscript written in an ex-slave's hand, which thus afforded the opportunity to analyse one slave's literacy and culture without the corrections of a white editor or printer. First, he argues that there was no advantage for a white in pretending to be black. (A dozen or so white writers did, however, and there could always be an artistic advantage or challenge, if not a commercial one.) Second, Hannah introduces characters first as people, only later as black. The norm is black. (But Harriet Beecher Stowe does just this for the whole of the first chapter of *Dred*, where Harry's identity as a black slave is not revealed until after he has been established as a character.) Third, the novel gives the houseslave's derogatory view of the fieldslaves (pp. 133, 203) without deodorising in the name of black unity or censoring honest reactions. (This may establish that the book is not targeted at an abolitionist reader, but can also be read as the author's internalisation of plantation hierarchies.) Fourth, there are real historical figures in the story, notably John Hill Wheeler, famous in 1855 when his slave Jane Johnson escaped from him in Philadelphia with the help of abolitionists, leading to a court case and considerable publicity. Wheeler, who held various political offices, had 25 slaves in 1850 and estates in North Carolina, much as Hannah describes. Crafts says that she was bought by him to replace an escaped slave called Jane. The problem with this argument is that the Jane Johnson case was well known, and almost anyone with a fair knowledge of slave history (or contact with Jane Johnson) would have been able to use this material. Moreover, it seems distinctly unlikely that a man who had just lost one slave and her two children in a fashion which established him as an abolitionist target would go right out and buy another. Wheeler replaced Jane with white servants in Philadelphia; in 1860 he had no slaves at all. Any white servant hired at this point would have known she was replacing a slave and that might well have suggested an assumed fictional identity as a slave.

The case for seeing Hannah as a white bondservant is therefore just as compelling as that for seeing her as a slave, and the intertextual features of the novel support this argument. Most of the literary influences are from the Brontë governess/schoolteacher novels, particularly *Jane Eyre* and *Villette* (the ghost story as cover for illicit lovers). The other major source, Dickens's *Bleak House*, also features a heroine (Esther) in a between-stairs position. Hannah is not just a house servant but an upstairs one, rarely seen below stairs. A snob, she is always positioned between her mistress and other slaves, and never gives any sense of the internal politics of a slave group. Indeed she hardly tells us anything of other slaves; her whole interest is in her mistress and to a lesser extent the soft furnishings. (She spends a lot of her time observing paintings and decor in an aspirational manner.) In addition, the lady doth protest too much. She makes a great deal of unnecessary justification of her closeness to her mistress (p. 150), because she anticipates the reader's doubts that she is a slave. She observes that Lizzy had a great memory for dates and names, unlike herself (p. 33), a handy note in a novel which clearly lacks the veracity of the slave narrative. Hannah is seen teaching children at the beginning and at the end, but has no children of her own, and never entertains the idea of marriage until the conventional happy ending, very much the position of the servant who delays marriage to hang on to economic security. When Charlotte's slave husband is detected in the house by night, Hannah wonders what he is doing there. Then she tells her mistress all about it. Would a slave do this, even with a kindly mistress? She describes Charlotte, a slave, as her superior, as if that were surprising (as it might be assumed to be if she were white). When offered the chance to escape with Charlotte and her husband, Hannah declines. Even more astonishingly, when her master is killed in an accident and there is no proof that Hannah is not free, she volunteers the information of her enslaved status. Essentially she then hangs about for some months, neither anyone's slave nor a servant. She describes her ambiguous situation: 'It would be a difficult matter to tell what station I filled … I was not considered a servant. Neither was I treated exactly as a guest' (p. 124). This is just the kind of between-stairs position that a governess, a nanny, or perhaps a superior lady's maid, would occupy. When Mrs Henry declines to keep her and suggests sale to the Wheelers, she hangs around some more (despite Charlotte's example), so that she can be enslaved anew. When she falls out with Mrs Wheeler following the gossip of a 'snaky' (p. 203) mulatto, she is worried that her reputation with her mistress has been 'blackened' (her term, p. 205). It is as if she feared dismissal without a character reference. The truth of her position is to be found in what Hannah's imagination unwittingly reveals in the unexceptional moments of her daily existence. In short, the deep structure of the novel, the unconscious evidence of Hannah's real life experience, is that of a servant not a slave, obsessed by her mistress, admiring of the great house, demarcating her territory as opposed to that of the slaves and with absolutely no sense of real solidarity with them. At the surface level of the text, the plot is so unlikely that it offers little evidence of any real life experience. After Gothic horrors and sentimental excesses it is not much of a surprise to learn that Hannah not only plays the harp but has brought it with her through all her adventures (p. 153). But at the subtextual and the intertextual level, as opposed to the paratextual and hypertextual, the novel reflects the experiences of an upstairs servant, not a slave.

Since its publication in 2002 the fanfare over the novel has muted slightly. A second volume of critical essays looked carefully at the evidence. None the less in the introduction the editors comment that

> Questions of Hannah Crafts's actual identity are put aside in most of the essays that follow. These scholars take it as a more or less settled matter that the author was a woman of African descent.[33]

William Andrews none the less argues that she was not a fugitive slave, though most likely to be African-American.[34] Robert Levine comments astutely that there are no real differences between reading the novel as the first novel by a former slave, or by a white abolitionist; the point of the novel is its entrapment of bookish readers 'who insist on working with essentialized racial categories in order to establish "authentic" identities'.[35] Gates also includes in the volume John Bloom's review, which challenged the assumption that Hannah was black, commenting that 'in this case we went from "uncertain that the work was written by a negro" to "first known novel written by an African American woman" in less than a year, and that includes the time the book was at the printer.'[36] None the less, as Bloom recognises, everyone wants Gates to find the evidence that proves that Hannah was black: 'you're rooting for him.'[37] Indeed the popularity of the novel remains high, and not just on college courses. In 2005, for example, the Indianapolis 'One Book, One City' award went to *The Bondwoman's Narrative*. The 2005 theme was 'The Spirit of America: Representing Some of America's Finest Hours, Darkest Hours, and Sometimes Both', and the story of 'a young North Carolina slave' triumphed easily over 155 other nominated titles.[38] Described on the city's website as 'a CSI mystery of the literary kind', the book was vigorously promoted. Indianapolis bought 3,000 copies to lend to its citizens, produced a 'Discussion Guide' to the novel for book groups, and envisaged the novel as a means to produce unity among city dwellers of different generations and backgrounds – a handy icebreaker with co-workers, a great conversation topic on the bus or plane, and a means to have 'that rare "real" talk with your teen'. If not quite such a global phenomenon as *Roots*, the novel was certainly following in its footsteps.

In the face of such instant commodification, what resistance is possible? One African-American novel engages directly with the issue, Zora Neale Hurston's prescient *Their Eyes Were Watching God*, first published in 1937. This may seem a surprising assertion to make about a novel which has been canonised almost to extinction. In 1990, analysing ways in which Hurston had been appropriated by later scholars, Michele Wallace asked the question: who owns Zora Neale Hurston? Wallace's pungent comparison of later critics to so many 'groupies descending on Elvis Presley's estate'[39] in their haste to turn Hurston to their own purposes strikes a cautionary note for any subsequent writer. As she notes, the risk of canonisation is that the work will be misused to derail the future of black women in literature and literary criticism. For Wallace, Harold Bloom's introduction to his *Modern Critical Views* anthology of 1986 is a case in point. Bloom prefaces a collection of African-Americanist and feminist essays with an introduction which essentially erases them; in which, ignoring race almost entirely, he concentrates on the novel as a story of sexual repression, compares Hurston's protagonist successively to Richardson's Clarissa, Dreiser's Carrie, Lawrence's Ursula, and finally moves from character to author to propose Hurston as The Wife of Bath. Writing anything further about Hurston must strike one as a dubious proposition, for if any one novel has been commodified and fully incorporated into the new canon of American literature it is *Their Eyes Were Watching God*. As Hazel Carby argues, the boom in Hurston studies, which has produced a snowstorm of books, papers and dissertations, ever since Alice Walker rediscovered her in the 1970s, is the result of a variety of factors: MLA support, the book trade, special courses on women's and on black writing, Afrocentric strategies of analysis, nostalgia for happy rural blacks (as opposed to inner-city violence), political activism of different types and the quest for literary ancestors.[40] Gloria Cronin observes, however, that amidst all this variety of motive, the criticism has none the less been largely dominated by one type of essay – reading the novel as a feminist triumph tale, unshaded by any less than affirmative vision of the heroine. 'Readings of the book have been overdetermined by feminist, multi-cultural and Africanist political imperatives of the last twenty years.'[41]

What has escaped attention in this debate is the degree to which Hurston herself focused on these very questions of ownership and appropriation in *Their Eyes Were Watching God*, in the backbone structure and plot of her novel, in the characterisation of the heroine's three lovers, in the frame tale and in such incidents as the 'mule story', Tea Cake's gambling activities and the rabid dog. *Their Eyes Were Watching God* brings cultural analyses together from very different locations, and represents a creative appropriation by a black woman of an anthropological discourse first analysed by a white Jewish male, Franz Boas, and associated with a Native American people – the discourse of gift exchange. Hurston studied with Boas, one of her principal mentors, whose major work *The Social Organisation and Secret Societies of the Kwakiutl Indians* concerned Kwakiutl 'potlatch', a form of gift exchange which became famous as the exemplification of the theory of conspicuous consumption advanced by Thorstein Veblen.[42] The Kwakiutl had a variety of gift-giving ceremonies involving the giving away of quantities of possessions or their wilful destruction. A man might destroy or disperse all his worldly goods in an attempt to maintain status or to eclipse a rival. While in theory the gift was spontaneous, in practice it was based on political or economic self-interest: the gift of property implies an obligation on the recipient – which, if not fulfilled, results in loss of face. The 'Indian giver' gives in order to establish credit, since the recipient must return the gift at a future time, with interest. The destroyer forces his rivals to destroy in their turn. As a cultural form, therefore, potlatch prevents any one individual from monopolising material goods, prevents the build up of economic surpluses and subtly maintains social order. Potlatch is none the less fundamentally aggressive (described by the Kwakiutl as 'fighting with property'). Originally potlatch meant 'to nourish' or 'to consume', and it has been seen as a sublimation of cannibal rites.[43] Gift exchange as aggression is of course a cultural phenomenon as old as the War of Troy. The idea of the fatal gift (for example the Rheingold, Scott Fitzgerald's 'The Cut-Glass Bowl') survives even in etymology. As Marcel Mauss noted, the semantic history of the German word 'Gift' contains the idea of the present or possession that turns to poison. 'Gift' in German now means poison. Modern survivals of gift exchange include gambling, which is commonly considered not as contractual but as involving honour and the surrender of property, even when it is not absolutely necessary to do so; philanthropic giving (for example the rivalry and competition of a pledge dinner); and intellectual property, where the donor retains an interest in the object given. (Artistic ownership is often considered to survive beyond the sale of the actual work of art.) Academics preserve gift exchange in the form of the scholarly offprint.

As a collector of folk material, over which proprietary rights remained with her patron, Mrs Rufus Osgood Mason, Zora Neale Hurston was intensely aware of the ambiguous nature of such ownership. Indeed her relationship with her patrons – those who gave her gifts – was clearly an uneasy one, as more than one critic has noted. Robert Hemenway sums it up: 'What Hurston possessed during the Renaissance decade was a career in patronage.'[44] Essentially Hurston had major financial support from three white women (Annie Nathan Meyer, Fannie Hurst and Mrs Mason) beginning in 1925 and spanning the years while she graduated from Barnard and conducted fieldwork in African-American folk culture. She met Mrs Mason in 1927 and signed a contract for $200 a month, a motion-picture camera and a car, in order to collect folklore in the South for two years. The folklore collected was to be Mrs Mason's property. Mrs Mason finally cut off funds in September 1932, having reduced the stipend by half in 1931. Hemenway notes that Hurston was unable to write creatively while under the influence of personal patronage, and suggests that 'Hurston sensed, later in the patronage period, that something about the gift-giving had inhibited her talent.'[45] Mrs Mason gave Hurston the money to carry out her work, but in return she had to give back to a white donor (and culture) the materials of her own people. Instead of beginning studies in general ethnology in 1935 Hurston used the time to write her novel. In *Their Eyes Were Watching God* she gives without being passive, placing those who 'take' (the readers) under obligation to repay, in what amounts to a meta-anthropology, turning the anthropologist's tools on himself.

How does this work? As Sherley Anne Williams has noted, by the end of the novel, 'Janie has come *down*, that paradoxical place in Afro-American literature that is both a physical bottom and the setting for the character's attainment of a penultimate self knowledge.'[46] In outline the story is that of a woman who swaps status and prestige of an empty material kind (running a store as the wife of the town mayor) for erotic happiness 'on the muck', picking beans in a booming farming area of Florida, at her lover's side. From an initial loveless marriage, arranged by a grandmother (Nanny) whose sole motivation is to preserve Janie from being like other African-American women ('De nigger woman is de mule uh de world'[47]) Janie becomes a field labourer, a participant in a world which originally seemed beneath her, willingly working at her man's side and finally at one with her community. As Williams argues, the differences between the image of the mule and its final reversal are obvious. On the muck, Janie is working only in name; she converts hard toil into play. Tea Cake has asked, not ordered:

> his request stems from a desire to be with Janie, to share every aspect of his life with her, rather than from a desire to coerce her into some mindless submission. It isn't the white man's burden that Janie carries; it is the gift of her own love (p. 297).

One might wonder, however, how this romantic vision squares with the Tea Cake who steals Janie's money and spends it on a party; beats her; and attempts, in a rabid frenzy, to kill her. Williams's unconscious use of the term 'gift' is telling. In Hurston's world the gift is always also a threat, a potential act of aggression, and the structure of her novel draws out all the tragic ambiguities involved in the safeguarding – and the voluntary loss – of prestige.

Janie's story (profoundly economic in emphasis, as Houston Baker has argued) focuses on three representative husbands. The first, Logan Killicks, is selected by Nanny, purely in order to safeguard the budding Janie's honour and security. As Baker comments, Nanny's history under slavery dictates her strategic manoeuvres in the wars of property and propriety. 'Having been denied a say in her own fate because she was property, she assumes that only property enables expression.'[48] The African-American community bear silent witness to their own awareness that Janie has been *given* in marriage, rather than choosing her own fate. Nobody gives any wedding gifts to the couple (p. 39) and they depart empty-handed from the feast. By not giving presents, the community demonstrate solidarity with Janie and a fundamental distrust of her commodification as a bride. To Janie's protests that she wanted a husband to love and to be loved by, Nanny can argue only that she should be glad of the organ in his parlour, his house and his 60 acres. Nanny assumes that Janie is hankering after 'some dressed-up dude dat got to look at de sole of his shoe everytime he cross de street tuh see if he got enough leather dere tuh make it across' (p. 42). For Nanny, Janie's property is much more important than her feelings, as assuring her status and security. 'You can buy and sell such as dem wid what you got. In fact you can buy 'em and give 'em away' (p. 42). In the mouth of an ex-slave, the comment on the commodification of a person as property to be bought or disposed of at will is particularly chilling. It takes Janie only a short while to realise that Killicks has given her nothing, as her final words to him reveal. 'You ain't done me no favor by marryin' me. And if dat's what you call yo'self doin', Ah don't thank yuh for it' (p. 53).

In contrast, Janie's second husband, Joe 'Jody' Starks, apparently establishes at the outset that she is a gift all in herself, and recognises the fact by showering her with presents: 'he bought her the best things the butcher had, like apples and a glass lantern full of candies' (p. 56). Yet as his dealings with the townspeople reveal, Joe Starks gives only to establish credit and 'take'. Eatonville has been founded as a town by the gift of land from Captain Eaton, a gift which Starks derides as far too small in size to assure economic prosperity. By buying 200 acres from Eaton, Starks 'gives' the people of Eatonville a town – though it is a town which they then buy from him with their own money. To celebrate the town's foundation he offers a 'treat' of crackers and cheese, followed by a barbecue. (They provide most of the food.) He uses their labour to cut drains and streets, and establishes Janie as a conspicuous object of display, dressed up to the nines in his store. Whenever Joe gives, it is for the purpose of assuring his own prestige and status, and ultimately seeing the gift come back tenfold. In the famous mule story, for example, Joe establishes his prestige by the destruction of property. He buys Matt Bonner's bony, cussed yellow mule for five dollars, to Matt's astonished delight. Joe, however, humiliates Bonner by destroying the mule as an object of economic value. He sets it free.

> 'Beatyuh tradin' dat time, Starks! Dat mule is liable tuh be dead befo' de week is out. You won't git no work outa him.' 'Didn't buy 'im fuh no work. I god, Ah bought dat varmint tuh let 'im rest. You didn't have gumption enough tuh do it' (p. 91).

While Starks gains the respect of the townspeople Janie, sensing the potential parallel between woman and mule, is more pointed in her comments

> 'Freein' dat mule makes uh mighty big man outa you. Something like George Washington and Lincoln. Abraham Lincoln, he had de whole United States to rule so he freed de Negroes. You got a town so you freed a mule' (p. 92).

In a capitalist economy, freedom becomes an ambiguous gift. Just as the original gift of land for the town was too small to assure its prosperity, so the gift of freedom without economic equality becomes ambivalent. Like the vultures later seen feeding on the mule's carcass, like Starks feeding off the townspeople, the gift lays obligations on the recipient and nourishes the giver. Janie is displayed by Starks as a 'lady' – just as he displays the retired mule. Above all, Jody's gifts – like the salt pork he apparently donates to Mrs Tony – are carefully calibrated. After Mrs Tony has begged for a piece of meat for her starving children, after she has poured scorn on the tiny piece which he cuts for her and flounced out of the store, Starks comes back to his seat on the porch, after a moment's pause. 'He had to stop and add the meat to Tony's account' (p. 116). Mrs Tony has shamed her husband by accepting the gift; Starks has maintained his own prestige at no cost whatsoever. As Houston Baker argues, Starks is intent on imitating the economics of Anglo-America.[49] He clearly represents an aggressive, white-identified capitalism, consuming Janie. As textual evidence makes explicit, Hurston evidently understood the dynamics of the relationship in terms of gift exchange. When Starks slaps Janie (over a ruined dinner) the text in manuscript reads 'she began to fold in on herself and to take without giving'.[50] Janie has become emotionally dead. When she retaliates, destroying Joe with an emasculatory insult, she realises that the fatal blow has been to separate the man from his possessions. 'When he paraded his possessions hereafter, they would not consider the two together. They'd look with envy at the things and pity the man that owned them' (p. 123). When Joe sickens (kidney disease) the rumour immediately runs that Janie is responsible. Poison is suspected. The accusation is symbolically appropriate. As the only person to see through his gifts, Janie has understood how gifts can turn to poison, property to a source of pity and danger. Meanwhile the townspeople bring gifts of broth and sick-room dishes to replace Janie's suspect cooking. They nourish Starks without recognising the extent to which he has made them consumers and consumed them. When Joe dies, the system lives on. He is replaced by Hezekiah, seen refusing credit with the ringing phrase, 'dis ain't Gimme, Florida, dis is Eatonville' (p. 142). But in a sense the town is 'Gimme, Florida', founded on and entrapped within the economics of the gift.

In contrast Tea Cake appears to be a subtler manipulator of gift exchange. From the beginning of their relationship Tea Cake is established as a games player prepared to take Janie's king at checkers (p. 147), a taker on equal terms with her. For the townspeople his gifts to her are motivated by the inheritance which she possesses from Joe. 'Dey figger he's spendin' on her now in order tuh make her spend on him later' (p. 168). The community, for whom an older woman can only lose prestige when in erotic association with a younger man, foresee a fate for Janie similar to that of Annie Tyler, who lost her pride and all she possessed to her younger lover, Who Flung (p. 179). Although Janie may argue that 'Dis ain't no business proposition, and no race after property and titles. Dis is uh love game' (p. 171), the reader may feel similarly uneasy when the pair marry and Tea Cake promptly disappears with the $200 which Janie had secretly pinned inside her shirt. Janie has imbibed enough of Joe Starks's views to conceal the existence of the cash from Tea Cake, as well as the $1,200 which she has in the bank. In order to demonstrate his lack of interest in material things, Tea Cake takes Janie's money and gambles it away, in the context of a stupendous feast, a ritual destruction of property. At the feast he gives ugly women money to stay away, a form of gift giving which destroys female status. Janie is also excluded. Ostensibly Tea Cake is motivated by his perception of the crowd at the party as of a lower class to Janie's. 'Dem wuzn't no high muckty mucks' (p. 186). In reality he uses her money to teach Janie her place in his community, destroying her assumed class prestige in the process. Appropriately, Tea Cake gets the money back – with interest – in the course of gambling. He is careful to let the losers have a chance to win back their losses – etiquette even today in gambling. The men grumble, but, with one exception, agree that the game was fair. But the aggression just below the surface culminates none the less in a furious fight, in which Tea Cake gets knifed. Tea Cake's involvement with money is as dangerous to him as it was to Joe Starks.

On the surface it may appear that Tea Cake is able to provide Janie with a better place in a more authentic, less money-driven world than Joe Starks, offering her an open, giving form of love and treating her as an equal. Indeed the workers on the muck are distinguished by the celebratory nature of their existence, replete with parties, dances, games and music, without apparent reference to the world of commerce. 'They made good money ... So they spent good money. Next month and next year were other times' (p. 197). When one woman does attempt to establish her own separate prestige (based on intracommunity colorism), arguing that she and Janie, both 'light-skinned', should 'class off' from the darker members of the race (p. 210), Janie is unpersuaded by Mrs Turner's arguments. 'Us can't do it. We're uh mingled people and all of us got black kinfolks as well as yaller kinfolks' (p. 210). Mrs Turner pays no attention to her protests. She is quite content to live off the workers' money (profits from her restaurant business) while deriding them in private. (She consumes as she apparently nourishes.) Tea Cake promptly takes a hand, arranging to 'rescue' Mrs Turner from a disturbance in her restaurant. While loudly proclaiming that Mrs Turner deserves respect, Tea Cake succeeds in orchestrating a riot which entirely destroys all her property. To add insult to injury, the prime movers appear the next day and make Mrs Turner a ceremonial present of $5 apiece.

Yet for all his apparent open-handedness, his lack of interest in prestige on white terms and his ability to function on a footing of equality with Janie, Tea Cake is still mired in the world of money. The process of destruction of property culminates when the idyll on 'de muck' terminates in a hurricane which lays waste the whole area. The hurricane functions as a great leveller, reducing animals and men to one common society. In their flight Tea Cake and Janie pass a dead man entirely surrounded by snakes and other animals. 'Common danger made common friends. Nothing sought a conquest over the other' (p. 243). Significantly, given the gift exchange motif, Tea Cake's tragic mistake had been to ignore Indian folk knowledge. He discounts the warnings of the local Seminoles that there is a hurricane on the way, in the first place because they are not property-owners ('Indians don't know much uh nothin' ... Else they'd own this country still', p. 231), and second because of the lure of money. 'Beans running fine and prices good, so the Indians could be, *must* be wrong. You couldn't have a hurricane when you're making seven and eight dollars a day picking beans' (p. 229). As the dyke bursts, he sees his error:

> he saw that the wind and water had *given* life to lots of things that folks think of as dead and *given* death to so much that had been living things (p. 236, my emphasis).

The gift comes also to Tea Cake, and is fatal. Tea Cake's death by rabies offers a horrendously appropriate image of the consumption of the human being, his identity eaten away by the saliva of the rabid animal until he can no longer consume, eat or drink. The image of contagion by saliva is significant. Nanny arranged Janie's marriage so that she would not become 'a spit cup' (p. 37) to others. Starks provided her with a luxury spit cup, painted with sprigs of flowers, but a spit cup none the less. Tea Cake becomes the cup himself, catching the disease from canine spit. Rabies appears to present the spectacle of a man turning into a dog, becoming possessed by the animal, until he snarls and bites – just as in totemic possession. It is as if the totemic animal is eating the man. In addition Tea Cake's paranoid jealousy when rabid transforms him into a mirror image of Jody, the arch-capitalist, devotee of consumer exploitation and finally himself consumed. More specifically (and an answer perhaps to critics such as Peter Messent who have found the mad dog plot melodramatic and forced[51]) rabies associates Tea Cake with the Kwakiutl cannibal dance in which the initiate bites a piece of flesh from an enemy's arm, identifying with the totemic animal. Tea Cake's last action, falling from Janie's bullet, is to sink his teeth in her arm. The position of the snarling dog, standing on a cow's back, above the floodwaters heaving with fish, snakes and people, recalls the animal hierarchy of the totem. Kwakiutl totems often depict animals biting a 'copper'. As the imagery suggests, gift exchange thus goes some way to account for the difficulties posed for modern critics by the character of Tea Cake. Tea Cake's last gift to Janie was a packet of garden seeds. She gives away all their other possessions, keeping only the seeds to plant back home, for a living remembrance. Tea Cake remains a giver, seeding the future with a promise of growth, rather than leaving a legacy of material objects. But Tea Cake is also a warning to the future, his fate admonitory. As the gift exchange structure demonstrates, Hurston did take account of an Indian warning, not least in the fashion in which she frames her tale.

At the close of the tale, prestige and hierarchy are reasserted. The black victims of the hurricane are tipped into a mass grave, carefully sorted from the whites, for whom all the coffins are reserved. Janie's love-affair with Tea Cake has been underwritten by the store and she can go home again. As Baker comments, Janie's freedom with Tea Cake was enabled by Starks's property. 'Her position derives from the petit bourgeois enterprises she has shared with her deceased husband.'[52] For Baker, therefore, *Their Eyes Were Watching God* is, ultimately, a novel that inscribes, in its very form, the mercantile economics that conditioned a "commercial deportation"'.[53] The comment, however, applies at best only to Janie's story and not to Hurston's. In Janie, Hurston focuses upon the possibility that her own work (fiction, folklore, anthropology) could allow others to 'buy safely into' African-American culture, to appropriate and own its material without considering the fundamental institutional and economic structures which inscribe it as valuable material, rather than as ongoing, living process. If the themes of the novel underline the dangers of the donor-as-taker, the frame of the story is equally strategic. The story is framed by a gift – Pheoby's nourishing (and appropriately creole) dish of mulatto rice, a sly, ambivalent gift which makes reference to Janie's white blood. It is in return for this gift that Janie tells her story. The process of storytelling, the manner and occasion of the story's delivery, is as significant as the content. Hurston goes to some lengths to underline the nature of the storytelling as a form of gift exchange. When Pheoby offers the gift, Janie is swift to underline the impossibility of repaying in terms of material exchange. 'You must think Ah brought yuh somethin'. When Ah ain't brought home a thing but mahself' (p. 14). Pheoby's comment, 'Dat's a gracious plenty', is met by teasing denigration of the gift of food, 'Ain't you never goin' tuh gimme dat lil rations you brought me? … Give it here and have a seat' (p. 15), followed, once the plate has been well and truly cleaned, by the instruction to 'take yo' ole plate. Ah ain't got a bit of use for a empty dish' (p. 15). In the distance the people of the community remain on the porch, clearly discussing Janie's return as if *she* were a meal to be feasted upon. 'Ah reckon they got me up in they mouth now' (p. 16). Janie refuses to satisfy their appetite for her story directly, on the grounds that they will not understand. They are 'puttin' they mouf on things they don't know nothin' about', and 'so long as they get a name to gnaw on they don't care whose it is, and what about, 'specially if they can make it sound like evil' (p. 17). Instead, to avoid her gift becoming poison, she tells the story to Pheoby on the grounds that when the latter repeats it, it will remain Janie's story. 'You can tell 'em what Ah say if you wants to. Dat's just de same as me 'cause mah tongue is in mah friend's mouf' (p. 17). As she tells Pheoby, 'you got tuh *go* there to *know* there' (p. 285). A story is not simply transferable from one teller to another, context-free, like an object in a collection of folklore. It needs a reader with understanding, knowledge of its meanings. Janie warns Pheoby that 'tain't no use in me telling you somethin' unless Ah *give* you de understandin' to go long wid it' (p. 19, my emphasis). And what she gives is an awareness of the nature of the donor relation. Hurston's story is designed both to nourish the folk and to liberate it from the property wars of capitalism. The exchange between Pheoby and Janie establishes the story as a gift – but a gift which lays obligations on both the black community and the reader. The frame tale transforms the gift into a moral transaction, maintaining human relationships rather than exchange relations, and preventing the transformation of authenticity into a marketable product. Folk elements in the novel – verbal contests, the buzzards dancing a call-and-response over the mule's carcass, folktales and games – are carefully positioned inside a frame which establishes the importance of context and highlights folk culture as a dynamic relation and process rather than a reified object. By employing African-American, Native American and white (Jewish) sources, Hurston provides the reader with a very creole rice indeed. In its implicitly hybrid form *Their Eyes Were Watching God* defends a 'mingled' culture as against essentialist 'authenticity'.

In a postcolonial context Trinh T. Minh-ha has remarked on the dangers posed by authenticity as opposed to hybridity.[54] Just as anthropologists want to study 'primitive' (non-state, non-class) societies, so the Third World representative whom the modern, sophisticated public ideally seeks is the 'unspoiled' original African or Asian, thus remaining preoccupied with the image of the 'real' native, the truly different, rather than with issues of economic hegemony, racism, feminism and social change. Similarly, in the African-American context there is a risk that 'authenticity' becomes a product to be marketed, bought and sold, displayed in a museum or on an academic's bookshelves. Anachronistically Hurston had recognised the possibility of functioning as an 'otherness machine manufacturing alterity for the postmodern trade in difference'.[55] Janie only 'goes folk' once she has made her money, rather as a modern-day millionaire may choose to collect art objects from the oppressed past of his ancestors. But her story is framed and structured in such a way as to prevent the reader functioning in any naïve fashion as a mere consumer of another culture. Hurston has too easily been celebrated in 'folksy' terms, even though the novel includes within it a clear example of the ways in which folk material can be exploited. When Matt Bonner's yellow mule finally dies, Joe Starks participates with all the townspeople in a grand 'dragging out' celebration, from which only Janie is excluded. Eulogies are spoken over the carcass, matching the exuberant tales featuring the mule as hero which have entertained the porch sitters for months. As mayor, Joe milks the folksy occasion for all it is worth, and his eulogy on the mule as a great departed citizen contributes to his own popularity and makes him 'more solid than building the schoolhouse had done' (p. 95). Joe feeds on the mule and on the folksiness of the occasion as much as any baby-kissing politician at an election picnic. When the townspeople leave for home, they are followed in Hurston's account by equally ritualistic buzzards, who wait decorously for the signal from *their* leader ('the parson') before 'picking out the eyes in the ceremonial way' (p. 97). Rather than telling a folk story, Hurston tells a global story, African-, Jewish- and Native-American in its direct challenge to appropriation and commodification. Restoring the international and cosmopolitan nature of this novel reminds us that it is possible for a novel to be both specifically local (authentic in terms of the folk) and globally significant. An increased awareness of the novel's insistent language of commodity and exchange implicitly combats romanticised readings of it as a feminist triumph tale. Triumphalism has itself been located within a dubious rhetoric of status. As a result, *Their Eyes Were Watching God*, a creole mixture drawing syncretically upon the cultural work of White-, Jewish-, African- and Native-American, constitutes a literary gift which makes the nature of cultural appropriation problematic.

4 Local life, global death
David Bradley's surrogate stories

Where Bharati Mukherjee creates an Indian ancestor for an American canonical heroine, or Octavia Butler sends a surrogate mother back to birth her foremother, John Washington, the hero of David Bradley's *The Chaneysville Incident* goes one better: he claims that his ancestors are not actually dead. In one of several Melvillean digressions, John firmly rejects an economic approach to the trade in slaves. According to his apparently fantastic logic, historians may have argued that the trade was 'something to do with economics, or with greed, or with lust', with its effects seen in shifts in the worldwide balance of power, the development of the British Industrial Revolution, or the growth of the European cultural tradition, but all were wrong in one respect: their agreement that however long-lived its effects, the trade itself is at an end.[1] To think otherwise involves

> dealing with something so basic, so elemental, so fundamental that it can be faced only if one is forced to face it: death. For that is what the Slave Trade was all about. Not death from poxes and musketry and whippings and malnutrition and melancholy and suicide; death itself. For before the white men came to Guinea to strip-mine field hands for the greater glory of God, King, and the Royal Africa Company, black people did not die (p. 208).

In African belief systems, according to John's analysis (amply supported by anthropological scholarship), ancestors do not die; they merely take up residence elsewhere. Even when the enslaved accepted Christianity, the deceased may have 'gone home to Guinea' (p. 211) or 'passed away', 'but never died' (p. 213). Christianity emphasises death as final; African belief systems do not. John argues that, as a result, African-Americans are caught between European knowledge and African belief.

For if European knowledge is true, then death is cold and final, and one set of our ancestors had their very existence whipped and chained and raped and starved away, while the other set ... forever burns in hell for having done it to them. And if the African belief is true, then somewhere here with us, in the very air we breathe, all that whipping and chaining and raping and starving and branding and maiming and castrating and lynching and murdering – all of it – is still going on (p. 213).

In *The Chaneysville Incident* the haunting sound of fugitive slaves in 1859, panting as they run for their lives, is a recurrent motif, dramatising their continued closeness to the narrator in 1979. Bradley, however, is not primarily arguing for the primacy of African belief systems over European, or redirecting the reader back to 'folk' or oral knowledge, as opposed to Western rationalism, as some critics have argued.[2] The primary charge of the novel is to engage with the relation of slavery to modernity, particularly figured in communication systems and in the relation of local to global. As the novel opens, a sound rings in the narrator's ears, a telephone call summoning him home to the deathbed of a surrogate father, Old Jack. The description merges the modern telephone with the 'call' from the fugitive slaves: the wire, freighted with 'the phantom sounds of someone else's conversation', is described as 'whining, crying, panting, humming, moaning like a live thing' (p. 1). Though John's mother, Yvette, has made the modern call, the opening suggests an African-American traditional 'call', to which the novel is in large measure the 'response'. Initially John's response is terse; he is estranged from his mother. When his girlfriend Judith appears, his account of the telephone call takes the form of a sizeable digression, entirely couched in terms of the history of modern communication systems. 'The telephone is popularly believed to have been invented' (p. 2), he begins, rehearsing its technological history (from Alexander Graham Bell to the invention by Almon B. Strowger, a Kansas undertaker, of the electromechanical selector switch) to deflect her from probing questions. John uses a discourse on modern communicativity to avoid actually communicating. For good measure he adds an account of the corporate development of unified telephone systems, by nationalisation in England, by a licensed monopoly in America, following up with a lengthy dissertation on the relationship of American communications systems (air, rail and bus) to economics, to demonstrate the classed nature of American society, in a lecture which segues into his account of the local history of his home town (recognisably Bedford, Pennsylvania, close to the Mason-Dixon line) as he travels there by Greyhound. Bedford clearly subordinates the memory of death to modern communications. The Town Square, 'the political heart of the town' (p. 169), was formerly presided over by a granite soldier on a monument; now it has been displaced to one side in favour of a traffic light.

Although giving a lecture (even to himself) is something John obviously does to avoid confronting his own emotions, 12 pages essentially devoted to historical and socio-economic analysis are something of a challenge for all but the most Melvillean admirer of the digression. Information functions here as surrogation, a substitute for feeling and action. In little, this deflection of the reader from imaginative narrative to essayistic prose is typical of the overall strategy of Bradley's novel – in which a variety of digressions stand in for the central subject. Getting to the core of the story is exceptionally problematic. Readers make their way through garbled or misleading communications in order to reach the one that really matters. To return to the opening metaphor of this book, it is as if the ball were deliberately fouled as it was passed across the field. Bradley has stated that the inspiration for the novel came to him from his mother's account of the 'Chaneysville Incident' in the local history which she co-wrote to celebrate the bicentennial of Bedford County.

> On the Lester Imes farm below Chaneysville one can still find the markers for twelve or thirteen graves of runaway slaves. Mr Imes relates that when the slaves realised that their pursuers were closing in on them they begged to be killed rather than go back to the Southland and more servitude. Someone obliged.[3]

In the novel, John realises that his ancestor, C.K., a conductor on the Underground Railroad, had died by his own hand with these slaves, and that the eccentric behaviour of his father, Moses, and his death in his turn at Chaneysville, was explained by his knowledge of C.K., on whom he had modelled himself. At the close of the novel John and Judith locate the graves, and John imagines the group back into life, to construct an account of their last hours. This is not, however, a straightforward fictional recovery of an episode of African-American history. Before any reference is made to the location of the slaves' deaths there is an account of a completely different incident at Chaneysville, a lynching in the 1930s, which the floundering reader may well take to be 'the' Chaneysville Incident of the title. The central incident is first surrogated, before being fully performed at the close in John's oral narration to Judith. Before John can reach the truth about the slaves, he has to engage with a substitute tale of the near lynching of Josh, narrated by Jack. Jack, as a surrogate father, stands in for the dead Moses, just as Moses has taken the place of C.K. In the background stands the shadowy presence of Bill, John's brother, dead in Vietnam, and a glaring absence. In narrating the story of the slaves John is also narrating a surrogate story covering the death of Bill, in a novel which moves towards its final resolution through a whole series of rehearsals and surrogates. The point is that miscommunication, the wrong story, precedes the delivery of the right story; modern communication governed by economics and politics has to be replaced by local, imaginative tale-telling. Modern communication networks, constrained by class, are replaced by an older communication network, designed for liberty, in the Underground Railroad.

At the centre of the novel, controlling its action, lies a racialised death metaphor. Bradley draws upon a close association between modernity and the changed relation of the living to the dead. In his wide-ranging anthropological commentary, *Dancing on the Grave*, Nigel Barley notes that differences in burial practices relate to differences in social organisation: 'the placing of the dead is never arbitrary. It is a clear act of classification and a statement of where they belong.'[4] In Europe the decline of the notion of purgatory after the Reformation encouraged an increasing separation of the living from the dead, and a new sense that the living (on this side) could no longer affect the dead (on the other). Importantly Barley also notes the ubiquity in African belief systems of the notion of death as not part of the original state of affairs, but in some ways a later development, the result of a garbled story or a miscommunication between gods and men. Telling the wrong story is the source of death. As Barley points out, it is now fashionable to see death as intimately linked to the faults that occur in the copying of DNA in cell reproduction. But this is merely 'a reworking of an old motif – the message that failed. In Africa, death is often the result of a garbled and misdirected message.'[5] In East Africa, for example, the hare is the intermediary who gets things wrong and so man ends up dying, in West Africa, the chameleon; the wrong story gets in the way of the delivery of an original 'right' story, in which death is not final. As will become apparent, Bradley's novel sets out to reverse the process, taking the reader back through 'wrong' modern communications to the 'right' story, which will annul the mortality engendered by modernity.

In American terms, Joseph Roach offers the fullest discussion of the relation of death to modernity and to race. For Roach, modernity may be understood as involving the segregation of the dead from the living, in his particular examples of the New Orleans 'Cities of the Dead' (cemeteries). Modernity is understood as a new way of thinking about and handling the dead. Formerly the dead (black or white) were perceived as omnipresent, their spirits hovering near to their descendants, and their bodies hard by in the churchyard, itself a social space where meetings and markets took place. By the eighteenth century, however, Western burials were no longer taking place in the churchyard, but outside its wall, in specified locations. As a result the formerly gregarious dead were relegated to a separate sphere, expected to retire from the space of the living to isolated cemeteries, to be remembered by monuments rather than by the invocation of spirits. The separation in modernity coincides with the racial separation of white free from enslaved black, the condition of the latter memorably described as a state of 'social death'. [6] In Orlando Patterson's argument, slavery is conceived as a substitute or surrogate for violent death, with execution suspended as long as the slave acquiesces in powerlessness. Because the master has 'ransomed' the slave, buying his life, the slave has no socially recognised existence beyond his master, and is a socially dead person, alienated from claims of rights. Just as the particular horror of slavery is that it is conceived as a kind of living death, so there develops the treatment of the dead as a race apart. Roach makes the point that the belief in continuous dynamic, intimate communication with ancestors may appear strange to Western modernity, but in world-historical terms is entirely normal. In the circum-Atlantic world since the late seventeenth century 'the peculiarity of the development of European memory with regard to ancestral spirits is conspicuous'. [7] The concept of a circum-Atlantic world insists upon the centrality of the diasporic and genocidal histories of Africa and the Americas, North and South, in the creation of the culture of modernity. Drawing on Paul Gilroy's formulation of the 'Black Atlantic' Roach focuses upon the interculture created by the peoples of the Atlantic rim, to argue that the scope of that interculture is most visible in its performances, which carry within them the memory of forgotten substitutions. Two related concepts are central to the argument: the effigy and surrogation. The effigy 'fills by surrogation a vacancy created by the absence of the original'; not merely as a wooden or cloth effigy may replace a corpse, but in the sense of fleshly effigies, made by performance. [8] Performed effigies include the obvious (actors, priests, celebrities) but also, and especially, corpses. Celebrations of death function as rites of social renewal, as the community, affected by a strong sense of affiliation, holds open a place for a successor. When actual (or perceived) vacuums occur in the social fabric, survivors swiftly fit in an alternative, often making several attempts to get the fit right. A loss therefore triggers a doomed search for originals, by the continuous auditioning of stand-ins. Performances carry the memory of otherwise forgotten substitutions, as they propose candidates for the succession.

Roach's thesis informs readings of minstrelsy, of revolutionary Americans impersonating Indian 'braves', and of the various impersonations of the New Orleans Mardi Gras, and appeared some 15 years after Bradley's novel. Its major concern is with impersonation of the Other carried out in order to empty the Other of threatening power, rather than with sympathetic auditioning. None the less it is intensely suggestive in relation to *The Chaneysville Incident,* a novel profoundly engaged in theme and narrative strategies with the ambiguous relation to modernity. John's return to his surrogate father's deathbed, his restoration of his brother's place in the community, and his negotiations with Judge Scott, the executor of his father's will, take place in a narrative which organises itself around a staged series of funerals, and focuses upon an oral performance of story, which subtly renegotiates the relations of the living and the dead. John has suffered a complete separation from his brother Bill, buried subtextually in the novel and only slowly exhumed, a figure whose absence is initially figured as other absences, part of a series of ancestral losses. John has been elected as his father's successor, inheriting his father's research materials and re-enacting his father's quest, moving back through Moses and Jack to the dead of the Chaneysville incident, as communication is re-established. When John returns to Bedford, called by Jack, he also claims his inheritance from the executor. As Carroll Smith-Rosenberg notes, the term surrogate is also used in some American states for the court officer given jurisdiction over the estates of the deceased.[9] A surrogate stands in for or replaces a lost or absent other, as an officially appointed successor or deputy, a person given authority to represent the lost and to exercise his rights. John is in a process of moving back to re-establish contact with the dead through a series of surrogates, restoring Bill from a white effigy to a place in African-American memory, claiming the inheritance, and finally recreating a past in which (in the final graveyard) black and white are buried together.

In the opening pages of the novel, the black corpse is concealed, a subtextual presence beneath a lecture on modern history. In this sequence John treats the reader to a short account of the history of Bedford, from the arrival of the Thomas Powell expedition in 1625, through the establishment of a settlement in 1751, the mustering of a force to attack the Indians in 1757, the War of Independence, the Whiskey Rebellion 1791–4, the Mexican and Civil Wars, and nineteenth-century prosperity based upon the Mineral Springs and Buchanan's Summer White House.[10] The alert reader, however, will recognise a subtext. In 1757 the plan to do battle with the Indians is dropped ('for lack of funding', p. 10). In 1758 100 'Provincial' soldiers are mustered, but 100 are reported 'down with the flux' (p. 11) and therefore *hors de combat*. In the War of Independence 300 men are mustered locally, but the local gunsmith has only been asked to make 25 muskets and is behind schedule. Antipathetic to the government troops during the Whiskey Rebellion, the locals fail to react to the presence of Washington, lodged in the Espy House. While heroism is somewhat more apparent in Mexico at the storming of Chapultepec, 30 of the 80 volunteers are detailed on other duties, and John salutes the 'discretion' (p. 12) of those who survived. After this it is no surprise to learn that county participation in the Civil War was 'somewhat ambiguous' (p. 12). The history which John rehearses returns obsessively to the fact that sensible men do not fight in wars, that the heroic dead of Bedford County are fairly few and far between. The exception is of course his brother Bill, who was unable to follow their example. The Espy House later became the office of the local draft board, which sent Bill to Vietnam. His is the corpse subtextually buried beneath the public discourse; he is the dead man separated from the living by modernity.

In essence, therefore, John's apparently factual, objective history has a deeply personal subtext. In their youth the two brothers had fantasised about foreign travel, Bill's imagination flying off to Paris, Hong Kong and Tokyo, while John, a more plodding fantasist, struggled to imagine getting out of the state: 'he flying from place to place while I crawled, making local stops' (p. 14). Bill flew off to Vietnam and never came back, while John is now returning through Blossvale, Hireling, Dry Run, Burnt Cabin and a whole catechism of small towns, to a place which, although once 'the watermark of westward expansion' (p. 13), has now been bypassed by rail and road routes, and left behind by the modern world. In these opening pages the novel sets up an opposition between a global modernity allied to death and the life-giving local which refuses it. Bill's death is emphatically aligned with the modern and with slavery; he is as much separated from John as the dead slaves appear to be. He did not make it to Canada and freedom, but was caught and impressed into service (military). Bill had been entranced by modernity, an All-American boy, passionate about football and his Chevy, milkshakes and French fries, 'the first black in the history of the County to call and have a pizza delivered' (pp. 132–3). A high-school sports star, he was the King of the Pigskin Hop and the Winter Sports Dance (p. 279), elected to fill the role of harmless black hero, as he garnered football trophies for the school teams. Once all the trophies had been won, however, the school which had repeatedly passed his failing performance, flunked him. With no college place (unlike his brother, saved by greater literacy) he was promptly drafted. America makes Bill a representation of its official national values; now he exists only in effigy. His mother has removed all photographs of him from her personal family display, and placed them with the citation, gallantry medal, condolences and telegram on a flag-draped table in the dining room. 'She had got him killed and then she had enshrined him' (p. 134). His funeral service, with its 10 different eulogies, is attended by the mayor, lieutenant-governor, town council, TV and newspaper journalists. Then they all leave, because in Bedford 'white people and black people aren't buried together' (p. 75). Like the fugitive slaves, Bill was heading north to Canada. John had given him $1,000 and a bus ticket to Montreal. Betrayed by his white-identified mother, Bill agreed to enlist to avoid jail. In the fantastical psychologic of the novel, without the slave trade, Bill would not be dead, because there would be no death. The trade lives on, in a sense, in Bill's failed escape, and in the finality of his death. Tellingly, his father's will made provision for the funerals of both Bill and his mother, both allied with modernity. But as the Judge notes, there is 'no provision made for your funeral, John. In fact there is no mention in the document of the possibility of your death' (p. 190).

In contrast to Bill, his father Moses Washington is situated in the realm of African belief systems. His funeral is governed by his own specifications, which pointedly exclude the Church (p. 21); the words of his chosen spiritual ring out, 'before I'll be a slave I'll be buried in my grave, and go home to my Lord, and be free' (p. 21), as a direct reference to the escape from both slavery and death by slave suicide. At the wake Jack appears, charged to take over as surrogate father and rescue John from the clutches of the Church. Jack lives on the side of the Hill (the black area of settlement), abandoned because supposedly populated by ghosts (p. 271). At one point both sides of the Hill had settlements, until an epidemic swept the far side in 1904, with Jack and Josh White the only survivors. The local black population, fearing economic ruin if news of the contagion reached the women's employers in the white townhouses, hushed up the epidemic and kept their children away from the area by telling them that Jack and Josh were 'boogeymen' living with ghosts (p. 273). 'Dead' to the modern world, Jack remains intensely alive, even after his apparent decease. When John decides to take the mortally ill Jack to the white hospital, he describes how he carries Jack from his cabin, carefully cradling him in his arms, protecting his arms and legs from collisions on the trail up the hill, and apologising when he slips in the snow and bangs his shoulder. In his mother's house, he seats him carefully in a chair, his head propped up on a cushion. The fact that Jack is dead dawns upon the reader only when John's mother enters and finds him 'sitting in the parlor in company with a stiffening corpse' (p. 116). When he tells Judith that the funeral is on Wednesday, he realises 'She did not understand – she thought he was dead' (p. 160). Preparing him for burial, John buys him new overalls, shirt, gloves and boots ('all he would need with the weather turning warmer', p. 214), laying his old boots beside him ('in case the new ones hurt his feet', p. 214), and adding tobacco and corn whisky to the coffin, grave goods ready for his life in some parallel universe of hunting and drinking.

The presentation of Jack's funeral also emphasises the connections between modernity and death. In the past, messages had been sent by a human chain, a grapevine. Each woman would have two others to get word to, and so on. But when the telephone came, the system died. For Yvette the telephone poles mounting the Hill initially represented progress. But when Jack dies she has trouble transmitting the message. In the past she could have told everybody by telling two people, but now it involves 20 phone calls. 'Those poles marching up the Hill weren't progress, they were death' (p.

152). They got in the way of the 'right' communication, rather than facilitating it. Jack's funeral marks the beginnings of a process of reintegration of the dead and the living, black and white, and is marked by a return to a traditional 'call'. At the funeral the call and response versions of spirituals include the expected repertoire, but also 'I ain't gonna study war no more', sung by the entire congregation, black and white. Judge Scott sings as one of them, and is also expected to contribute, though his response is ambivalent. He recites part of Tennyson's 'Ulysses', quoting 'Death closes all' (p. 218) and associating death with Westward expansion – 'to sail beyond the sunset', 'to seek a newer world' – in a fashion which links the West to death and modern empire. John strikes a compromise. His words are biblical 'but not their Bible' (p. 220). He quotes from Ecclesiasticus 44 (a text accepted as biblical by Catholics, but which is not fully recognised by Protestants as the 'right' message) and counters the finality of death with the verses 'Their offspring will last forever, their glory will not fade' (p. 221).

John's return to honour Jack also brings Bill back towards the forefront of memory. When Yvette welcomes John home she sets out to cook him his favourite meal. Yet when she places the lovingly prepared dinner before him he realises, 'it was not my favourite meal, it was Bill's' (p. 154). His mother is converting John into a surrogate, to occupy the gaping absence left by Bill. John has already noticed his mother's tendency to fill every available domestic space. She cannot see an empty space without filling it with junk (p. 123). In contrast his father constructed his house with an abundance of open spaces – seven exits, two entrances and plenty of exit routes. Both parents are reacting subconsciously to the slave past, either filling absences, or leaving escape routes open. Wearing Bill's clothes (pp. 150, 222), John becomes something of a willing surrogate, who fills Bill's place and brings him back to life. Clad in Bill's field jacket, he is mistaken for Bill by one of the town worthies:

> 'You that Washington boy, ain'tcha?' he said.
> 'That's right.'
> 'Thought so.'
> After a minute he took his face away, and looked at one of his companions.
> 'Told you he was that Washington boy.'
> 'Thought he was kilt,' one of the others said.
> 'That was the other one' (p. 225).

In contrast to the association of Moses and Jack with the continued existence of the dead, the white version of the Chaneysville incident, the near-lynching of Josh, features whites as utterly dead, as ghosts.[11] This is the 'wrong' story about Chaneysville. In fictional time this Chaneysville Incident comes first, a surrogate for the account of the one from which the novel takes its title. The first mention of the 1859 incident merely notes that the slaves died 'somewhere in the lower reaches of the county' (p. 62). The reader has no sense that it takes place in Chaneysville. The tale is narrated by Jack, who has discovered that John is seeing Judith, a white woman, and therefore recounts a cautionary story concerning the dangers of interracial love affairs. The story concerns Jack's closest companion, Josh White, an albino. Since the children don't understand his lack of pigment it is popularly assumed that 'he had been dead for some years' (p. 25). Josh has been courting a white farmer's daughter, and intends to marry her and pass for white (p. 87); the Ku Klux Klan mobilises to lynch him. Although essentially operating by naked violence and threat, whippings and lynchings, the Klan played upon superstition from its inception during Reconstruction.[12] Ghost riders muffled their horses' feet, covered the horses with white robes and dressed in flowing white sheets, their faces covered with white masks, posing as spirits of the Confederate dead returned from the battlefields for revenge. Jack's narration is serio-comic, emphasising the Klansmen as ridiculous buffoons, performing a role for which they have no real aptitude. In their white garments they are easily tracked: 'Fool runs around in a white sheet on a moonlit night is gonna stay in sight' (p. 97). Moses saves Josh by taking the place of the thirteenth member of the group, disguised in bedlinen, an extra ghost among the impersonations of the sheeted dead. In a Keystone Cops sequence Jack lures the Klansmen after him, into the woods, where they are hampered by their sheets: 'they was all the time gettin' their hems caught' (p. 107), comic ghosts in fancy dress. As a performative display of white authority based upon the impersonation of the dead, the incident reveals white powerlessness. The white loss of spirituality is being performed in effigy, the performers impersonating the spirits whom they have renounced in a ceremony designed to separate the living from the 'race apart', the dead, as figured by Josh. Although he is rescued, Josh is so traumatised by the girl's betrayal that he loses the will to live; he is 'living dead', refusing to hang on to his horse or to save himself from pursuit. Moses, aware that they will not outdistance their pursuers with 'a Goddamn dead man to cart around' (p. 108), resurrects him by an empowering fiction (the girl had tried to save him, had provided the sheet as a disguise, did love him) which restores him to some degree of heart and life.

This is a complicated inset story. In the first place it stands in for the later Chaneysville Incident, which has yet to be narrated, functioning almost as its proleptic mirror image, with 13 white 'ghosts' in the place of 13 black. In its content it suggests the deadly consequences of assuming white identity; Josh almost becomes white and almost ends up dead. It displays a white dramatisation of a threatening Other, designed to reinforce white power, which is subsequently revealed as entirely performative. Later in the novel John hears the story of the near-lynching (p. 232) from Judge Scott, who reveals that the 'sheets' were merely pretending to be Klansmen, acting out a role. In a political struggle the local Party members had hatched a scheme to impersonate the Klan and lynch a black man, in order to discredit their opposition. Surrogates are substituting for others in a chain of politically motivated substitutions. Finally, the story is itself an oral performance by Jack in which he tells John the story which Moses told to Josh. It is never clear whether the girl was part of the plot, or merely innocent bait. Moses' story to Josh creates the fiction of a helpful white woman – but when the story is told by Jack to John it is designed to warn him away from a white girl. The intermediary narrator alters the charge of the story, once again, away from the original intention. John has yet to learn how to perform the story which will unite black and white, the living and the dead, and to negotiate a better relation between past and present.

The additional surrogate in the chain is Judge Scott, the executor of Moses Washington's will. John's mother had been supposed to tell him that at 18 he could claim his inheritance, but instead kept silent. A deceptive intermediary, she did not transmit the message. John could not claim his real inheritance because nobody had told him that it existed. After Jack's funeral the Judge presents John with a Folio: 'Your legacy, John' (p. 164). Once 'the most feared artifact in the entire County' (p. 162), a record of Moses' boot-legging and the local worthies whom he bribed, it is reputed to be sufficient to ruin any of the local white politicians. John had assumed that this was why the local whites, particularly Judge Scott, were prepared to pay for Jack's funeral. In Judge Scott's office, however, he discovers that under the terms of Moses' will, the funeral costs were met from a trust administered by Judge Scott. The Scotts offered to pay merely to avoid John looking into the costs and discovering the terms of his father's will. The question of who pays for the funeral is thus crucial, for if John had left the white lawyers to it, rather than arranging an African-American funeral himself, he would not have received his inheritance, the books, papers and records which allow him to uncover the story of the Chaneysville Incident; the Folio; and the land on which the town's African-Americans live. The inheritance unifies the realms of the dead and the living, by bringing together the two sides of the Hill. Moses left the town side to Bill, and the far side (with its ghosts) to John, who now owns both. Acting as the surrogate for Moses, the Judge passes power back into John's hands. The chapter ends as John breaks the seal on the Folio. Yet when the reader turns the page, what appears is not the contents of the Folio but John's lengthy digression on the slave trade and the nature of death, almost as if that were the story hidden in the Folio. In a sense it is.

When the Folio is opened it turns out to be empty. It actually denotes an absence of records, a blank page that has been controlling the motives and actions of the white townspeople, an image of an absence which is enormously powerful. John now fills that space with the story which lies behind all the events of the novel, the story of slavery. There is an empty space to fill with a story, and it is John's choice of story which closes the novel. As Bradley commented, 'To me the story is what version John is going to come up with.'[13]

Once he has decoded the evidence left by Moses, John is able to establish the facts of his ancestry. Modern communications are replaced by older models. While Bedford has now been bypassed by modern rail and road routes, it was previously a central station on the Underground Railroad, on which C.K. Washington was a conductor. The Underground Railroad, the system of clandestine routes, safe houses and sympathetic abolitionists, borrowed the language of the steam railways in its myth-making, with 'stations', 'depots', 'conductors' moving slaves from one waystation to another, 'agents' who pointed fugitives towards the stations, 'stockholders' who financed them, and messages passed in code, often referring to slaves as cargo or passengers. One major route went through Pennsylvania, and bottlenecked in a narrow valley to the south of Chaneysville. C.K. died with the escaped slaves at Chaneysville, after a lifetime helping slaves to escape. Moses' apparently eccentric life-choices are made clear by his attempt to understand the absent C.K. He went to war in his fifties purely to understand dying; he married and had sons because C.K. did; he studied theology only to be sure that Christianity was wrong. 'You don't throw your whole life away if you're not sure that the dead really are there, waiting for you' (p. 389).

At the close of the novel, John and Judith follow the clues to Chaneysville to find the graves. Significantly the rounded gravestones of the white Iames family give way to triangular stones 'dark in color, almost black' (p. 379). Moses had built his house out of triangular stones, modelled upon the memorials at Chaneysville. How to read a burial ground becomes the key to re-establishing identity and family belonging.[14] The graves allowed 8 feet for one male grave, a wife's grave beside that and 5 feet for children, at the foot of the mother's grave. John is able to read the stones' spatial positioning to decode them as commemorating one man, four women and seven children, arranged in family groups. There is also one more marker, close to the southeast corner, for C.K. 'It wasn't a death that somebody had marked, it was only a grave' (p. 381). Judith poses the vital question: 'Who buried them?' (p. 430). John's answer brings white and black deaths into renewed contact. The slaves were buried next to a family graveyard, with the same spacing as the family stones, and the only conclusion is that the white farmer had taken the time 'to bury them like that, to figure out who loved who' (p. 431). In this image of the common graveyard of black and white, in intimate proximity to the white home, and a model for the black, John erases the racialised death structures of modernity, motivated by his love for a white woman. Historical facts will not yield the whole truth of the past, which is absent. Instead John performs an oral story, imagining the slaves back into life, filling the empty spaces of the past by assuming a succession of roles. Telling the story depends upon him taking up the role previously played by Jack, the storyteller. John describes the moment as if Jack were alive: 'And suddenly I heard his voice' (p. 392). John has run out of facts and research trails to follow and has to use his imagination. Turning to Judith he begins with the time-honoured opening phrase of Jack's stories 'You want a story, do you?' (p. 393), and follows his instincts and emotions. Around him he hears the slaves, as if alive. 'They're running quietly ... You couldn't hear them at all if it wasn't for one thing: the breathing' (p. 394). John's story is carefully designed to be reparative, as its plot indicates. In his account C.K. sets out to help the group to freedom, only to spot a famous slave-catcher, F.H. Pettis, lying in wait.[15] C.K. attempts to warn the two conductors, the historical Crawley and Graham, away from the rendezvous point, but cannot make contact or intercept the slaves in time. Instead he draws the slave-catchers away, acting as a decoy (p. 403) and leaping a local gorge to evade capture. It is only at this point that he realises from the deployment of Pettis's men that the slaves were substitute targets, bait for a trap aimed only at catching him. His capture would have been a huge propaganda victory for the South. Pettis was not concerned about the runaway slaves, 'just about one particular runaway slave' (p. 408). The design of the tale reflects John's awareness that he could not save Bill, and that the story he is telling is also that of the one individual always at the back of his mind. Unwilling to admit defeat, in a sudden twist John invents a new possibility. If C.K. leaps back across the gorge he can outdistance his pursuers, double his lead, reach the slaves and get them to safety, closing his career with a success. Filled with new emotional warmth, John empathises with C.K. ('I was no longer cold.' 'He was warm now', p. 413) and transfers his love for Judith to C.K., promptly inventing a romance.[16] C.K. finds among the escaped slaves his own lost beloved, Harriette. After a lifetime taking refuge in cold facts and digressive substitutions, John tells a tale of love, and weaves the slaves back into Bedford by sympathetic identification. Most importantly he invents for C.K. and Harriette a first-born son, William Washington, putting Bill back into the story, alive and restored to his family group. Even his mother's white-identification is partially revised. In this story Harriette has only posed as a docile slave in order to protect her son. She is a killer, but of a son who dies with her rather than return to slavery. In this version of the story the slaves do not beg to be killed; they commit suicide. C.K. has become an inspiring story and a symbol of hope, and in dying by his own hand, remains an empowering fiction.[17] At the close of his story John includes an inset tale of African origins, in which an old slave, Azacca, recounts how the sky god sent Legba to tell men that death was not an ending of things, merely a change of shape. Legba, however, passes the message to Rabbit to deliver, who passes it to the white men, who then tell the black men that death will turn them to dust and ashes and their spirits will burn in torment, unless they submit to white authority. Azacca's story emphasises that there is no death. It is an empowering story, designed to encourage the slaves to face their suicides, secure in the knowledge that death is only a big white lie. John has answered the opening 'call' with a response, a story of voices reverberating across time, finally achieving the communication with the dead which had been interrupted by modernity.

In this denouement the historical puzzle is triumphantly solved. None the less, at the close, John destroys his working notes, his files and his conclusions, carefully leaving only the original historical clues for the next family descendant to begin all over again investigating the story of the incident. In the staged erasure of the historical evidence – in admitting that it was 'only a story' and can be rubbed out – Bradley acknowledges both that the quest for originals is impracticable – and that it is not lightly abandoned. By burning the solution to the puzzle, but leaving the clues, John implicitly acknowledges the role of a 'next reader', and leaves a gap for that next reader to fill. Critics have debated the meaning of the ending of the novel, in which John burns his notes and in the process splashes kerosene on his boots, commenting fatalistically, 'But that would make no difference' (p. 430).[18] Judith has been sent away and he wonders as he stands by 'the pyre' (p. 432) if she will understand when she sees the smoke rising from the far side of the Hill. John is in front of Jack's cabin, in the area associated with death and ghosts; the suggestion lingers that he has immolated himself, a symbolically appropriate death, given the references to Vietnam. Bradley himself noted that the bimodal narrative of the novel (with John existing as both a child and an adult in the text) allows for him not surviving, and for a post-mortem narrative.[19] But the point is that if we follow the logic of the novel, the question of John's death or non-death cannot even arise. The line between life and death is no longer clear-cut. John has in a sense destroyed the notion of death, and made it redundant.

As John notes, 'to truly judge the importance of a given area on a total society we must look at the lines of communication' (p. 156). In *The Chaneysville Incident* these lines involve the substitution of the traditional 'call' for the modern telephone; the Underground Railroad for modern roads and railways; the right message truly communicated, for the wrong message, of death. Modern communications produce death and a mistransmitted story, a process reversed in the novel, in which garbled and surrogated versions of the story are ravelled back into a contra-mortem narrative. John's inheritance, withheld from him by the deceptions of intermediaries, is finally restored, and the surrogated story emerges from the shadows. Reading the novel is in some respects an exercise which recognises the ways in which surrogation operates to repair the damages of the past, even while it acknowledges the absences which will always remain.

5   Going global
From Danish postcolonial novel to world bestseller

Reviewing for the *Toronto Star*, John North asked:

> What are the odds of a translated novel by a relatively obscure Danish
> author and featuring a part Inuit female scientist/detective living in
> Copenhagen succeeding in the overcrowded North American book
> market?[1]

The question was rhetorical. The novel under review was Peter Høeg's
Smilla's Sense of Snow, first published in Danish in 1992, and by 1997 a block-
buster US and world bestseller in translation. The novel's success was even
more surprising given its focus on the history and afterlife of Danish colonialism, not an immediately topical theme. With the exception perhaps of
the Caribbean islands of St Thomas, St John and St Croix, a Danish colony
sold to the United States in 1917 (now the United States Virgin Islands),
American awareness of Danish imperialism has not been noticeably acute. A
roster of Danish colonies would add some holdings in India (passed to the
British in the nineteenth century), 200 km of the Guinea Coast of Africa
(ditto) and a few trading posts. Without wishing to underestimate Danish
colonial activity (which included involvement in the slave trade), the international general reader is unlikely to have been drawn to the novel by fascina-
tion with the topic. And yet, Denmark has one territory which is still part of
North America: Greenland. Situated geologically as part of the Canadian
Shield, Greenland became a Danish colony in the eighteenth century, a
province of Denmark in 1953 and gained home rule in 1979, remaining part
of Denmark (though not, now, of the European Union). It is also host to an
American settlement. When Germany invaded Denmark in 1940 the
United States invoked the Monroe Doctrine and made an agreement with
Denmark allowing the establishment of American military bases. Thule
(massively expanded during the Cold War) remains the United States's most
northerly base, hosting a unit of the Ballistic Missile Early Warning System.

In Høeg's novel, the plot turns upon the existence of this US presence, a colony within a colony, and its relation to its hosts, in a narrative foregrounding metaphors of pollution and parasitism, in relation to translation. *Smilla's Sense of Snow* offers a fascinating case study of the ways in which translation functions to create a world literature; the extent to which it fosters domination of minority language cultures by more powerful linguistic communities; and the degree to which translation may erase local differences, homogenising culture or pandering to the demand for the exotic while safely domesticating it. Translation may be said to lie at the heart of any transnational system which moves across cultures and languages. In literary critical terms, working with a translation is suspect, impure. Atwood's Professor Pieixoto, translating the handmaid across time and space, into the assumptions of his own culture, and getting her altogether wrong, offers an object lesson to the current writer, not a Danish-speaker and dealing with work in translation, with all which that implies of interference and disruption of cultural messages. Translation, however good, is never an innocent activity. The relation between translation and postcoloniality has become a focus for contemporary critics, kick-started by the appearance of Eric Cheyfitz's *The Poetics of Imperialism* (1991), Vicente Rafael's *Contracting Colonialism* (1988) and Tejaswini Niranjana's *Siting Translation* (1992).[2] Douglas Robinson's *Translation and Empire* (1997) offers a succinct and discerning introduction to the ways in which translation has been understood: as a channel of empire, assisting in the colonisation of subject peoples; as a lightning rod for cultural inequalities after the collapse of colonisation; and as a potential channel of decolonisation, primarily as a means to decolonise the mind.[3] Robinson draws attention to the power differentials which control what gets translated and how. As Lawrence Venuti argues, 'Translation is uniquely revealing of the asymmetries that have structured international affairs for centuries.'[4] Translation is deeply implicated in relations of domination and dependence, a powerful tool in the formation of cultural identities, and in the creation of representations of foreign cultures which simultaneously construct a domestic subjectivity. Venuti notes the dominance of English-language cultures. English is the most translated language worldwide, but one of the least translated into. In 1987, he points out, only 1,700 books were translated from Italian into English, 5,000 from German, while 32,000 were translated from English into other languages. Translation thus occupies a marginal place in Anglo-American cultures. A great deal of money is made translating from English; very little is invested in translating into it. In addition, translations are expensive and tend to be designed to serve domestic interests. 'A best-selling translation tends to reveal much more about the domestic culture for which it was produced, than the foreign culture which it is taken to represent.'[5] In a special issue of *Public Culture*

(2001) devoted to translation in a global market, Emily Apter highlights the role of translation in globalising the canon, to create 'Global Lit'. In her view the increased motility of global culture may foretell a time when national labels will become obsolete, as an international aesthetic emerges in which location has become increasingly meaningless. For Apter,

'Global' signifies not so much the conglomeration of world cultures arrayed side by side in their difference but, rather, a problem-based monocultural aesthetic agenda that elicits transnational engagement.[6]

In this connection, the drive towards a transnationally translatable monoculture reveals itself in the ways in which linguistic superpowers call the shots, marginalising former healthy cultures. Translation elides the situatedness of texts, dehistoricising and depoliticising them. As Venuti argues, the result may be that translation 'makes ideas and forms appear to be free-floating, unmoored from history, transcending the linguistic and cultural differences that required … their translation in the first place'.[7] Conversely, of course, improved translatability may be a good thing, improving connections between nations and unbordering zones of cultural production.

How then can a writer in a relatively powerless language community create a novel which both crosses borders and communicates beyond his own specific location, while embodying resistance to dominant cultural hegemonies? In Høeg's case, as the development of this argument will establish, translation may imply interference with the message but that interference may also be part of the message, and not necessarily an accessory to commodification. Although Høeg's novel is steeped in history, its major strategy is inscribed within its aesthetic and formal structures, in plot, character, imagery and language. Previous criticism has highlighted the thematic and historical freight which the novel carries, in accordance with the overriding tendency of postcolonial criticism – even when broadly understood as signalling a critical stance towards forms of empire rather than a concern with a narrow historical period – to analyse novels in terms of cultural and political themes and preoccupations, or contemporary issues. It would be relatively easy to take a thematic approach to Smilla, to note that she is a hybrid figure, part-Danish, part-Greenlandic; that she acts on behalf of an oppressed Greenlandic child, used as a guinea-pig by representatives of established scientific power; that her pursuit of the truth about his murder confronts readers with some unpalatable facts concerning Danish treatment of Greenlanders in the past, their transformation into 'Northern Danes', in 'Denmark's Northernmost county';[8] the history of mineral exploitation and so-called 'scientific' racism; and the uneasy contemporary relations between modern Europeans and their immigrant communities. More critically – but still essentially thematically – the critic might contrast Smilla's hybridity with her nostalgia for a constructed Greenlandic innocence, symbolised by the child Isaiah, who represents also her own past, a childhood spent hunting seals with her Greenlandic mother. Or, indeed, the novel might be interpreted as an exercise in exotic nostalgia, as a work that, for all its good intentions, never introduces its readers to any contemporary resident of Greenland, treating the Arctic territories as a land of fantasy and alien life. Reviewers commented that the novel began well but that its second half transformed it into a conventional thriller in which Smilla discovers that in Greenland a strange meteor (an energy source and apparently alive) has brought back to life a presumed-extinct Arctic worm, another alien life-form which Isaiah had carried with him to Denmark, and which was the focus of the scientists' plots and counter-plots. Alien life-forms thus appear to be located in the immigrant, the minority and the 'Other'. From this point of view the novel can be approached not as a rigorous confrontation with colonial guilt, but as an implicitly racist parable, involving the death of the dangerous infected – a very politically incorrect novel. Since the worm kills most of its hosts, these 'aliens' pose a severe threat not just to the Danes but also to all mankind. Dangerous imagery.

Like the fictitious worm, the novel displayed a capacity to spread rapidly, moving swiftly from Denmark on to a world stage. From its appearance in 1992 it had been published in 24 countries, from Brazil to South Korea, by 1997; at least 10 more countries had bought translation rights. As Eva Hemmungs Wirtén notes, it epitomises the status of the book as global commodity. Early expectations for the book were for a modest print-run of 5,000–7,000 copies, which swiftly rose to 40,000, with the mass-market version expected to hit 2 million. Reviewers hailed the book – and also applauded the quality of its translation, by Tina Nunnelly, of the Fjord Press in Seattle.[9] The book was assisted by a massive advertising campaign in the US of $50,000 dollars, a Book of the Month Club selection in 1993, and when it came out in paperback, promotional paraphernalia which included 'Think Snow' baseball caps and pillows, and a reader's companion. TIME voted *Smilla* 'Book of the Year'. Then the film appeared: *Smilla* had gone global. The film, *Smilla's Sense of Snow*, directed, in English, by Bille August, was released in 1997, cost $35 million and stars an international cast – Julia Ormond, Gabriel Byrne, Richard Harris and Vanessa Redgrave among others. Isaiah was played by a seven-year-old Canadian, who was already a veteran of the Toronto production of *Miss Saigon* – as if ethnicities were interchangeably performative. The only major role played by a Greenlander was that of Juliane, the stereotypically feckless 'drunk native', played by Agga Olsen. Predictably the film omits much of the novel's social criticism (no references to *Das Kapital* or to Smilla's political education with the Greenland Marxist Society), and in place of the original open ending, substitutes a conventional resolution, closing with an explosion which blows up villains, worms and meteorite in one blast and leaves only the romantic leads (Ormond and Byrne) alive. Greenlanders apparently welcomed the film, in the belief that it might increase tourism. August, however, wanted a bleak atmosphere and was annoyed by the strength of the Greenlandic sun. He therefore shot at dawn and dusk. Where the novel attacks the idea that Greenlanders are 'primitive' or timeless, as if at some earlier stage of development than Europeans, the film opens with an image described in the screenplay as 'a fur-clad Inuit hunter poised above a small opening in the ice – so still he seems as frozen as the landscape. A timeless image; this could be the present – or a thousand years ago.'[10] Seconds later the meteor hurtles through the air and an avalanche engulfs him. He is frozen, timeless, and then disappears in a flurry of snow as the screen turns to white. Høeg had disassociated himself from the view of indigenous people as unspoiled; but Bille August described Greenland in terms which emphasise a lack of culture, as 'a landscape totally untouched by the hand of man'.[11] Strikingly, then, the opening of the film erases the human presence, in favour of a vast whiteness, and the ending restores the landscape to the same emptiness as the wheel turns full circle. At this point we might say that any resistant content had been emptied from the novel, which had become a fully commodified product. The story has been translated from Danish to English to the screen, and in its content no longer carries any postcolonial charge. As a result it appears to exemplify that flexibility and adaptation which characterises the global – a flexibility of form which serves the interests of the trade in ethnic differences, and which informs the various degrees of complicity between local oppositional discourses and a global late capitalist system. As Graham Huggan explains it, keeping the margins exotic is the objective of the mainstream – policing its boundaries, and keeping the margins available to the mainstream, but on the mainstream's own terms.[12]

But can this flexibility and adaptation also be subversive? E. San Juan Jr would maintain that it cannot, that postcolonial discourse merely mystifies the political and ideological effects of Western hegemony by its linguistic and textual emphasis, ignoring the real resistance of the Third World to domination. For him, Homi Bhabha's emphasis on contingency and indeterminacy simply legitimises a new master narrative.[13] Bill Ashcroft, in contrast, argues that postcolonial cultures develop in ways which reveal remarkable capacities for change and adaptation, and for local engagements with global culture, using imperial culture for their own purposes, just as Smilla uses the system's own scientific records to outwit the system. For Ashcroft the experience of the postcolonial world demonstrates that change won't come by attempts to establish fortress societies or to abolish globalisation, but by strategies to transform it, by appropriation and adaptation.[14] In this connection Peter Høeg's use of the rhetoric of pollution, the trope of the parasite, of global interchanges and contrasting situated knowledge, creates a nexus of images informed by the work of Michel Serres, which offer a counter-argument, establishing the novel as not merely a critique of colonial and neocolonial domination, but also of the globalising impulse.

The image of the infected immigrant draws very obviously upon the rhetoric of pollution. One example is instructive. In J.M. Coetzee's novel *Waiting for the Barbarians*[15] a magistrate occupies a fort on the frontiers of an unnamed empire. A visiting colonel, Joll, has been torturing the native inhabitants, a group of fisher people whose condition is thoroughly wretched. They are dirty, diseased and disliked. When Joll departs the magistrate announces, 'I want everything cleaned up! Soap and water! I want everything as it was before.'[16] In his desire to erase the dirty story of empire, he is tempted to resort to the type of purification which today would be termed 'ethnic cleansing'. He considers making a fresh start by marching the smelly, diseased prisoners into the desert and simply burying them there. But he does not do so.

> That will not be my way. The new men of Empire are the ones who believe in fresh starts, new chapters, clean pages; I struggle on with the old story, hoping that before it is finished it will reveal to me why it was that I thought it worth the trouble.[17]

As the magistrate has discovered, there can be no clean pages in human history without some sort of violence. The lure of the 'purified' clean, empty space, the new beginning, the neatly bounded territory, is a dangerous one, in culture at large, as in literature. As Rey Chow argues, sanctification and defilement – the clean and the unclean – belong to the same symbolic order, and modernity (in trying to be new) 'must incessantly deal with its connection to what precedes it in the form of destruction', citing Paul de Man's comments on the 'desire to wipe out whatever came earlier'.[18] Cultures like to impose systems – scientific or everyday – on inherently untidy experience. As Mary Douglas puts it, 'It is only by exaggerating the difference between within and without, above and below, male and female, with and against, that a semblance of order is created.'[19] Douglas argues that human beings are likely to condemn as 'dirty' or 'polluted' any object, person or idea which is liable to confuse our cherished classifications. Culture will always evolve rules for avoiding anomalous things, in order to strengthen the definitions which they challenge. In biblical dietary taboos (her example) the principle of cleanness in animals is that they should conform fully to their class, occupy their right place. Birds fly and are clean. Four-footed animals that fly (flying squirrels) are unclean. Almost anything that creeps, crawls or swims, that moves between land and sea, is unclean because its place or movement is of an indeterminate nature. Margins are dangerous. People in a marginal state, placeless, left out of the social patterning, become 'dirty', sources of pollution and danger, because their status is indefinable. This can include social outsiders, or offenders against the bounded wholeness of the human body: the racial minority, the physically handicapped, the sexually ambiguous, the parasite which penetrates the bodily boundaries. The body is a model which can stand for any bounded system. Its boundaries can represent any boundaries which are threatened or precarious. Danger also lies in marginal states because transition is neither one state nor the other, but indefinable. To have been at the margins – in the disordered regions of the mind, say, or in 'unexplored' areas of the globe – is to have been in danger – and at the sources of power. Works of art may be understood in terms of their function of enabling us to go beyond the explicit structures of our normal experience, into areas of formlessness, indefinability, which can be credited with powers, some dangerous, some good. In ordinary society, however, any transgressor of a social boundary is treated as a dangerous polluter. The transgressor has crossed some line which should not be crossed, and society mobilises to reinforce the boundaries. Purity – the clean and bounded space – is the object and it is the enemy of change, ambiguity or compromise. Colonial enterprises frequently depict the space into which they are expanding as empty, a 'new world', a fresh start, an open prairie, on which clear lines and boundaries can be drawn. At the same time the native or marginal is characterised as dirty, unclean or corrupt – the drunken Juliane and her dirty child Isaiah spring to mind.

Two images are crucial to the action of *Smilla*: the white empty space and the polluted unclean body, and they come together in the event which initiates the action, Isaiah's death, falling from a roof. When Smilla reaches the roof she finds an empty, snow-covered place, shining with reflected light. Only Isaiah's tracks show in the snow, leading to the edge where he jumped to his death. There are no footprints except Isaiah's. 'No one has been across the surface of the snow except him' (p. 9). For the Danish police the verdict can only be accidental death. Dr Loyen tells Smilla, 'It was quite clear from the footprints that he was alone on the roof when it happened' (p. 22). The roof was empty. This is an emblematic image of unmarked, clearly defined space. It conjures up the one familiar image of Greenland in the popular mind. What everyone 'knows' about Greenland is that successive waves of settlers arrived – and died. The Norsemen came – and died. The Danes who went to look for them found nobody there. Greenland is empty; the pages of its history are blank. And that timeless emptiness is uncorrupted. 'The ethnographers have cast a dream of innocence over North Greenland' (p.

76). But Smilla can read the tracks. As a Greenlander she has 'a sense of snow' (p. 72). Because of the precise pattern of acceleration she can see that Isaiah, terrified of a pursuer, went back nine feet to the centre of the roof to get a running start, to try to jump to the next roof. Smilla benefits from situated knowledge. The Greenlandic eye can translate the markings and 'read' the page, even when it is meaningless, blank, to the Danes. Snow is not actually white smoothness; it is read in many different ways throughout the novel. It is almost as if Høeg set out to dramatise that cliché of all linguistic study, that 'the Eskimos have many words for snow'. For Elsa Lübing, snow is a symbol of inconstancy (drawing on the Book of Job); for Smilla it is a symbol of truth (drawing on Revelation). Smilla finds Elsa because Mrs Lübing wrote a note in the margins of the official letter awarding Juliane a pension – she left an illicit track on the page, a second message which interfered with the official one. When Smilla approaches Elsa for help the marginal writer turns out to occupy a place at the heart of power, the Cryolite Corporation. Elsa collaborates with Smilla because she opens her Bible at random at the very phrase quoted by Smilla. Elsa's reading is textual, docile to authority, bound to power; Smilla's is bodily and depends upon operating across disciplinary categories. 'Reading snow is like listening to music. To describe what you've read is like explaining music in writing' (p. 43). In literary terms Smilla's reading is a model for the reader. We tend to expect place to be bounded; we guard the boundaries of our own knowledge domains; we expect novels also to stay in their places – nationalistic or generic, Danish or postcolonial, social novel or thriller. But art crosses boundaries and exceeds our limited definitions. These include generic definitions. Høeg uses the detective genre to parody the mode of the 'expert investigator', the skull-measuring anthropologist of the past, pursuing the truth about the native. Smilla therefore risks contamination herself by taking on the role of investigator. She tracks Isaiah's killers, just as they tracked Isaiah. She is prepared to get her hands dirty in the cause of truth, just as she was prepared to take in Isaiah, a decidedly grubby, smelly child, deafened by recurrent ear infections and already a victim of the worm.

So much for reading the blank space. How do we read the worm? Inscriptions *of* the body (tracks in snow) are easier to decipher than those *on* the body. When Lagermann shows Smilla X-rays of the victims of another 'accident' in Greenland, the images are 'a chaos of black and gray nuances' (p. 243), almost unreadable. 'Do you notice anything?' he asks. Smilla peers. 'Even when he points it out I don't understand.' He tracks it for her. 'It's a needle-thin, whitish line, uneven, crooked. It wanders up along the smashed vertebrae, disappears up the ribs, reappears at the tip of one lung, vanishes and shows up again near the heart, outside and partly inside of it, in the long ventricle.' Moritz explains the line by showing a second photograph of a man infected by *Dracunculus*, the Guinea worm. 'A truly nasty parasite. Up to three feet long. Works its way through the body with a speed of up to half an inch a day. Finally sticks its head out through the thigh' (p. 244). The reader may, at this point, share the comment of Moritz's trophy child-bride, Benja, 'That's gross' (p. 244). The scene provokes visceral, bodily disgust in the reader; it displays what is inside the body, breaching its boundaries. The X-ray image is, in itself, penetrative, a violation of bodily limits. At the same time it reveals a prior penetration and pollution by an alien life-form, the unclean parasite. In the case of Isaiah and his father, the parasite is *Dracunculus borealis*, the Arctic worm, a parasite which, unlike all others, kills its host, and, given enough hosts, could expand to cover the globe. As such the image appears to play into the rhetoric of pollution as opposed to the clean white space, an image, drawn from the stock of anti-immigrant rhetoric, of the primitive alien life-form which expands from its proper place and destroys the cultures it penetrates.

But the genesis of this parasite enforces a counter-reading. In this case it is the colonial parasite which takes root in the indigenous host and exploits it. The Arctic worm is prehistoric, an image of the 'primitive' or 'timeless' just like the racist image of the Greenlanders as 'a transitional form of ape' (p. 18). When the scientists graft the worm larvae onto living human tissue they potentially unleash a parasite on all humanity. Propagating the timeless turns out to be a potentially deadly enterprise. The post-mortem reveals that Isaiah's body bears a puncture mark. It has been recently penetrated, not by the worm, but by the needles of the scientists, monitoring the worm's progress by regular muscle biopsies. The real parasites penetrating Isaiah's body are the Danish scientists. The villains are financing their planned expedition to Greenland by the manufacture of hard drugs. Smilla's ally, Jakkelson, also bears puncture marks on his body, those of the addict to heroin, another substance which takes over the body and coexists with it. As we are told, 'A good parasite does not kill its host' (p. 453). The scientists' drug-financed power base was on the borders of Laos, Burma and Cambodia, where they encountered the Guinea worm, which comes essentially from dirt. It lives anywhere where people depend upon surface, polluted water. The scientists have carried out their grafts in 'empty' Greenland where they will not be discovered. Up to now the worm has lived in balance with its hosts. Now it is going global, adapting and mutating from a parasite which feeds on its host, to a killer. The worm is linked to Africa (the Guinea worm), and to the East, to those borders where the scientists found themselves at war 'with support from the US' (p. 457), and to the Arctic territories where Isaiah's father dies. Empire is mutating here from a local, Danish power system to a worldwide killing machine. In its plot and imagery, therefore, the novel constructs a postcolonial critique of the imperial rhetoric of purity.

What of characterisation? Importantly the killer worm is female. Verlaine, one of the villains, explains that 'women are vermin' (p. 456) (i.e. parasites), thus placing women in a super-category of the unclean and polluting. The female worm is bigger than the male; when it penetrates the skin 'it pushes its womb out and emits a white fluid full of millions of larvae' (p. 457). (Disgust contorts the scientist's face.) Several critics have commented on the sexual indeterminacy and gender reversals of Smilla and her lover, the Mechanic.[20] Just as the female worm penetrates and emits its fluid so Smilla takes the male role in sexual activities. She defies easy gender categorisation. She loves clothes and mothers Isaiah – but she can't cook, is skilled at hand-to-hand combat, and keeps a screwdriver in her pants to stab/penetrate others. In contrast, the Mechanic loves cooking, weeps readily, blushes furiously and is passive to her suggestions. Traditionally, in Greenland a woman may hunt, but only if she renounces family life and dresses as a man. (The Greenlanders are also category-bound.) 'The collective could tolerate a change of sex but not a fluid transition stage' (p. 33). Smilla's mother hunts like a man, but she plays both gender roles; while hunting she breastfeeds Smilla. The characterisations of the novel, therefore, continue the emphasis on resisting fixed categories. Danger – and power – come from these boundary crossings, whether political borders (Africa, US, Laos, Denmark, Greenland); gender categories; or bodily boundaries. The reader is left perpetually unsure of any firmly bounded place. Smilla, for example, remembers at one point walking with a group across a hot plain, surrounded by flat, lifeless spaces, the only living creatures in an empty world, through saltpans, dunes and a sandstorm. When and where was this? 'The time was 11.30 at night, the burning light was the midnight sun' (p. 311) and the location was northeast Greenland, an Arctic desert. Both place and time are out of joint for the European reader. Smilla understands the attraction of imposing order on contingency. She contemplates the oil platform at Nuuk and says, 'What they want is to coerce the other, the vastness, that which surrounds human beings' (p. 360). She herself is drawn to the clearly delineated spaces and forms of Euclidean mathematics, and when she realises that her own frozen, empty existence is threatened by her love for the Mechanic, she resists change as long as she can, trying to keep him out of her space. As she notes,

> People perish during transitional phases … It's not difficult to coast along when things are going well, when a balance has been established. What's difficult is the new … The new feelings (p. 346).

Importantly Smilla makes this observation from the constricted space of a kitchen dumbwaiter in which she is crouching, using its lift shaft to travel surreptitiously between the decks of the Arctic ship. Like the worm, Smilla travels through a food-channel, moving through the bowels of the ship to enter the spaces which are supposedly off-limits, impenetrable, in order to reach the truth. To outwit the parasite she has parasitised herself.

Which brings me to Høeg's irresolute ending. At the end the novel returns to formlessness, an Arctic space in which fog obscures the outlines of objects. Smilla does not need to pursue Tørk onto the new, thin ice and kill him. The Arctic will do it for her, that very emptiness which Tørk sought to dominate, the emptiness which colonial fantasy projects onto the places which it plans to exploit. The surface of the ice is 'thin as a membrane, a fetal membrane. Underneath the sea is dark and salty like blood, and a face is pressing up against the icy membrane from below; it's Isaiah's face, the as-yet-unborn Isaiah' (p. 468). This is an image of death as penetrating a body boundary, but also as a passage towards birth. It is an image of a new beginning which is also a death, bloody and interstitial. Tørk is not yet dead but in a space between life and death; the unborn child is in a similar interstitial space, separated by only a slight barrier from the realm of life. The novel closes ambiguously.

> Tell us, they'll say to me. So we will understand and be able to resolve things. They'll be mistaken. It's only the things you don't understand that you can resolve. There will be no resolution (p. 469).

If you understand, in other words, you will understand the need to remain in the area of interstitiality.

In interview Høeg commented that he wanted at the end to have the realistic plane of the novel crack, to leave the reader uncertain: 'Are we inside the mind of the author? Is this simply a psyche making its presence felt, the characters merely slivers of this psyche? What's going on?'[21] In short, we don't know where we are, inside or outside, and the page is suddenly just that, a page on which the author is writing, not a realistic landscape. Although the crime has been solved the death has been deferred, the final meaning postponed. Homi Bhabha has argued that the deferred or postponed meanings in cultural translation are a guarantee that the postcolonial is not bound to any one fixed referent; contingency and indeterminacy are guarantees of freedom. E. San Juan Jr contests this view, arguing that Bhabha ignores the fact that 'utterance addressed to a specific listener in a specific situation is concretely determinate.'[22] Just as the ending seems indeterminate, the reader may feel that Høeg's novel is ambiguous, that the symbolism of the worm can slip from host to parasite, imperialist to imperialised. But in this case there is the possibility of a third term, resistance, which concentrates upon language, my final aesthetic focus. Throughout the novel there is a series of images of balked communication, or messages which meet with interference. The Mechanic stutters; Isaiah is deaf; Andreas Licht, already blind, is deafened by his assailants (penetrating his ear with a live electric wire); phone calls are cut off or overheard by different listeners from those intended; Miss Lübing's entry-phone drowns out Smilla's voice in static crackle. A similar phenomenon involves the presence of an interloper or third party in major scenes: Benja interrupting redundantly; Smilla commenting satirically on events; Miss Lübing's neighbour admitting Smilla, taking her for a florist; Lagermann's wife mistaking Smilla for the babysitter with a series of utterances at cross-purposes. One scene is particularly striking. Smilla discovers a cassette tape hidden by Isaiah, and can't make it out at all. The recorded voice is in East Greenlandic, a southern dialect incomprehensible to Smilla. The tape is interrupted by noises, the sound of an engine, electric noise from the cassette player, the palimpsestic hiss of a previous recording which has not been fully erased. The tape ends suddenly with jazz, described by Smilla as having 'a strange precision ... What takes the greatest precision is that it is supposed to sound like total chaos' (p. 121). When the acoustic expert deciphers the tape, the spoken message appears to be a description of a journey. But the significant sounds are located in the interference behind the voice – a motor, a prop-plane, a jet, a clatter of dishes, a waiter speaking Danish and American English, and a jazz pianist. The expert wonders where in the world you can have an East Greenlandic hunter sitting and talking in a restaurant where tables are being set, a Dane is yelling in American English, you can hear an airport in the background, and a famous jazz pianist playing in the restaurant. The answer is Thule American Air Base, specifically its club. This is the evidence which provides the story of the original accident in Greenland. This evidence is what Isaiah was killed for. The interference, the noise, is the message itself. The chaos is actually precision, identifying a precise location.

The scene opens the way to a more positive reading of the parasite. The truth about the parasite and the interference in the message come together here and return to the original starting point of this chapter, concerning the role of translation. In his book *The Parasite*, Michel Serres, the philosopher of science, has pointed out that in French *le parasite* also means noise.[23] A parasite is a noise in a channel. Noise is part of communication. It cannot be eliminated from the system. The speech utterance is not 'determinate'. In any communication we have three elements, a message, a channel for transmitting it and noise or interference which accompanies the transmission. Noise makes a reading of the message more difficult. But it is always there. There is therefore no message without resistance, no space without the parasite. Ideally noise is what is not communicated, a kind of chaos or third element to the message, the part of difference that is excluded. Every formalism (

mathematics, say) is founded on the exclusion of the third element of noise, to keep one area of knowledge separate from another. But in fact, different knowledge domains interpenetrate – postcolonialism and Danish literature, for example. The noise is the interesting part of the communication. The speaker or sender may see it as an obstacle, but for the reader it has its own informational value. The parasite is therefore a catalyst for complexity and interest.

> Whether it produces a fever, or just hot air, the parasite is a thermal exciter. And as such it is both the atom of a relation and the product of a change in this relation.[24]

The meteor, a foreign body and heat source from outer space, is almost too obvious a dramatisation of the notion of the thermal exciter. Serres himself uses the vocabulary of table manners and hospitality in his account, drawing on Horace and the fables of La Fontaine (who, he notes, uses rats as his examples of the parasites, as opposed to 'worms in the intestines').[25] The parasite feeds on another but also brings charm and interest to the table, information, energy and even (if the guest is a god) danger. Guest and host are conflated in the French term *l'hôte*, with the implicit recognition that the parasite is its own *pharmakon*, both the disease and the cure. (The novel's emphasis on food, drugs and the joys or hostilities of the table picks up the argument subliminally.) Above all, Serres makes the point that there is no exchange without the parasite, the third party who appears to be redundant noise.

Serres goes on to ask if there is a space outside parasitism, a pure or clean space, and his answer is that all culture depends upon the parasite, in its different meanings. In a conflation of economics and culture, he argues that to grow crops demands a cleared space, and therefore boundaries. Inside is empty; outside are weeds, bugs, interference. But something always comes in. There is always a hole in the fence. Thus, the real origin [of culture] is 'the making of a blank space and its simultaneous parasitism'.[26] The image is highly suggestive as a description of the scene of crime in the novel – an empty space which has been parasitised by Isaiah, his own space already parasitised by the worm, which provides the interference with emptiness, and offers the clues to all the revelations which follow. History begins with the parasitism of space, with deviation and diversification, so that the parasite, the boundary-crosser, the interfering noise, is also the motor of change and history.

History hides the fact that man is the universal parasite, that everything and everyone around him is a hospitable space. Plants and animals are always his hosts; man is always necessarily their guest.[27]

Or as the villain puts it in the novel: 'Human beings are the parasite. The worm is an instrument of the gods' (p. 457).

Without multiplying examples redundantly, it is important to note that in other significant ways the work of Michel Serres informs the novel. Bounded spaces are a constant focus. The novel opens with maps of Greenland and Copenhagen, spaces of fact which are parasitised by fiction, most obviously in the fictitious island of Gela Alta. Smilla is fascinated by Euclidean geometry, a frequent point of reference for Serres. A series of scenes feature Smilla breaching territorial defences, climbing the fence of the Cryolite factory (p. 81), passing through the hole in her father's hedge, escaping from her father's house past the police guard, escaping from the Casino, gaining access to the forbidden deck of the *Kronos* by dumbwaiter, entering Tørk's sleeping-quarters by subterfuge. External phenomena penetrate internal spaces. Smilla is surprised to find that it is snowing in Lagermann's living-room. (A flour bag has burst.) Serres's attention to the 'thirds' in any apparent binary is comically enacted, as Smilla (hiding in the shower) witnesses a sado-masochistic erotic encounter between two of the villains. In similarly voyeuristic fashion, the existence of the meteor was only discovered through the intervention of a third party, Benedicte Clahn, who was charged with reading mail going in and out of postwar Germany, as part of Allied surveillance, intercepting messages as a third party. Smilla figures in police records as having previously been denied access to Northern Greenland, following violation of Canadian territorial boundaries. (The polar bears which she was tagging showed even less respect for boundaries than Smilla.) Smilla is intensely claustrophobic, and when threatened with imprisonment at police HQ, caves in. 'The Greenlandic hell is the locked room' (p. 103). The police building is entirely featureless and empty, described through a succession of negatives – no sign on the door, no typewriters tapping, no nameplates, nobody in the corridors, nothing on the walls, tables or windowsills, and in the interview room, no coffee, cigarettes or tape recorder (p. 98). Yet when Smilla and Ravn enter the office she is surprised to find a third party already there, sitting in the dark. When Smilla herself responds to the threat by retiring in fright from the investigation, her own first reaction is to create a private fortress, walling herself off from her neighbours, disconnecting her telephone and her doorbell. Her space is none the less invaded by successive interlopers, including Juliane at the back door, the window cleaner at the window, and finally the Mechanic pushing a note through the letterbox, 'the last entrance that the world hadn't tried to force its way through' (p. 111).

Recognising that withdrawal behind fortifications is not a useful strategy, Smilla evolves from the fiercely independent, uncommunicative, anti-parasite to willingly parasitising herself. She takes a five-figure sum from her father, preying on 'his vital organs: his wallet and his checkbook' (p. 40). She accepts hospitality (she becomes the 'guest') from various hosts, enjoying the Mechanic's fish soup, Miss Lübing's spiced cookies, the delights of the Brioche D'Or (p. 156). She herself acts as a somewhat less elegant host to Isaiah (eating mackerel off newspaper on her floor) and serves food to the villains on the *Kronos*. She realises that an invisible hand 'has pushed me forth into a network of sewer pipes', running beneath the landscape of Denmark (p. 137). Penetrating the law offices of Hammer and Ving, joining the crew of the *Kronos*, she disguises herself in both cases as a cleaner, exploiting the desire for the clean space in order to further her own strategic pollution. Cleaners enter dirty spaces by right. On board ship she is able to interfere with the plotters' activities by repeatedly running noisy loads of laundry; the crew assume that Smilla is where the noise is. To gain access to the ship Smilla has to draw upon Birgo Lander, a ship's broker who describes himself as inhabiting a world of parasitic interchanges: 'a ship's broker lives off other ship's brokers who live off other ship's brokers' (p. 201). Lander owns part of the Casino Øresund, a fortress space. 'All the walls are decorated with rivets and the door frames are three feet thick and finished with bolts. The whole thing is designed to resemble a safe' (p. 220). A wall of glass, 'like a black barrier' (p. 220) faces the water outside. Officiously regulated, with an inspector for every two tables, the Casino actually propagates the gambling bug, 'one of the most voracious creatures in the world' (p. 221). As Lander describes it, 'The moment you buy your chips a little animal takes up residence inside you, a little parasite' (p. 221). Legalisation has merely increased the Casino's potential client base, 'like an infectious disease which was once under control, but has now been let loose' (224). Lander has also realised that the poison is the *pharmakon*. After losing everything several times he bought a share in the Casino deliberately. Owners are not allowed to gamble in their own casinos. The tables are turned as, to quote Serres, 'The host counter-parasites his guest.'[28] Captain Lukas is not such a lucky gambler: 'a parasite ... has eaten him up from the inside and now takes up more room than he does' (p. 222), which is why he takes up the captaincy of the *Kronos*.

In the image of the ship, Høeg constructs an extreme example of the opposition between bounded space and external threat. On a ship 'private space must be subjected to the severest discipline if it is to withstand the dissolution, destruction, and pressure to yield coming from all sides' (p. 277). The *Kronos* is 'ice-class', double-hulled to resist external pressure. Outside it, the sea represents Smilla's fear of formlessness and disorientation, a confusion that

> will work its way into the chambers of my inner ear and destroy my sense of orientation; it will fight its way into my cells and displace their salt concentrations ... leaving me deaf, blind, and helpless (p. 264).

Within the ship, however, every space includes a potential interloper; every room has an intercom from which orders crackle; spaces are penetrated by fire alarms and the sprinkler system, and the crew form different interest groups. As Verlaine notes, the ship may have rules (the Captain's and Tørk's) but 'They're dependent on us; we're just the rats' (p. 298). In the denouement, Tørk is defeated by a combination of Smilla, the Mechanic and Lukas. In a scene of poetic justice the latter takes revenge on Verlaine, using a harpoon gun to penetrate him in the same spot where Verlaine stabbed his brother to death. The Mechanic attacks Tørk when the latter tells a lie, saying that he shouted out to Isaiah to warn him away from the edge, and that Isaiah turned around but chose to ignore him. Isaiah was deaf; he could not have heard Tørk's cry, even if he made it. Smilla comments that 'The most important information always comes at the end. As if in passing. In a side letter. In the margin' (p. 382). Tørk's casual lie is enough to propel the Mechanic onto him and send him out onto the ice. Like Elsa Lübing's marginal annotation, it is a small phrase which provides entry to the truth, and changes the dynamics of the situation. Isaiah died because noise was eliminated from his hearing channels. 'Interference', the parasite as noise, might have saved him.

As, indeed, it provides a means for Smilla and the Mechanic to raise the alarm and get help. Laying out his theory, Serres's example of noise as a parasite concerns a telephone ringing at a feast, interrupting conversation at table, 'the noise interrupting the messages'. Once the individual answers the phone, 'the sounds of the banquet become noise for the new "us"'. The system has shifted.' Moving back to the table, the noise slowly becomes the diners' conversation once again. In the system noise and message exchange roles according to the position of the observer and the action of the actor. What is mere noise to those at table is a message for the recipient of the call; their conversation is merely noise to him.[29] When the Mechanic uses the ship's radio to call for help, it at first looks as if interference will get in the way. He picks up a Canadian classical music station, for example, not the station he wants. The conversation with Ravn is interrupted by 'the crackling of empty space' (p. 431); it fades, returns, clarifies, then is 'carried away through a tunnel of noise and vanishes' (p. 435). The Mechanic is perilously positioned between two conversations; he has the headset pulled away from him to listen for any noises in the corridor. When Smilla hears interference in the phone conversation, she assumes the noise is coming from the Mechanic, but in fact the sounds of distress are from Ravn, confronting the fact that Tørk murdered his daughter in Singapore. As Smilla comments, 'In some ways it has become easier to orientate ourselves in the modern world. Every phenomenon has become international' (p. 123), and 'There's nothing local left any more. Something happens in Greenland, it's connected to something else in Singapore' (p. 230). But where globalisation may be seen in terms of a Euclidean notion of space, defined by Serres[30] as a homogenous plane to be overcome, divided up and approached by calibration, the Mechanic has constructed the space of his message topologically, as a distribution of points in a complex spatial arrangement – a radio version of the West Coast offense. He is able to use interference to relay his message beyond the tracking devices of the criminals, hopping from the ship's location in the Northwest Passage, to Sisimiut, on to Reykjavik, to Torshavn and to Lyngby, creating a smokescreen which hides his position. Interference is used as a means to resistance. Where the villains attempt to dominate space, the Mechanic is able to use its tangled relations to his advantage, in short local hops and deviations which outwit the global system of surveillance. What this suggests is that patterns of communication cannot in themselves be understood globally, without following the series of displacements and transformations that occur between the points. Serres understands knowledge as an endless distribution of intricate shores connected by innumerable passages, using the example of the Northwest Passage

> with shores, islands and fractal ice floes. Between the hard sciences and the so-called human sciences the passage resembles a jagged shore, sprinkled with ice and variable ... Less a juncture under control than an adventure to be had.[31]

Smilla and the Mechanic are, of course, sending their message from the beginning of the Northwest Passage.

As Ruth Mayer has argued, in a time of globalisation it is unsurprising that the image of the parasite should be so widespread.[32] Popular films and novels are full of images of viruses and parasites, notions of infection, contagion, infiltration and contact. Today, she argues, people, goods, ideologies, patterns of consumption travel around the globe, and areas not yet in touch (empty areas) seem like a challenge to the smooth machinery of global translation and transformation. Mayer demonstrates that the parasite theme tends to be enacted in conjunction with images of global interaction, communication and contact, as in this novel in the contacts between Africa, America, the Arctic, Indochina and Denmark. The buzzword of our time is flexibility, through which we escape the confines of local culture, but our adaptive capacities are also those of unpredictable infection, 'the flip side of global contact scenarios'.[33] What Høeg does that is different from such films as *Alien* or *Outbreak*, is to embed the notion of resistance in the parasite plot. Crossing boundaries is both danger and power. The notion of the parasite, of interference with the message, exemplifies Mayer's description of the redesigning of cultural contact 'by messing up the poles of confrontation and forcing our attention toward the very channels between these poles',[34] making the parasite a 'mediate, a middle, an intermediary', as Serres describes it.[35] As a result Høeg's novel, centred upon the opposition of empty space and its simultaneous parasitism, offers a potentially revealing paradigm for literary studies in the age of globalisation.

6 Southern apes

McCarthy's neotenous killers

Globalisation has much in common conceptually with Manifest Destiny; each relies heavily on an inbuilt determinism founded on notions of technological or evolutionary progress. Manfred Steger has argued that globalisation's claims and political manoeuvres remain tied to a nineteenth-century narrative of modernisation and civilisation, presenting the West 'as the privileged vanguard of an evolutionary process that applies to all nations'.[1] The result, in Chalmers Johnson's analysis, is the creation of a spurious scientificity, so that one of the most deceptive aspects of globalisation is its claim to embody fundamental technological developments, inevitable and determined, rather than the conscious policies of Anglo-American political elites.[2] As the previous chapter indicated, adaptation and evolution are a frequent focus in contemporary narratives, exploring the human capacity for resistance and survival in a fast-moving world. Cormac McCarthy's *Blood Meridian* encapsulates the argument with American imperialism as destiny, in a mock-evolutionary scenario, satirising popular scientism.

Critical readings of *Blood Meridian* have tended to focus upon the novel as an *ur*-text of American anti-imperialism, its abundant historical detail deployed to condemn the American sense of divine mission or Manifest Destiny, and to reveal the violence concealed beneath the story of Western expansion and conquest.[3] With its flayings and slayings, sodomising and evisceration, scalpings and weltering gore, *Blood Meridian* makes the costs of imperial expansion all too evident. Set primarily between 1848 and 1861 (with a short final sequence 17 years later) the novel is situated between the treaty of Guadalupe Hidalgo (February 1848) in the aftermath of the Mexican War (by which the United States acquired the future states of Colorado, New Mexico, Arizona, Utah and California) and the final destruction of the American buffalo herd in 1878, ending as the Plains are fenced in. The year 1846 also marked the acquisition of the Oregon territory, and thus the American domination of the northern part of the continent.[4] The novel therefore apparently emphasises the moment when modern America assumes the mantle of destiny and takes on its essential form, acquiring coast-to-coast dominance. In the biopolitical transaction at the heart of *Blood Meridian* (scalphunting) genocide is commodified; the successive encounters between Americans and Mexicans, Comanches, Apaches and other peoples foreground genocidal violence as defining American history. Critical interpretations of the novel have tended to concentrate on genealogical readings, seeking the origins of American violence in its moment of formation, or focusing the events of the past through the lens of the present. Critics read the historical events of the novel as if framed by the moment of its inscription, highlighting contemporary politics. Published in 1985, the novel has been read in terms of Anglo-American hostility to an increasing Latino presence, potentially penetrating its permeable borderlands; in terms of the genre of the 'Vietnam Western', its scalphunters foreshadowing the similar trophy-hunting of their political descendants, the 101st Airborne Division in Vietnam; and in relation to increased awareness of renewed imperial ambitions in Latin America.[5] In philosophical readings, extending the time frame further, the novel has been understood as a critique of the Enlightenment tradition of appropriating nature to man's dominion, itself also a plank in any imperialist enterprise.[6] Yet for most critics, McCarthy's politics remain ambiguous: the image of the racially fluid borderlands may equally well be understood as catering to racist fears of invasion from 'down below', or as fostering a scare story of barbarians at the gates. Indeed, in the novel, Native Americans feature as 'the savages' *passim* – a term consonant with the rhetoric of 1848 but not with that of 1985.[7] While the ceaseless slaughter implies condemnation of the imperial mission, it also reduces imperialism to mindless violence, rather than to economically motivated plunder or even territorial expansion. (The scalphunters do not settle, squander their bounty, and appear to have no reason for their trade but the lust for killing.) As John Rothfork has commented, there remains no consensus among critics as to what the novel is about.[8] Why the huge casualty rate in successive – and repetitive – massacres? Why focus on scalphunters in the pay of Mexico? Why feature an unnamed central protagonist (the Kid) and his antagonist (the Judge), an enormous and enormously learned paedophile rapist? What are the bases of their antagonism? And why does the novel close as the Judge may or may not kill the Kid against a background involving the shooting of a be-crinolined dancing bear?

The answers to these questions – even the manner in which they are posed – depend upon an informed awareness on McCarthy's part of a series of debates in ethology, the science of animal behaviour, which have particular reference both to apes and to Africa. *Blood Meridian* is a novel which primarily engages not with the recent past, not with the nineteenth-century past, not with the legacy of Enlightenment thought, but with prehistory, in an explicit critique of the employment of a global genealogical scenario as an exculpatory fiction. As preceding chapters have indicated, the twentieth century is overpopulated with geneholics. Global flows of information and people have created both the desire and the resources for genealogical constructions, in literary criticism and in ordinary life.[9] Tracing ancestry, however, is an activity usually designed to connect back to innocent (or victimised) forebears, those who are inspirational in some respects, or at least deserve to be rescued from the obscurity to which history's victors have consigned them. The attraction is to forebears who exemplify radical or adventurous pasts (*Holder of the World*, S.), to whom a moral debt is owed (*Wuhu Diary*) or on behalf of whom the modern investigator restores a past which has been erased (neo-slave narratives, Høeg). It is a truism of the quest for ancestry that nobody seeks to trace his or her story back to the village thief – or the village slave trader. And the ancestral reach has to be limited: taking ancestry too far back to its earliest origins replaces the noble ancestor with the prehuman or subhuman.

Blood Meridian is the exception to the rule. This is a novel which traces its protagonists' antecedents back to ancestors convicted as killers in the popular account, the neotenous killer apes of prehistory. Where previous chapters of this study have focused on novels in which children are victims, *Blood Meridian* centres upon the child-as-killer, in a global line of descent. In *Blood Meridian* McCarthy exploits a pseudo-scientific hypothesis, engaging with the 'discovery' in the late 1960s and 1970s that the family of man traces its descent from a violent progenitor, a killer ape-child. For all its careful local detail, the novel ostensibly relates its protagonists not to a national family or imperial nation but to a global genealogy, in the process descending Americans, including Native Americans, from African origins. In evolutionary terms, as far as the current archaeological record demonstrates, man did not originate in America. North America is notable for the absence of apes or their remains; McCarthy therefore supplies them to satiric purposes, transforming the founders of the modern nation into Australopithecines, 'Southern apes'. McCarthy's parodic transnationalism works by expanding and simultaneously diminishing his characters, as actors on a global stage, fictionally Africanised, implicitly suggesting that the whole South is immigrant and African, while at the same time undercutting the claims of genealogical origins. Readings of the novel in terms of national political origins are thus undermined by McCarthy's deployment of a strategy of ethological pastiche, in order to challenge genealogical notions. The action of *Blood Meridian* begins with the image of the unnamed Kid, crouching by the fire, unwashed and illiterate: 'in him broods already a taste for mindless violence. All history present in that visage, the child the father of the man.'[10] The child becomes the ancestral figure, not in any sense of Wordsworthian innocence, but purely on the grounds of his violence. Wandering south, divested of family ties, meeting men 'whose speech sounds like the grunting of apes' (p. 4), the Kid joins a band of similarly simian scalphunters and slaughters his way westward, until the close of the novel, by which point his character has become generalised in a country filled with 'violent children orphaned by war' (p. 322). The Civil War (a shrieking absence in the novel) refounds modern America not on founding fathers but on orphaned children. Along the way the Kid meets the Judge, a figure repeatedly described as childlike, with tiny, skilful hands, a particular nimbleness on his feet, a huge head (and apparently well-developed brain), the capacity to produce weaponry from thin air, and a strangely hairless body. Both in a sense children, the two figures step out of the pages of popular ethology.

Primates, whether ape, monkey or chimpanzee, have been a focus of attention since the 1960s, when a spate of books appeared which claimed first to describe man's 'real' or 'natural' behaviour in ethological style, and second to explain how this behaviour evolved. Robert Ardrey's *African Genesis* and *The Territorial Imperative*, Desmond Morris's *The Naked Ape* and *The Human Zoo*, Konrad Lorenz's *On Aggression* were all popular bestsellers in the 1960s; all purport to document the idea that man is an animal, that there is little we can do but accept our instinctive natures, and that we are naturally aggressive creatures.[11] Ethological ideas were given special impetus by archaeological discoveries in Africa. Until the 1920s the hunt for early man had focused on Asia. Then in 1924 Raymond Dart discovered the Taung skull in South Africa. Furious controversy broke out when Dart claimed to recognise features in the skull which took it out of the ape class and placed it in that of the *Hominidae*, the group which includes man and his early ancestors. Dart christened his find *Australopithecus*, the Southern ape. Resistance to the idea that all human beings are descended from Africans was strong. When Dart's paper 'The Predatory Transition from Ape to Man' was published, the editor of *The International Anthropological and Linguistic Review* preceded it with the disclaimer that the Australopithecines were 'only the ancestors of the modern Bushman and Negro and of nobody else'.[12] Americans were clearly excluded from this low-growing branch of the family of man. Subsequent discoveries in the 1930s in caves near Johannesburg apparently confirmed Dart's thesis, since when hundreds more such remains have been found on African sites.

Not all Dart's ideas, however, have proved so acceptable. Until his discovery it had been assumed that our primal ancestors resembled the shy, vegetarian ape of the forest. Observing fossilised baboon remains with head injuries, however, Dart concluded that his 'Southern ape' had killed them with an antelope humerus, and that the hominid hunters lived in bands, systematically killing for a living. Their evolution of upright posture had made possible the dextrous hand and the efficient killing. In his paper Dart argued for continuity across the centuries:

> The blood-bespattered, slaughter-gutted archives of human history from the earliest Egyptian and Sumerian records to the more recent atrocities of the Second World War accord with early universal cannibalism, with animal and human sacrificial practices or their substitute in formalized religions and with world-wide scalping, head hunting, body mutilating and necrophiliac practices of mankind in proclaiming this common bloodlust differentiation – this predacious habit.[13]

McCarthy's novel begins with an epigraph which emphasises the same long history of scalping, quoting an account in the *Yuma Daily Sun* of an expedition by J. Desmond Clark and Tim D. White (major figures in the Middle Awash project) to the Afar region of northern Ethiopia, where 'a re-examination of a 300,000-year-old fossil skull found in the same region earlier shows evidence of having been scalped'.[14] McCarthy omits Clark's additional comment that 'it's impossible to say whether this [evidence of grooves on the skull] constitutes cannibalism or ritualistic scalping.' In what follows, in the details of the Comanches sodomising the dead, the headhunting involving the heads of Captain White and the putative Gomez, the description of the Comanches with armfuls of human viscera, McCarthy picks up on Dart's points. Essentially, Dart argued that man had emerged from the anthropoid background for one reason only – because he was a killer. As he learned to stand erect, to run in pursuit of game and to use weapons, he made new demands on the nervous system for the coordination of muscle, touch and sight. Bipedalism freed the hands to hold a weapon. The result was first the enlarged brain, and then man. In other words, the weapon had fathered man.

It was to be a view taken up enthusiastically by Robert Ardrey, American playwright and novelist, in *African Genesis*, a work which popularised the 'Killer Ape' theory. *African Genesis* begins with a fantasy of birth as melodramatic as the moment in a horror film when the 'thing' awakes:

> Not in innocence, and not in Asia, was mankind born. The home of our fathers was that African highland reaching north from the Cape to the Lakes of the Nile. Here we came about – slowly, ever so slowly – on a sky-swept savannah glowing with menace.[15]

Ardrey's final chapter is entitled 'Children of Cain' and in between he paints a dismal picture of man. In accepting that the carnivorous, predatory Australopithecines were the unquestioned antecedents of man, Ardrey appeared to accept violence as the source of progress, arguing that man's best cultural efforts were spent, not on the tool or artefact, but in the perfecting of weapons. Hunting was basic to our characters; the long period of human existence dominated by hunting left us with habits of behaviour which were deeply inscribed in our nature. For Ardrey, the most significant of our inherited traits – territoriality, hierarchy, dominance – came from the killer apes, our forebears. He noted the popularity of Westerns and of television violence as evidence of our primitive instincts, and acclaimed *West Side Story*, with its rival gangs in New York, as a vivid portrait of the natural man. For Ardrey, juvenile delinquency was not the result of social deprivation; it was entirely normal. Untouched by cramping civilisation, the citizen of the streets found his rank and security in the gang, defending his territory and enjoying the blood and loot of the predator. Rejecting any romantic or liberal thesis of human behaviour, Ardrey found hope for the future, not in the soul or innate goodness, but in the image of man as a bad-weather animal, designed for storm and change

Desmond Morris added a further dimension to the image of the killer ape, arguing that the transition from ape to man depended upon neoteny. 'The hunting ape became an infantile ape.'[16] Neoteny is the process by which juvenile characteristics are retained and prolonged into adult life. It is in the long period of childhood dependency that complex relationships develop, and thus language and culture. The absence of hair on the body of man (as opposed to apes) may be part of the process of neoteny. Similarly, paedomorphic characteristics in women are widely acknowledged as desirable by men and are attractive also in domesticated animals. (The dog shares many of the characteristics of the immature wolf, for example.) If McCarthy's Kid represents Ardrey's juvenile delinquent, finding his gang and getting his weapons, killing out of instinct, the hairless, childlike Judge, frequently unclothed, with his well-developed brain, bipedal skills and sexual attraction to the immature, is clearly Morris's naked ape. Throughout the novel the Judge is linked to the deaths and disappearances of young children, a reminder of the neotenous condition of the naked ape with its long, vulnerable childhood. Power also comes from neoteny, in the development of cultural knowledge. It is no accident that the Judge's status with the scalphunters is assured by the manufacture of gunpowder for their weapons. When their ammunition runs out, the scalphunters are unable to hunt, or to mount any resistance to the Indians who are pursuing them. Man without fire swiftly becomes man the scavenger (an alternative evolutionary thesis, dismissed by Ardrey in *The Hunting Hypothesis*), feeding off antelope meat left behind by wolves. The Judge, however, gathers charcoal, nitre and sulphur, the whole mixture aerated by urine, to make gunpowder and save the day.[17] Naked and urinating gleefully into the mixture, he is the naked ape incarnate (p. 131). Throughout the novel, weapons of a particular sophistication or design are a continual focus – from the gunrunner Speyer's Colts, to the lavishly decorated and mounted English shotgun which Brown takes to a farrier to be cut down. The farrier's comment, 'You can't pay me to butcher that there gun' (p. 267), reveals the degree to which the weapon is fetichised and revered, as opposed to the butcherable quality of human life.

The killer ape thesis has, of course, been attacked on good scientific and moral grounds. If Ardrey's 'Territorial Imperative' merely revives the old 'Instinct of Property' in modern dress, his emphases on competition, biological nationhood and violence as the source of progress are all deeply objectionable.[18] Ralph Holloway has described *The Territorial Imperative* as 'an apology and rationalization for Imperialism, Pax Americana, Laissez Faire, Social Darwinism and that greatest of evolutionary developments, Capitalism'.[19] In the world at large, however, 'naked apery' remains popular, despite its flaws, perhaps because it offers absolution to its readers, a means of shifting our guilt onto 'natural inheritance' or 'innate aggression'. Naked apery has an exculpatory function; it provides us with 'attractive excuses for our unpleasant behaviour toward each other'.[20] It is important to note at this point that these theories emerge just as the European empires established in the nineteenth century were perceived to be ending, yielding place to American global domination. Ethological theories are thus intimately related to social anxieties at the moment when empire reaches its furthest expansion, and promptly goes into decline. Ardrey, short of money since a play of his had failed on Broadway, only went to Africa because he had a contract to write feature articles about the Mau Mau anticolonial insurgency. Boyce Rensberger comments that the story which Ardrey tells of Africa 'has its roots not in evidence and not in Africa, but in Ardrey's own emotions about Africa'.[21] Ardrey saw the African independence movements as converting a continent into a state of nature, and described Nairobi as a place embodying the 'primal dreads of a primal continent'.[22] Ethological theories represent a retrojection of the postwar world onto the whole of the past, by claiming that analogous patterns of cultural violence have always existed. Naked apery and its related theories are exculpatory fictions for guilty imperialists and Cold War warriors alike.

Without multiplying examples redundantly it is demonstrable that McCarthy draws upon ethological material in *Blood Meridian*.[23] The ethological emphasis also explains the prevalence in the novel of archaeological notations and evolutionary material. Simian imagery abounds; head injury (whether crushing with clubs, scalping or decapitation) is a particularly common feature. The men dig graves with antelope bones (p. 44), camp amidst bones, eat raw meat, hide in caves (p. 57) and are described as 'without fire or bread or camaraderie any more than bonded apes' (p. 148). Imprisoned, they 'picked at themselves like apes' (p. 74); the Mexicans take one look at the Kid and laughingly 'pummel one another like apes' (p. 65).The bones of children are 'like the ossature of small apes' (p. 90); Mexican women paint their faces 'gaudy as the rumps of apes' (p. 200). Finally the scalphunters have 'nothing about [them] to suggest even the discovery of the wheel' (p. 232), and the last survivors of the band are reduced to fighting over waterholes 'like rival bands of apes' (p. 284), the Kid moving warily on the heels of his hands (p. 291), chimp-fashion.

As that last image suggests, Man the Hunter rapidly becomes Man the Hunted. McCarthy exploits a rival view of the remains which fostered the killer ape theory to set up the central dynamic of the novel. Dart and Ardrey argue that animal remains were found with prehistoric human remains because men were hunters killing both men and animals. C.K. Brain, however, argued that the men's skulls showed that they were killed by leopards, and that both men and animals were prey to larger animals.[24] Barbara Ehrenreich notes the widespread currency of the museum cliché of 'Man the Hunter' but argues that theories of man as a bloodthirsty carnivore do not account for the human tendency to sacralise killing.[25] In her view the significant point is that sacrificial rituals celebrate or re-enact the human transition from prey to predator, teaching the lesson that human beings are meat. Before the supposed age of Man the Hunter came long aeons of Man the Hunted.

> If we seek an 'original trauma' that shaped the human response to violence, we have no need to postulate some primal guilt over hunting and killing. The original trauma ... was the trauma of being hunted by animals and eaten.[26]

In Ehrenreich's argument, human culture is heavily marked by the fear of becoming prey. A mark of human society is the practice of burying or cremating the dead – not leaving corpses to be eaten by animals. To bury the body is to cheat the beast, to refuse even in death to accept the status of prey.[27] In *Blood Meridian* funeral processions or rites are frequently set in counterpoint against the violence of the scalphunters and their rivals, with unburied bodies *passim*. Scalping has been understood as one of a complex of practices (all involving the mutilation and removal of a body part) which prevent the whole body moving to paradise, and thus convert it into prey. A particular horror in the novel is the recounted desecration of the Lipan Apache tomb, a cave in which a thousand Indians are preserved (pp. 77–8).

Stripped of their regalia and robes, their corpses swiftly disintegrate once outside the cave air – and their mummified remains are promptly scalped. The Lipan become prey even though long dead. Their status can be reversed, as can the tide of history. At another point in the novel, the scalphunters discover a diligence in which three dead bodies are 'enhearsed' in their own stink (p. 112), but rather than laying the remains decently to rest, whip up the horses to propel them across the plains in violent motion. Notably the scalphunters don't bury their dead, or anybody else's. They establish themselves as predators by converting others into prey.

Ehrenreich points to the myriad cultural features which revolve around this anxiety concerning the beast: folk tales in which smaller animals defeat larger ones; the cultural transmission of predator anxiety from parent to child; blood rites that mime predation; blood sports; commercial entertainments that feature human beings devoured by ghouls, flesh-eating monsters, vampires; the cultural heroes of Greek myth, all hunters and killers of wild beasts; even modern-day 'predator porn' (Fox TV) in which real-life footage of animal attacks on human beings is shown. Ehrenreich connects sacrifice to the human need to appease the predatory beast, to give up one member of the human group to be eaten, in order to protect the rest. As Ehrenreich notes, leaving a trail of blood attracts predators, hence the isolation in many cultures of menstruating women in one hut at some distance from the others. Plains Indian mythology associates scalping with menstruation, linking the scalped man (bloodied hair above) with the menstruating woman (bloodied hair below).[28] McCarthy describes one group of mutilated victims, 'in their wigs of dried blood' (p. 153) as having 'strange menstrual wounds' (p. 153). Scalping explicitly transforms men into prey, and associates them with women. The scalped also draw the predators away from the victors. In the aftermath of the massacre of the filibusters, wolves are seen moving towards the scalped men. When the Kid encounters a group of penitents, flagellants leaving a trail of bloody footprints behind them, he wisely takes a different path. Later he discovers all of them dead, presided over by an old woman. The Kid approaches her in friendly terms as 'abuelita' (grandmother, p. 315) only to find that she is an age-old mummified corpse. The bloody trail leads to mass death, presided over by an ancestor from the long ago past.

McCarthy emphasises that Man the Hunted is no more admirable than Man the Hunter. One incident, in which the Kid appears to be affected by a sudden unaccustomed access of mercy, makes that clear. A running fight with General Elias and a party of Sonoran cavalry leaves four scalphunters wounded and unable to ride. The men draw lots to decide who will remain behind to administer the *coup de grâce*. The Delawares simply club each of their two wounded comrades to death with one skull-crushing blow apiece. The third man, a Mexican, is already in the throes of death. But the fourth,

Shelby, his hip smashed, is conscious and otherwise unhurt. Although it is quite clear that a fate worse than death awaits Shelby once Elias catches up with him, the Kid is unwilling to kill him, and leaves him behind, alive. Inevitably, readers desperate for some sign of morality, however vestigial, in McCarthy's gorefest, have clutched at the suggestion that the Kid's action demonstrates mercy, if misplaced, as opposed to the Darwinian action of the Delawares, who simply slaughter those who can no longer keep up and thus delay the others' escape. The prey hypothesis makes the scene legible in a more chilling sense. The horrible possibility is that the Kid's decision is not motivated by compassion, or even by moral cowardice. Rather the Kid acts out of strategy: he leaves Shelby as bait, to delay Elias's pursuit, a sacrifice to ensure the escape of the others. The scalphunter is left to be prey for the Mexican hunters, already visible upon the horizon.

Throughout the novel McCarthy emphasises the fear of the predator. Sproule awakens to find a vampire bat drinking his blood (p. 66). One of the Delawares is carried off by a bear, dangling from its mouth 'like some fabled storybook beast' (p. 137). The precarious dominance of man over beast is repeatedly celebrated. Jugglers juggle with dogs; chickens, hogs, and in one particular scene two puppies, are wantonly shot. But in a small circus, amongst the display of caged vipers and lizards, the Kid confronts in one container, a pickled human head. 'It was Captain White. Lately at war against the heathen' (p. 70). The rest of him has been eaten by hogs. The message that man is meat is frequently repeated. Entering Chihuahua, the Texans are pelted with offal and driven like cattle (p. 72), while vultures perch on the cathedral, itself ornamented with scalps. The men ride past 'the carnage in the meatstalls' (p. 73), the guts and flensed skulls. In prison, the Kid hails Toadvine with 'I'd recognize your hide in a tanyard' (p. 73); forcing down tough bullmeat from the corrida, the Kid describes it as if it were still alive and an adversary: 'Don't let it feel ye to weaken' (p. 76). In contrast, the scalphunters demonstrate that they are not meat but meat-eaters by wearing trappings of human skin and hair (p. 78), ornamenting themselves with human ears and teeth as if they 'fed on human flesh' (p. 78). Meat fascinates. A group of Indians initiate trade purely because they have never seen sawed bones in a stew before (p. 87). Hunter and hunted change places repeatedly. The scalphunters encounter *ciboleros* (Hispanic buffalo-hunters) hung with dried meat and dressed in skins sewn with the animals' ligaments. When they enter a meat camp (p. 104) they promptly scalp the inhabitants, turning them from meat-hunters to meat, against a backdrop of 'butcherpaper mountains' (p. 105). Near the close the Judge appears, stark naked, but 'bedraped with meat' (p. 282), steaks hanging on his body in bandoliers.

The peculiar resonance of scalphunting is that it conjoins Man the Hunter with Man the Hunted, the predator become prey. The most striking moments in McCarthy's fiction are those points where prey suddenly becomes predator, and vice versa, as destiny and evolutionary progress apparently reverse. In *No Country for Old Men*, Llewelyn Moss is hunting antelope when he makes a fatal error of judgment and becomes a target to Anton Chigurh, the avenger of a drugs cartel, whose weapon of choice, a stun gun, implies that men are cattle, animals bound for slaughter.[29] Wells, a freelance investigator, is sent to track Moss but ends up himself tracked and killed by Chigurh, as hunter becomes hunted. In *Blood Meridian* the reader is often left uncertain who is chasing whom, as the roles of hunter and hunted criss-cross. The text repeatedly forces us to ask ourselves whether we are dealing with Man the Hunter, or the Hunted, with predator or with prey. In itself the historical detail of the conflict in Mexico also gives plentiful examples of hunters becoming hunted and vice versa. The historical Glanton fought against General Urrea in Texas. Despite the fact that Urrea massacred 330 surrendered American prisoners at Goliad, Glanton (one of the Goliad survivors) later served Urrea as an Indian fighter.[30] The Kid hunts Comanches who then hunt him, is pursued and taken prisoner by the Mexicans, becomes a scalphunter for the Mexicans, preying on Indians, and is preyed on again in his turn. When the gang camp at the Hueca tanks, the ancient rock paintings left by hunters of the past include images of 'men and animals and of the chase' (p. 173), one of which the Judge promptly erases, a hunter erasing other hunters. When the Indians pursue Glanton's unarmed men, tracking them relentlessly, the Judge's expertise with powder-making suddenly turns the tables, as hunted become hunters, promptly massacring the Apaches. At another point the men ride in the tracks of the Indian war-party in order to make it less easy for the Mexicans to track them. And the Kid and the Judge play out the roles of prey and predator in various ways, alternating as allies and enemies until their final embrace at the close of the novel establishes the intimacy of the prey–predator relation.[31]

In plot terms the emblematic moment in which hunters and hunted change places is the Comanche attack upon Captain White's filibusters, a scene which satirises the attractions of a genealogy of violence. Captain White, secure in his sense of the American civilising mission, dismisses the Comanches as 'a parcel of heathen stockthieves' (p. 51), and looks forward to 'a little sport' (p. 51). Suddenly there arises 'a fabled horde of mounted lancers and archers' (p. 52) attacking out of their ponies' dust, massacring the Texans, scalping, sodomising and eviscerating them as they lie dying. McCarthy bases his description upon the Battle of Plum Creek (1840), which followed the great Linnville raid in which the Comanches, 700-strong, under Buffalo Hump, raided the coastal warehouse settlement of Linnville, carrying off an enormous amount of loot, including some 3,000 horses and a large number of pack-mules. McCarthy describes the warriors, their horses' ears and tails worked with bits of brightly coloured cloth, as wearing all manner of costumes, including dragoons' uniforms, cavalry jackets, a blood-stained bridal dress, a head-dress of crane feathers, the armour of a conquistador, with one man in a stovepipe hat carrying an umbrella, and another in a pigeon-tailed coat worn backwards. All the historical accounts of the Battle of Plum Creek include these details. The Comanches had looted a warehouse full of red cloth, stovepipe hats, umbrellas and ladies' finery, and galloped off, umbrellas aloft, in tall hats with trailing bolts of red cloth tied to their horses' tails. John Holland Jenkins (who fought at Plum Creek) notes 'a huge warrior who wore a stovepipe hat', another 'in a fine pigeon-tailed cloth coat buttoned up behind', others wearing buck and buffalo horns and one with a head-dress consisting of 'a large white crane with red eyes'.[32] At Plum Creek, the Texas militia were heavily outnumbered. Buffalo Hump's entire strategy was merely to delay battle and distract them long enough to get the remuda and the loot past them. The wheeling braves followed the usual pattern of a Comanche attack, which involved the circling and weaving of independent warriors, swirling, breaking, gesticulating obscenely, dissolving and regrouping, making difficult moving targets, so that 'The net effect sometimes mesmerised the waiting enemy.'[33] Theirs was a deliberate theatricality, designed to distract their opponents.

In history, however, as opposed to the novel, the tactic failed. When General Houston gave the order, the Texans attacked, stampeding the horses, which ran into the booty-laden mules. Bogged down in marshy ground, a mass of frightened animals trampled each other and trapped the Comanches. The battle turned into a rout, as the Comanches abandoned their loot and fled for their lives, pursued by the Texans, who eventually mounted a punitive mission to hunt them down and massacre them. In strong contrast to the historical account, McCarthy reverses the roles of hunters and hunted, rewriting history. In converting Native American loss to victory, McCarthy testifies first and foremost to a broader historical truth, the often forgotten fact that a relatively small number of Comanches kept an exploding culture at bay for years by sheer ferocity.[34] There was nothing manifestly destined about American expansion in the area. In the 1840s Comanche terror tactics had intensified; regular raids into Mexico went unchallenged by a Mexican army which had been almost destroyed; and the Comanches succeeded in denying the Anglo-Americans possession of their hunting grounds for some 40 years. As Fehrenbach argues, the Civil War exacerbated the situation so that in 1864 the true frontier had actually retreated by some 100–200 miles, back to the settlement lines of the 1840s.[35] The apparent tide of history had reversed, if temporarily. The period of the novel, identified by critics as the founding moment of American empire, is actually a moment where empire goes into reverse. The apparent moment of its highest expansion is also that of its sudden decline, betrayed by its own 'predacious' nature. As the Judge puts it, wolves may be savage but 'is the race of man not more predacious yet?' (p. 146). For man, 'the noon of his expression signals the onset of night. His spirit is exhausted at the peak of its achievement. His meridian is at once his darkening and the evening of his day' (pp. 146–7). As the subtitle of the novel indicates, as American territorial domination increases so, in Yeatsian fashion, it spirals out of control. Ethology undermines cultural triumphalism, and is associated with the moment of imperial decline.

In McCarthy's invention, the Comanches win the battle because they mount a theatrical spectacle which involves the display of men as beasts, and of a dramatised genealogy of slaughter. The exhibition of wildness and of historical violence is put to strategic, dazzling purposes. To the musical accompaniment of flutes made from human bones, the Comanches attack, and the Texan response stalls, fatally, for a breathless page of description, mesmerising reader and victims alike. Through the dust the painted designs on the ponies appear 'like the shade of old work through sizing on canvas' (p. 52), like an archaeological trace or palimpsest. The warriors are described in terminology drawn from military campaigns and cultural identities going back thousands of years. They are lancers, archers, 'a legion', 'clad in costumes attic or biblical', riding down 'the unhorsed Saxons' (p. 54) as if 'Mongol hordes' or conquistadors, leaving their scalped victims like 'tonsured' (p. 54) monks. Violence is Viking, Asian, Biblical, Greek and Roman, with the Comanches advertising their status as predators not prey in their trophies of buffalo horns and crane feathers. The emphasis on different historical periods, races and cultures disseminates an image of animals and human beings merged as one, in some mass genealogical fantasy of predation. The theatricality of these 'funhouse figures' (p. 54), their painted faces 'grotesque with daubings like a company of mounted clowns' (p. 53) forms a fascinating, but deadly, spectacle for the Texan onlooker. By the time the watching sergeant comes bathetically to his senses ('Oh my god. Said the sergeant.', p. 53), men are already dying around him. McCarthy's depiction portrays the Comanches not as beast-men who turned the clock back, but as clever strategists exploiting the theatricality of violence to their own ends. In a sense they are doing just what Ardrey does – exploiting the image of a long pedigree of human violence to their own advantage. The reader, sucked into McCarthy's mesmerising, headlong description, its catalogue of copulative phrases and its anachronisms ('shields bedight with bits of broken mirror glass', p. 52) is forced to confront the dazzling nature of the genealogical spectacle of violence, as itself a form of and cover for violence.[36] These 'beasts' in horns and feathers are careful strategists engaging the eye to mesmerise and dazzle, their display of past ancestry spellbinding the sergeant to his ultimate destruction. Far from indulging in primitivism, McCarthy reflects it back upon the reader, in deconstructed form, shards of mirror glass.

The Comanche attack is something of a rhetorical *tour de force*, but throughout the novel theatrical displays of beastliness recur, undermining the essentialist nature of ethological theory, and often also drawing attention to such displays as popular entertainment. The action begins in a circus tent, when the Judge accuses the Reverend Green of a history of bestiality, specifically sexual congress with a goat. Significantly this bestiality turns out to be entirely fictional; the Judge has never laid eyes on the churchman before. The tent, collapsing in beastly fashion ('like a huge and wounded medusa', p. 7), conflates the celebration and condemnation of the beast into one paradigm of prey and predator. Circus animals recur, when a small group of circus people join the Glanton gang for safe passage. In the gang there are two men called John Jackson, the one white, the other black. Black Jackson is the enemy of White Jackson and figures initially as resentful but non-aggressive. Then Black Jackson becomes a member of the circus and is seen performing 'strange posturings' (p. 99) under the light of torches, displaying himself half-naked as an exhibit. When next he encounters his racist white counterpart and is refused room at the fire, he has gained sufficient courage to decapitate him on the spot. As Adam Parkes has argued, in the hostility between White Jackson and Black Jackson, the novel gives the victory not to the white racist (the essentialist) but to the black performer.[37] Theatricalised wildness is what makes Black Jackson able to strike back. Later he is himself attacked in a scene of reverse minstrelsy by the Yumas at the river crossing, their faces painted black, as if in an 'atavistic drama' (p. 274). The point here is not that 'all the world's a play', that selves are merely performative, and ethnic and racial identities fluid. Rather McCarthy underlines the fashion in which atavistic drama licenses and enables violence, as ethology excuses and perpetuates it in culture. One episode demonstrates McCarthy's separation from the tenets of naked apery in quite specific terms. Arriving in Tucson, Glanton and the Judge spot a rude tent with a sign, 'See The Wild Man Two Bits'. Within a crude wooden cage crouches 'a naked imbecile' (p. 233) peering at them with dull hostility. When his 'owner' joins Glanton's company, alone, Glanton asks, 'Where's your ape at?' (p. 238). In fact the imbecile is the man's brother. The scene deliberately parodies the popular image of evolution from wild hairy ape to naked ape. Originally the idiot's wildness was enhanced by an animal costume, but according to his brother, the idiot saw it as meat. 'I had him a hair suit made but he ate it' (p. 238). Neotenous, hairless, almost brainless, the imbecile has shucked off his ape costume only to become a parody of the naked ape. The Judge, however, finds his older brother an equally interesting specimen, carefully feeling his skull to check the degree of his humanity. According to the brother, the idiot has always been like this. 'He was born that way.' Glanton's response, 'Were you?' (p. 239), registers his distaste for a man who would exhibit his faeces-smeared brother for pay, to make a profit out of the attractions of the wild-man myth. The scene asks the reader to consider who is the 'primitive' specimen – the idiot, or the brother who makes theatre out of the idea of a regressive image of man, an image which people will pay to see? The Judge is of course instantly attracted. He not only saves the idiot from drowning, but makes him his familiar, a reflection of his own naked apery. In his last appearance, accompanying the Judge, the latter festooned with slabs of meat, the idiot's 'simian' steps (p. 273) lend him a resemblance to a 'naked species of lemur' (p. 298).

In the course of the novel McCarthy embeds his moral in an interpolated story which sketches the central theme. Around the campfire the Judge tells the story of a man, a harness maker, who begged by the roadside, impersonating an Indian in feathers and beads, until a young traveller recognised him as a white man and rebuked him. The harness maker, ashamed, offered him hospitality, continued to wheedle money from him, then for no apparent reason killed him, burying him by the roadside and inventing a fiction of attack by robbers. On his deathbed he confessed to his son, who 'went away to the west and he himself became a killer of men' (p. 145). The audience reaction to the story is telling; the men burst forth with rival claims to know or be related to the protagonists, to exonerate the killer or to relocate him in their own familiar landscapes. Everyone claims a connection, genealogical or otherwise. The Judge then adds a rider to the tale: the traveller also had a son, born posthumously, in whose memory his father's image shines bright. Which son is most disadvantaged? The son who knows his father to be a wanton killer? (And therefore, unburdened by the need to live up to a parental model, feels perfectly free to be anything at all.) Or the son for whom the father is 'the idol of a perfection to which he can never attain' (p. 145)? For the Judge the traveller's death has 'euchered the son out of his patrimony' (p. 145). In his argument it is not in fact a good thing to have an ideal vision of the past. It is actually more attractive to have an image of hereditary evil, to know one's progenitor as a killer, and thus to be excused from the moral obligation to emulate a previous perfection. The harness maker masqueraded as an Indian – making a fictitious 'savage' ancestry pay. For the Judge, American to the core, 'savage' ancestry also pays dividends psychologically, in the son's freedom to make himself without a paternal model. The Judge uses the incident to argue for the nature of man as 'predacious' (p. 146), a term which is imported from ethological discourse, to offer an image of human existence as dominated by Darwinist survival of the fittest. But what the anecdote primarily demonstrates is the exculpatory attraction of a genealogy of violence. The story is told in the setting of the ruined dwellings of the Anasazi people, now lost to memory, whose artefacts surround the camp, a visual reminder of a people who did not survive. Importantly, the interpolated story also focuses on the proper disposal of the dead; how we handle our ancestors in specific physical terms, as opposed to psychologically. While the traveller is rebuking the harness maker, a hearse passes by, drawn by a black man and containing a black body. Although the African-American is dressed gaudily, even clownishly, and the hearse painted pink, he is, in the Judge's words, 'a man among men' (p. 143) for whom a place must be made. In contrast to this ritualised disposal of the dead, the harness maker's son exhumes and scatters the bones of the murdered man. The African-American is burying his dead with due ceremony; the white American leaves the bones for animals, an apparently minor detail which underlines the contrast between traducing our ancestors with ethological theory, and paying them due honour as men among men. White America exhumes the decently and previously buried, scalps the living, scatters remains, in order to maintain its predatory self-image. And it leaves a place for the black man only as a mythical savage. In these scenes and images, McCarthy's novel signals itself as a pastiche ethological work which overtly declares itself as theatre, in mocking reference to Ardrey. Near the close of the action, McCarthy refers back to the story of the harness maker. Elrod is an orphan; 'His granddaddy was killed by a lunatic and buried in the woods like a dog' (p. 323). Elrod has not learned, however, by his ancestor's example. The final argument between Elrod and the Kid hinges upon the desire for savage origins for men's cruelty. The Kid has kept the necklace of black ears worn by his friend Brown, Apache ears turned black by time. But Elrod is not interested in historical facts; he refuses to believe that these are American trophies and argues that they are 'niggers'' ears, and potentially those of 'cannibals or any other kind of foreign nigger' at that, like the shrunken heads available in New Orleans (p. 321). Ironically, as a result he is shot dead by a killer much more dangerous than any mythic African primitive. Elrod is a hunter of buffalo bones, one of a party dressed in skins or 'green hide boots peeled whole from the hocks of some animal' (p. 318), but he is no match for the Kid, who turns the tables by a decoy manoeuvre, evades his ambush and shoots him.

But what of the dancing bear in the novel's final scene? In the last pages of the novel, the Kid and the Judge meet again in a saloon, against the background of a performance by a dancing bear, who is suddenly shot by a drunken bystander. Wounded, blood running down his groin, wearing a crinoline, the feminised bear bleeds to death with his head in the lap of a little girl, covering the front of her dress with blood, 'like some monster slain in the commission of unnatural acts' (p. 327). After his death, his place is taken by the Judge, dancing naked. Apparently the ending offers an image of the relentless desire of man to hunt, to kill and to annihilate the predator. The bear was harmless, yet even though men have tamed him and forced him to dance, converting him into a triumphant image of the predator under control (here, moreover, under the control of a small child) one of the men still cannot resist shooting him. The bear and the girl together form an image of the scalped prey, the bloodied lap, as the apparently triumphant Judge is left alone on stage, the naked ape incarnate. The little girl is soon being sought for – another of the Judge's putative victims (p. 327), as indeed may be the Kid, apparently murdered offstage. Events appear to support the popular Social Darwinist moral that there can be only one tiger to a hill – or as the Judge puts it,

> There is room on the stage for one beast and one alone. All others are destined for a night that is eternal and without name. One by one they will step down into the darkness before the footlamps. Bears that dance, bears that don't (p. 331).

The Judge occupies the evolutionary stage alone, dancing and saying over and over again that he will never die.

McCarthy may, however, be offering a sly insider joke to the informed reader. When the ethological thesis of man the killer emerged, it was countered satirically by the image of man the dancer. Anthropologists have discussed the human propensity for keeping together in time, as in dancing or military drilling, and suggested that it can be traced to the primordial sociality of the hominid band confronting a wild animal. Thus the exigencies of antipredator defence may owe as much to dancing as to anything else. As several commentators have playfully pointed out, the evidence for dancing as the vital trait that transformed ape into man is as persuasive as any other. The titles of Leonard Williams's *The Dancing Chimpanzee* and Frank B. Livingstone's 'Did the Australopithecines sing?' speak for themselves. In proposing the theory of Man the Dancer, Robert Sussman argued that using the cultural-survival approach, the evidence for dancing is as good as that for hunting.[38] Men and women love to dance; it is a behaviour found in all cultures. A variety of social systems could have developed from the dance (square, line, riverdance, war). It is difficult to dance on all fours (hence bipedalism). Leaving the trees, cooperating, singing (a human trait) can all be related to man the dancer.

The story does not end, however, in the dance. McCarthy closes with an epilogue in which the facts of real history replace the timeless myths of naked apery, as the posthole-makers advance across the plains to fence them in, followed by bone-pickers collecting buffalo bones. The workers' creation of postholes to contain or exclude the beast takes place against the background of the extinction of the US buffalo herd, the last great American beasts. Now, however, man no longer eats their meat; their bones are being collected for fertiliser. All the preceding chapters have consciously archival 'playbill' headings, summarising the main action in advance, a technique which overtly aligns the novel with nineteenth-century forebears. The epilogue, however, merely features an empty space, fenced off by ornamental lines from the italicised text which follows. In visual terms it replaces the scene settings with a blank stage curtain. Previous chapters encouraged the reader to read forwards while simultaneously referring back to the chapter headings, for clarification of the action. For example, the heading to Chapter IV includes 'pursued by cholera' (p. 42). In the chapter, the reader learns only that two men fall sick and die; cholera is never mentioned. 'Old Ephraim' (p. 136) appears to have no relevance to the story; it is actually the name of a fabled monster bear in folktale, referring to the ursine abduction of the Delaware. The chapter headings offer the reader a trail to follow, though often a misleading or baffling one, in which there seems little logic to the clues. 'Herdsmen on the plain' (p. 42), for example, gives the reader no sense of the Comanche horde to which it refers. 'Death of Juan Miguel' (p. 151) precedes a chapter in which there are many deaths, but no character is so named. And what reader would connect 'The ogdoad' (p. 204), referring to eight deities of Upper Egypt, with a circle of decapitated men's heads (p. 220)? As hunters we are lead astray and fail, falling into the ironic traps set by the chapter headings. At the close, however, the trail ends in blankness; in the epilogue, movement is entirely forwards, into modern time. The empty space fenced in at the close, in its half page of blank paper, is suggestive of the counter-narratives of Manifest Destiny in nineteenth-century literature, generated by apparently empty spaces, tales of the emptiness or hollowness of the West.[39] Far from emphasising the moment at which the United States apparently realises the continentalist dream, McCarthy both expands onto another continent entirely, and shrinks empire down to the empty space of an animal boneyard.

7 Priority narratives
Bharati Mukherjee's *Desirable Daughters*

Nobody will deny that this is an age of connectedness, in horizontal terms, with simultaneity of time and the borders of space erased. How are we to avoid being swamped by an overload of connections, a homogenising mass? How do we establish meaningful connections in the general soup of signs in which the modern individual swims? In an internet world, story links to story, windows open on new stories, and no overall authority establishes priority. James Lull poses the question succinctly:

> The challenge for people today is to navigate and combine an unprecedented range of cultural territories and resources, ranging from relatively unfamiliar terrains imported to the self through technological mediations and human migrations of various types, to territory that is far more familiar and stable, such as that offered by religion, nation and family, in order to invent combinations that satisfy individuals' changing needs and preferences.[1]

One temptation in such a world of rapid change is for people to group 'around primary identities: religious, ethnic, territorial, national'.[2] In the absence, however, of a dominant code or master narrative, Lull argues that culture is becoming an individualistic enterprise, in which people create their own super-cultures or cultural matrices, becoming in a sense their own 'cultural programmers',[3] not merely as consumers or as members of an audience but by actively fusing near and far, traditional and modern, in order to create worlds which transform life-experience and reconfigure the meaning of cultural space. Lull's comments are highly suggestive in relation to Bharati Mukherjee's *Desirable Daughters*, and especially to its narrator Tara, whose attempts to centre the story upon her individual experience are repeatedly frustrated by a whirling centrifuge of other stories, alternative models, involving different territories, migrations and mediations.

Mukherjee's novel takes as its starting point the heroine's most American of impulses, a 'roots search'.[4] The action ranges widely across time and space, in a murder plot which links India, the Indian community in Jackson Heights, and the present-day existence of the narrator, Tara Bhattarcharjee (formerly Mrs Bish Chatterjee, from Calcutta), living, as the action opens, in San Francisco with her lover, Andy Karolyi, Hungarian refugee, ex-Hells Angel, and now 'Zen Master of the Retrofit', proofing Californian homes against the threat of earthquake. As Tara comments, 'I saw my life on a broad spectrum, with Calcutta not at the centre, but just another station on the dial.'[5] Tara is both a protagonist and the narrator, the author of the book which we are reading, composing her own story, based upon the history of her family. Her ex-husband Bish is a different type of author, a writer of software programs who now enjoys semi-mythological status among Indians as the Stanford college student who, with his equally penniless friend Chet Yee, made a fortune overnight in computer bandwidth routing technology. Bish's globally operating connections threaten to dwarf Tara's individual existence. As Amitava Kumar comments, 'It is the software writers from India rather than the fiction writers who are wired to the circuits of global production.'[6] In the novel, the central question concerns the usefulness or redundancy of narrative in a globalised world. Is there a use for the novel when primary myths have been superseded by internet connections and software writers? Tara grants the proposition that story has a traditionally adaptive function, in the example of her grandmother's stories.

> When you are armed with Hindu stories, every earthly tragedy is a shadow of something greater, from a previous time. Consolation comes from comparison … Had a bad day at the office? Well, at least you didn't get decapitated and have to go through life with an elephant's head replacement (pp. 149–50).

Hindu stories are lurid, shape-changing, gender-bending, involving grand-scale slaughter and polymorphous sexuality. One example is the story, told by her grandmother, of Shitala, the goddess of smallpox, laying waste a kingdom. Her grandmother grew up before vaccination became routine, hence her ability to comfort herself with story (p. 57). Now the narrative is redundant. Tara's Buddhist lover Andy tells very different stories, 'plain and everyday. Traveller Po came across a fork in the road … Farmer Jiang had three beautiful daughters' (p. 148). Andy's stories, minimalist rather than maximalist, shrink the individual into insignificance. Tara has no time for Andy's stories, in which nobody is a hero or heroine; only nature has a starring role. Instead she writes the novel in order to place herself centre stage, arranging the materials around herself. As Mukherjee commented, 'In writing up history, she is going to reframe it, to tell herself a myth to survive by.'[7]

One mark of the effect of globalisation upon the novel is the resurgence of interest in theories of the novel which might be termed 'Darwinist', 'evolutionary' or 'sociobiological', reacting to the perception that our old stories may no longer be a good fit for us. Edward O. Wilson is the major figure in the field, arguing in straightforwardly Darwinian terms that literature has a profoundly adaptive function, part of the human urge to create scenarios, reading ahead into distant places or times. Stories thus enable human beings to survive and reproduce better in their environment. In Wilson's example, myths and tales of serpents improve people's chances of vigilance and survival in societies where snakebite is an important cause of mortality.[8] Through myth and story, snakes acquire additional meanings which reinforce their power and danger. Wilson also highlights the fashion in which stories frequently focus upon 'cheater detection'. Contractual agreement pervades human social behaviour and as a result the capacity to detect cheating has developed to exceptional levels of sharpness and rapid calculation. Both points are suggestive in relation to a novel which explores the consequences of snakebite across the centuries, and focuses upon true and false claimants. Wilson's points are, of course, of a broad, general nature and therefore in some ways blindingly obvious. In *Beyond Ethnicity* Werner Sollors makes a more specific case for considering the function of American stories in relation to family and migration. Sollors emphasises the complicated fashion in which narratives of descent (inherited family and ethnic ties) intersect with narratives of consent (chosen identities, contractual relations and imagined communities) in the making of an American self, in which a new identity is shaped. In the American national character, notions of legitimacy and privilege based upon descent are repeatedly denied in favour of the newcomer's rebirth into a forward-looking culture of consent. *The Scarlet Letter* is again the national psychodrama: Chillingworth the representative of an old-world arranged marriage, Dimmesdale the representative of consensual love and modernity.[9] This model might well be applied to Tara, whose arranged marriage breaks down in America, as she claims American liberties, only to be challenged subsequently by a representative of the world she has left behind.

What kinds of story are adaptive therefore in a broadband world? What are the 'right' stories for globalised women? Mukherjee's exploration of this question is novel in that she explores the oppositions of tradition and modernity, descent versus consent, through the microcosm of a sibship, three sisters, as its members adapt to different environments, thus setting up a series of oppositions between 'family' stories and 'global' plots, as they jockey for position as priority narratives. The desirable daughters of the title, Didi, Parvati and Tara, are part of an apparently doomed social group, teasingly described in Darwinian terminology, as 'homo bengalensis, subspecies Hindu Calcutta, subbreed Ballygunge' (p. 245), a middle-class, conservative, Calcutta-bred clan, 'already extinct in our native habitat' (p. 245). The plot turns upon a case of attempted identity theft, when Tara finds a stranger, 'Chris Dey', claiming to be her nephew. 'Chris Dey' addresses Tara in terms which emphasise family intimacy and sisterly kinship. He calls her 'Tara-mashi' (maternal aunt, p. 34). In India every word relating to family carries a special meaning, and indicates place in relation to sibships (lateral branches of the family) as well as place in terms of descent: Padma-didi (oldest sister), Parvati-di (middle sister); mashi and mesho for maternal aunt and uncle; pishi and pishemashai for paternal aunt and uncle. In *Desirable Daughters* Mukherjee uses the dynamics of a group of sisters to explore the way in which a story is claimed, transmitted or denied, how even in the apparent homogeneity of three almost identical sisters divergent roles are created, and what the political consequences are of a place in a sibship – envisaged as a literary and social model largely replacing 'vertical' lines of descent.

Mukherjee's model of relationships also builds notions of rebellion and revolt into the lines of descent and consent. Unknown to her sisters, Didi had given illegitimate birth to a son, Christopher, fathered by Ronald Dey, an Anglo-Indian Christian. Tara's attempts to excavate the story, verify or disprove the identity of the claimant, and engage in wholesale cheater detection, expose the lack of real connections between the apparently intimate family, in the context of the political contest between tradition and modernity. In the novel, the illegitimate child is doubly bastardised and twice rejected. As the illegitimate offspring of a Bengali Brahmin's eldest daughter, conceived in passion with an Anglo-Indian Christian, Chris Dey's existence goes unrecognised, his mother refusing ever to admit to his existence. His descent is utterly denied. Before the adult Chris can claim his heritage, his place is usurped by an interloper who kills him, steals his name and attempts to take his place in the family. By the time Tara establishes the existence of the illegitimate child, the real son is already at the bottom of San Francisco Bay. The claims of descent are not validated. The point of the novel is not to re-establish contact with a denied male line, but to focus on a sibship. Or rather, two sibships: the three sisters of the present and their distant relation, the Tree Bride, also one of a sibship of three. Mukherjee's plot sets up two models of connectedness: the global (embodied in both the apparent master of connectivity, Bish Chatterjee, the software genius, and the criminally networked 'Chris Dey') and the three sisters whose connections are traditional, intimate and lateral. In the action there is a continual tension between the two stories, alternately prioritised.

The novel begins with the story of the Tree Bride. In its opening epigraph Mukherjee evokes tradition – both as impossible to follow, and as a felt necessity.

> No one behind, no one ahead
> The path the ancients cleared has closed.
> And the other path, everyone's path,
> Easy and wide, goes nowhere.
> I am alone and find my way.

In interview Mukherjee commented that this Sanskrit verse, adapted by Octavio Paz, translated by Eliot Weinberger, and passed to her by a Bolivian graduate student in Berkeley, embodied 'the globalization that we really want to prize ... that we can take from each other's heritages what we need and sew it together into our heritage.'[10] The opposition between the narrow traditional path (closed) and the broad, easy, pathless present (without a connection back to the past) is embodied in the contrast between the opening scene of the novel and its broadband present. The novel opens onto a path disappearing into the dense fog of the Sunderbans, 'a distant wall of impenetrable jungle' (p. 3) in a scene which explicitly engineers an encounter between tradition and modernity. To an American reader this opening could hardly be more remote; to any reader the action – the arranged marriage of a five-year-old girl – is likely to evoke unease. Ostensibly everything suggests the horrors of past 'darkness' and absence of consent, as opposed to present-day enlightenment. The scene is set on the darkest night of the Bengali month of Paush. On the narrow raised trail the wedding procession wends its way from Mishtigunj in 1879, lit by flickering oil lamps, through flooded fields where banks of fog and smoke from cooking fires obscure the moon and dim the man-made light 'to faintness deeper than the stars' (p. 3). This is a world of corruption, stagnation and disease: 'Tuberculosis is everywhere. The air, the water, the soil are septic' (p. 3). Such enlightenment as there is, is European and modern. The procession is preceded by servants holding naphtha lamps. 'No one has seen such brilliant European light' (p. 4). But in a plot device which suspends lines of descent in favour of sibship connection, Tara Lata, the bride, is not about to be transferred to a human bridegroom to continue an ancestral line. She is headed deep into the forest to marry a tree. Her family tree is just that – a large hardwood. Indian lack of light (metaphorically and literally) is apparently the cause; the groom has died of snakebite in the dark, and Tara Lata has become unmarriageable, a bearer of ill fortune. For a solution her father turns to Hindu custom. In marrying her to a proxy-husband, a tree, he permits her to occupy the respected position of married woman, within the family home.

What appears to be a bizarre practice is in fact a highly efficient adaptive strategy, given the surrounding circumstances. The return to tradition is also a revolt against modernity. Tara Lata becomes famous for acts of rebellion. Her dowry gold finances Gandhi's salt march; her house offers refuge for dissidents fighting the British Raj; she becomes a freedom fighter and ultimately a martyr. As the memorial plaque informs us, 'She rallied the Cause of an Independent India and United Bengal and protected Young Freedom Fighters from British arrest' (p. 20). Dragged from her home on the night of 12 October 1944 by colonial authorities, she is hanged in a police cell as British forces attempt to quell the Bengal insurgency. Paradoxically, therefore, in pursuing Indian tradition and confining his daughter to a life without the distractions of husband, children and mother-in-law, Jai Krishna transforms her into a freethinker. Immobile in the home, 'the world came to her' (p. 17). An act apparently out of step with any evolutionary goal is socially instrumental. As an opening sequence, therefore, the story which Tara tells of the Tree Bride raises a host of questions concerning the relation of tradition to modernity, conformity to rebellion. Faced with rapid change, the father has opted for an apparently 'primary' identity. In an era when fundamentalists are attempting to redeem a 'pure' Hindu past, the image of a return to tradition as a valuable nationalist step has a disquieting resonance. In little the Tree Bride's story appears to validate the glories of a nationalist past against the diminished claims of the modern present. 'Enlightenment' is apparently discredited; the inventive traditionalist secures his daughter's place in the world by a fiction of marriage which returns her unscathed to her sisters, to live out her life in the family home. Tara Lata becomes 'Tara Ma', an honorary mother to the nationalist family – and an inspirational foremother to the narrator, whose apparently Utopian modern life in California comes under threat in the course of the novel.

But why has Tara chosen to tell this story? What needs does it fulfil? Tara's own story is ostensibly that of an entirely untraditional Bengali-American who has rebelled against the enclosed life of an Indian wife, divorced her husband, and set up home with a lover in a multi-ethnic neighbourhood almost synonymous with revolt: the Haight. She has recently campaigned for a gay Chicano candidate, wears blue jeans and works in a school. If the Tree Bride's path is narrow and traditional, and her world circumscribed, Tara's is quite the reverse. Hers is emphatically a broadband world. As students at Stanford her husband Bish and his partner Chet Yee discovered a process for allowing computers to create their own time, instantaneously routing information to the least congested lines (p. 24). As an architect of globalisation, Bish is none the less exceptionally traditional. 'A first son from an outstanding family' (p. 23) of Calcutta conservatives, Bish lives up to family expectations, becoming an engineering student in India 'because his father told him he would be an engineer' (p. 44). Bish is part of the process of globalisation, the process by which people become increasingly interconnected across natural borders and continents. His mobile phone routing devices connect the whole world. Yet he is also the product of complete loyalty to tradition. As previously mentioned, Bish's discovery was prompted by a football game in which the players exploited the 'West Coast Offense', a tactic in which short passing plays replace the running game, to control the ball – a process invented by Bill Walsh of the Cincinnati Bengals.[11] The bandwidth system, called CHATTY, is 'about width, using the whole field, connecting in the flat, no interference, a billion short passes linked together' (p. 24). It also exemplifies the method of Mukherjee's novel. In interview Mukherjee said that

> The aesthetic strategy of the book was using the width of the field – of history, geography, diaspora, gender, ethnicity, language – rather than the old-fashioned long, clean throw.[12]

So what happens in the novel is that the reader is passed from story to story across a broad geographical and historical sweep; the narrative passes from one controller to another, at times appearing to be misdirected or displaced, with the story moving forward through changes of direction, side-passes, misdirections and feints. The straight trajectory of a story based on descent is replaced by a model which involves many side connections, sibships and horizontal or lateral moves. Connections are made through a process which also underlines the problems of connection. Arguably, through the connectedness of information, and the shrinking of space and time, all our histories intersect in the modern world. We can no longer move back onto the traditional narrow path; we are in the same time with interconnecting histories, and an awareness of time as space. Bish's discovery underlines the sense in the novel of a complex network of connections in which people are both receivers and senders across a very broad field, where routers are as important as roots. As Paul Harris argues,

> Narrative no longer seems to work by imposing the telos of plot on the contingencies of the world, but by sifting through dispersed bits of discrete input and rendering them intelligent and coherent.[13]

The risk of loss of aesthetic value is a real one. In this vision, what differentiates the novel from a form of information farming? Cultural synthesising or programming does not facilitate cheater detection, the seeking of truth.

Bish's connectivity also has its darker side. On the one hand the mobile phone figures repeatedly as a security device. When 'Chris Dey' appears,

Tara relies on the phone; she has both her lover and the police on her speed-dial. She uses the internet to locate Ronald Dey and check the intruder's claims. But 'Chris Dey' located her on the internet, and is himself part of a worldwide criminal network. Manuel Castells has highlighted the emergence of global crime, the networking of powerful criminal organisations across the planet, as a relatively new phenomenon; in his argument, criminal penetration of financial markets constitutes a critical element in a fragile global economy, and an essential feature of the Information Age. While basing their management and production firmly in low-risk, controllable areas, such cartels habitually target areas of affluence, exploiting allegiances with other cartels, their 'business practices' closely following those of the network enterprise of the Information Age. Immigrant networks are often used to penetrate First World societies; contemporary cartels exploit cultural identity to hold their enterprise together. 'Criminal networks are probably in advance of multinational corporations in their decisive ability to combine cultural identity and global business.'[14] Mukherjee herself has good reason to be aware of the transnationality of crime. Her non-fiction work, *The Sorrow and the Terror*, explored diasporic fundamentalism, sleeper cells and cyber-terrorism. In a painstaking investigation of the 1985 Air India bombing in which a Khalistani (Sikh secessionist) group blew up a Canadian flight bound for India, killing 329 people, Mukherjee drew attention to the worldwide fundraising for terrorist activities in Sikh temples, and to the laxness of airport security. Before 9/11, she commented, the white establishment assumed that any violence would be exported back to immigrant homelands. What she learned (as she explained to Bill Moyers on PBS) was the strength of the terrorist fear of modernisation, particularly as it affected religion and women's willingness to follow religious rules.[15] As a result of the book she found herself stalked and under death threat for two years, publicly denounced in Sikh temples in large American cities. In interview she described the sense of finding oneself scripted into other people's stories, as her heroine is.

> It wasn't until the World Trade Center was demolished that the average citizen began to realize how, like Tara, you can be living your life, immersed in your own personal conflicts – Should I go back to my husband? Why did my Hungarian lover leave me for someone else? *etcetera* – while unknowingly you are enmeshed in someone else's incredible fantasies.[16]

Those who combine and select their own materials to form their own cultural syntheses enmesh others in the resultant scenarios, whether modern or traditional. Globalisation connects the Indian Dawood gang across the globe, threatening security and destroying identities. Fundamentalism can exploit the same networks and synergies. If traditionalism can be transposed into radical revolt (in the example of the Tree Bride), modern globalisation can do the reverse, hand-in-glove with the forces of coercive and fundamentalist tradition.

As the narrator, Tara is caught between different stories. On one level (as Dragana Obradovic has argued) she is faced with a variety of shared histories and has to reconfigure her own cultural space, becoming to some extent at least a cultural programmer, navigating a range of cultural territories.[17] Just as technology may give us the sense of being in two worlds at the same time (in a chatroom, a real room, on a cell phone) so the novel gives the reader the bewildering sense of having jumped from one story to another, of being deflected, off-balance, led astray by another seductive linkage. Is the novel a story of America? Or India? Or the British empire? Of parents and children? Or of sisters? In a metaphor drawn from anti-earthquake technology (as practised by Andy, Tara's lover) the story concerns the problems of how, given the seismic shifts in people's lives, we can 'retrofit', making for a secure structure, without embracing either rickety traditions or a simplistic fundamentalism, how we relate tradition and modernity in the new, networked world.

Tara's connection to the Tree Bride is not, therefore, a connection back to a secure, primordial identity, steeped in religious tradition, but to a rebel. She feels a profound connection to the Tree Bride, as a member of a sibship. 'She had two sisters, as do I. Perhaps we learned the same nursery rhyme. We are sisters three/as alike as three blossoms on one flowering tree' (p. 16). To an external eye, Tara's sisters are very alike. All share a birthday (at intervals of three years); all have played the same roles in the same Gilbert and Sullivan operettas at the same convent school; all are exceptionally attractive. But the apparent homogeneity of the sibship is an illusion. The novel excavates their histories in explicit relation to theories – not of descent through the generations – but of sibship and birth order, to place the emphasis on rebellion rather than conformity. It is not for nothing that the Tree Bride, her father and Tara Chatterjee are all third children – or that dutiful Bish is a first son. What I want to suggest is that Mukherjee deliberately casts her discussion of the relation of tradition to modernity in the context not of vertical lines of descent and consent but in terms of sibships and lateral familial connections, a model which is suggestively related to a networked world. Writing in 1996, Frank J. Sulloway made the following statement:

> To understand why some women rebel, we must answer the question, 'Why are sisters so different?' The answer involves the ways in which

family niches promote sibling differences in risk-taking and openness to experience.[18]

Alfred Adler, the originator of birth order theory, argued that a major determinant of personality is birth order.[19] However apparently alike, siblings are not actually born into the same family. By birth order children will hold different positions, and their quest for identity, power and attention is influenced by their sequential positions as siblings. Adler argued that all children were striving for superiority, struggling to get attention and affection from parents, competing and engaging in sibling rivalry. To Adler, each child is born onto a different 'stage' in the family home and learns to perform a script with the help of parents who try to direct the play. The firstborn is born into a small family and receives a great deal of attention; laterborns have to find different ways to earn centre stage and parental applause. A laterborn may therefore choose different hobbies, different personality traits, in order to get attention and find a place on what may be becoming a crowded stage. But, because they are not so strongly watched and disciplined by parents, laterborns may have more freedom to create an individual personality. Firstborns tend to be given a great deal of discipline and attention, thus becoming high achievers, concerned about performing dutifully for parents. They tend to be conservative and rule-bound. They arrive first and then use their superior power to defend the status quo. For laterborns the rules are less rigid and they have to look within themselves for latent talents that can be identified through systematic experimentation, in order to find a niche. They are thus more open to experience, more imaginative, prone to fantasies and unconventional – all tendencies which increase the likelihood of finding an unoccupied space on stage.

Although Adler did not spell out the political implications, Frank J. Sulloway's bestseller, *Born to Rebel*, advanced the argument that during socially radical revolutions, laterborns have been much more likely than firstborns to adopt revolutionary alternatives.[20] In his hypothesis, laterborns opt for radical rebellion; firstborns try to preserve a waning orthodoxy or at best opt for reforming the existing system. During the Protestant Reformation, for example, he argues that laterborns were nine times more likely than firstborns to suffer martyrdom for the new faith; whereas firstborns were five times more likely than laterborns to suffer martyrdom for refusing to abandon Catholicism. In the American abolitionist movement, the most radical reform movement in American history, a very high proportion of laterborns featured, including Harriet Beecher Stowe (seventh of thirteen children) and Angelina Grimké, a fourteenth and last child. The process continues today. Sulloway notes that Democratic presidents show a consistent tendency to nominate laterborns to the Supreme Court. All appointments made by Kennedy and Johnson were laterborns. 'At the level of the US Supreme Court, sibling differences determine the laws of the land.'[21] Firstborns are more likely to rise to power in war (or to take a country into wars): Roosevelt, Mussolini, Churchill, Stalin. Middle children, who cannot resist older siblings and cannot be aggressive to the 'baby' below, are flexible and favour compromise, cultivating diplomacy, coalitions and non-violence: Martin Luther King, the second of three. Trotsky, Castro, Danton, Lenin and Yasser Arafat are all laterborns.

Siblings are thus very different politically and philosophically despite similar backgrounds. To sum up, birth order theory is a Darwinian story. Birth order introduces the need for differing strategies in dealing with sibling rivals in the competition for parental investment. 'Siblings become different for the same reason that species do over time; divergence minimises competition for scarce resources.'[22]

Tara's son Rabi is completing a school science project, to 'illustrate a panel of Galápagos finches' (p. 155). Darwin studied the many closely related species of Galápagos finches, each with a niche in the foodchain, feeding differently upon seeds, cactus, leaves and insects. In like terms, siblings become increasingly diversified as 'the brainy one', 'the family diplomat', 'the sportsman', 'the family baby'. Darwin's principle of divergence underlines diversity as a useful strategy. Species diverge in order to become adapted to a variety of places in the economy of nature. Different species find different spaces and avoid competing for food. Similarly children develop different interests and abilities to minimise direct competition.

Tara Lata, the rebel, is the third child of a third child. Bish is a dutiful eldest son. The three Bhattacharjee sisters occupy different places on the family stage. Didi, the eldest, earns her living as a traditional Indian performance artist. Parvati shares her family space with a constantly changing cast of extended family members and consequently lives in a world of compromise. An important encounter for Tara involves a casting director who compliments her on her ability to fill up a space and offers her a film role. Although she refuses the offer, she recognises that on one level the casting director held 'the only key that could fit my complicated lock' (p. 85). Tara has diversified, rebelled, travelled in order to find a space for herself, to place herself at the centre of the stage. The attraction of the Tree Bride also consists in her centrality. She has become 'the quiet centre of every story' (p. 289).

In contrast, in the novel, Tara repeatedly finds herself displaced, her own story spiked in favour of somebody else's more compelling narrative. Her successive attempts to get to the truth and confront her sisters with the emergence of Chris Dey are ignored. Like a sibling being pushed aside, her story is repeatedly dismissed. In the present, the eldest sister, Didi, occupies centre stage, performing in a conventional drama. Laterborn Tara, unable to rival Didi, experiments instead with modern living and modern men. But every time that Tara is about to take hold of the story she is upstaged, or recast by more powerful directors who briskly absorb her into *their* cultural plots. In the quest for truth she is continually deflected by a more able cultural programmer, making sense of the world by telling a different story, or (in a metaphor repeated at several reprises) running a different movie. The novel thus replaces an Oedipal narrative in which the yoke of parents, colonial history or tradition, has to be thrown off, in favour of a sibling story, less vertical and more horizontal. Siblings are like broadband, occupying different positions in the field.

In India Tara's identity was fixed by father's religion (Hindu), caste (Brahmin), subcaste (Kulin), mother tongue (Bengali), place of birth (Calcutta) and region of origin (East Bengal) (p. 78). Arjun Appadurai has commented that, in the past, social experience was in many respects inertial; tradition provided a finite sense of possible lives, fantasy and imagination were residual practices.[23] In contrast our lives are now no longer the outcome of the givenness of things, but as much acts of projection and imagination as the enactments of known scripts. In America Tara enjoys the ability to invent and reinvent herself, as a 'border-crashing claimant of all people's legacies' (p. 79). But the arrival of 'Chris Dey', another border-crashing self-inventor, destroys Tara's certainties. Now she sees herself as part of a story that is all too modern, in which her role is scripted according to stereotype and genre. 'It's soap opera, it's too corny for soap operas, but it's happening to me' (p. 45). Tara's reaction is not to challenge Didi directly, but to first seek an ally in her middle sister. Settled in a luxurious high-rise in Bombay, Parvati speaks to Tara by telephone once a week. 'The whole point of these phantom family reunions is to stop time, to when we were the Bhattarcharjee sisters' (p. 53). There is no face-to-face communication, merely a fantasy of electronic propinquity.[24] Indeed when Tara telephones to tell her story, she finds Parvati in the midst of a much more engrossing modern event. Robbers have broken into the building and beaten a neighbour to death. The three sisters had been brought up in a protected enclave in Calcutta, ignoring the dangers outside and seeing poverty and misery only through bulletproof glass. Now their world has been invaded. Fantasy closeness gives way to real invasions. Suddenly the story is really about Parvati and her burglar. The emphasis falls on the opposition between different scripts or types of movie. Parvati dismisses Tara's fears as a paranoid fantasy, scoffing at 'a conspiracy of Christian orphans' (p. 111). In the past Tara had enjoyed classic Hollywood movies, along with her father, particularly their insistence on the restoration of order and harmony. For her father, 'Hollywood values were Bhattacharjee family values' (p. 112); Hollywood plots would allow love and truth to triumph, order and harmony to be restored (p. 113), as opposed to the implausible and repetitive nature of Bollywood productions. Now, however, Tara regrets her sanitised upbringing. 'The plots and the participants in my San Francisco drama belonged more to Bombay than to Calcutta, and the India that had stayed on, not the one I had left' (p. 114). Her mind turns to less reassuring plots: the sinister doubles of *Rebecca* and the identity theft of *The Talented Mr Ripley*. 'Which movie was playing around me in San Francisco?', she wonders (p. 114). The large repertoire of images and narratives on offer to her provides little reassurance. She has too many stories to choose from, too many potential scenarios.

Getting no support from Parvati, Tara visits Jack Singh Sidhu, to get police help, and is infuriated to realise that he sees her use of her maiden name as an attempt to conceal her real identity. She, too, is an impostor in his eyes. For Jack, the story is about Bish. The plot can only be aimed at Bish, not at Tara or Didi. The family story of the sisters is irrelevant; Tara's only identity (p. 143) is as Mrs Bish Chatterjee. The global story is the priority story. Millionaire Bish is the real target, and the others merely surrogates. The real force behind the interloper, the real threat, is the internet and the crime syndicates which it has spawned (p. 144). The story moves almost immediately towards Tara's son Rabi. He, too, is concealing a real identity. Visiting his school, Tara is given a letter from her son, who makes it clear that while Tara has seen 'Chris Dey' as the interloper at the heart of the family, Rabi sees things differently. 'This is not about him, either the real one or the fake. It is about me, another kind of fake' (p. 163). The title of Rabi's play ('Ma, I am gay', p. 165) says it all. Rabi's story takes immediate priority over that of Chris Dey, just as Bish had displaced Tara in Jack's version of the plot, just as Parvati's story of robbery and murder eclipsed Tara's story of the nephew. Tara has been competing ineffectually in the family sphere, waved into the wings by voluble sisters whose stories are always centre stage. Her story is redefined as 'about' her sisters, 'about' her husband and now 'about' her son, never about her. In the culmination to this series of sidesteps, deflections, surrogates and plot usurpations, Tara actually finds herself a character in a play scripted and directed by Rabi. In the play two Indian sisters speak on the telephone. As she leaves the school Tara sees Rabi shouting at the girl on stage who plays the role of his mother, telling her not to overact. Tara is under direction in her son's script. Rabi has learned from the finches. He is versatile and adapted, and uses art to control his mother's role.

A final irony concerns Andy, the retrofitter. Tara wonders what Andy's reaction will be: 'did he have a story for it? *When it came time for his marriage, farmer Zhang's son declared himself repulsed by every woman in the village*' (p. 167). But when Tara rushes home to reveal the news of Rabi's sexual orientation, she finds Andy packing, furious because she had contacted the police against his wishes. Tara pleads with him that Chris Dey is 'no big deal' (p. 169). For her the priority story, the big deal, is Rabi's story. Just as the communications through which most of the story is told – phone calls and letters between India, California and New Jersey – move across a vast field, so the stories jockey for position. For the reader the question asked is which story has priority here? Which comes first? Who is centre stage? How can the truth be detected (the real identity of 'Chris Dey') in this welter of competing storylines and syntheses, all apparently coherent on their own terms? The first movement (Part One) of the novel poses the question of priority among narratives, exploiting birth-order position in a sibship in order to stage a battle between global and family stories. And the implication is that individual cultural synthesising has got Tara no closer to the truth.

So should Tara opt instead for a return to supportive tradition? In her next role, Tara appears to regress, featuring in a sari in an expatriate Indian enclave in Jackson Heights, with Didi, apparently returning to a primordial identity. As a 'multicultural performance artist' (p. 94) Didi stages Indian mythological evenings with readings, recitations and music. She is now 'more Indian than when she left Calcutta' (p. 94), entirely as might be expected of a conformist firstborn. A conventional success story, she is on the invitation list when Indian dignitaries arrive for UN functions or when Indian film stars come to New York, and she appears on Indo-American television channels. Just as her role as a child was to act out the parental script, so now she has adopted even more traditional roles. She appears to have found an individual place on the stage which successfully unites family and nation. Didi's new job in Queen's for a tycoon with a community channel involves a role in a vernacular soap opera for North American, thirty-something Bengalis, 'full of the vicissitudes of life from an Indian perspective' (p. 175). Do these, wonders Tara, involve 'murderous stalkers, gay sons, and break-ups with Buddhist carpenters? (p. 175). The Bengali soap opera looks decidedly non-adaptive to Tara. Nothing more exciting is envisaged in the plots than dealing with old in-laws, wives working outside the home, stopping daughters from wanting to date and maintaining respect for tradition (p. 175). Didi's dramatic role is only a shadow of what might have been, had she been more radical. As a teenager she complied with her father's refusal to allow her to take the lead in Satyajit Ray's film, *Asani Sanket* (*Distant Thunder*).[25] The film deals with the 1943 market-manipulated East Bengal famine, the famine that caused the Tree Bride to take up arms against the British. Didi was not even allowed to impersonate a radical. Tara may see Didi as big sister, centre stage, but Didi never got the main part. Instead she sold theatre tickets, and finally reached the heights of a recurrent slot on *Namaskar, Probasi*[26] and a voice-over for a Jackson Heights tandoori mahal (p. 179).

Deprived of a leading role on stage, however, Didi can still claim that in the sibship. She invites Tara to a party ostensibly thrown in her honour, promptly beginning 'the ritual, big sister dismantling of my self-confidence' (p. 185) by engineering a complete makeover, new hairstyle, manicure, 'museum quality' designer sari and extremely expensive traditional gold earrings and necklace. Tara revels in the situation, overtaken by the appeal of being at the centre of attention. Failed rebellion gives way, apparently, to museumised tradition. What Tara does not realise is that Didi has actually inserted her into quite a different script. En route to the party, Didi rehearses the guest list, thus preventing Tara from having any opportunity to broach the subject of Chris Dey. Surrounded by Indian faces, which could be Muslim or Hindu, Tara is bewildered. 'I felt as though I were lost inside a Salman Rushdie novel, a once-firm identity smashed by hammer blows' (pp. 195–6). In fact she *is* inside a staged drama of a type – though it is less Rushdie than Scott Fitzgerald. It takes all of the 45-minute bus ride to rehearse the guests' biographies. In a *tour de force* scene clearly modelled on the 'schedule' scene in *The Great Gatsby*, Didi describes the scandalous tale of Sujit Roy Chaudhury and the French consul's wife; Dr Prafulla Nag (parents dead in an automobile crash for which he was not to blame, insurance fraud implied); the snobbish Sinhas and boring Sen family; pushy Mr Basu from Hackensack; Dr Gautam Dutta (Medicare fraud cases pending); and Arun Mehta, whose bride has died under mysterious circumstances. Narrating other people's scandals conveniently allows Didi to avoid discussing her own; prioritising these stories is an adaptive strategy. They also suggest that in addition to her 'Indian role', Didi has made a place for herself in a classic American narrative. With the mysterious gaps in her story (like Gatsby's lost years) and her sudden re-emergence, her ambiguous connections to gangsters, movie producers and society figures, her 'son' who repeatedly employs Gatsby's key expression 'old sport', and above all the stupendous party in a former mafioso's faux-Tuscan villa, Didi is explicitly constructed as a female Gatsby – an impostor with a gift for staging social events for her own purposes. Ostensibly playing a family role, Didi is actually maximising her investments. The party has its own economy. The sari which Didi loans Tara is actually for sale, as is the 24-carat gold jewellery. As the star of a TV shopping channel, Didi is an icon to the Indian community and her parties are 'a kind of home shopping service for upscale Indians' (p. 231), essentially the rich equivalent of Tupperware parties for housewives. Tara's hair was cut, the better to display the earrings to busy businessmen and their normally stay-at-home wives; the sari is designed to expose sufficient cleavage to show off the necklace. It dawns on Tara that she is performing in an advertising stunt. It is as if Gatsby's shirts were actually for sale. By party-end, the disgraced Chowdhury has bought the earrings, and Mehta the necklace. Like Cinderella, Tara is stripped of her finery in a dark corner.

On one level the sequence embodies the kinds of questions raised by the end of a 'national' literature. Mukherjee's skilful parody of Fitzgerald – the dreadful party, the scandalous guests, the capitalist agenda beneath the commodified sociability – places the scene in relation to an American filiation. Didi conforms to an American model, but with a difference. The director is a sibling and the roles played are performed in accordance with a family script. The guests' concern to keep business in the family and to socialise only within the home is the reason Didi can sell to them. Her own family structure and conformity enable her to manipulate Tara. Family is exploited to consumerist ends. Tara is at her most 'Indian' when most commodified and scripted by her elder sister. She is happy (for once) to fill the space vacated by big sister, centre stage at the party, and for a moment yields to the illusion of centrality. Throughout the scene the reader, just like Tara, is continually misdirected, wrong-footed or mystified, and like Tara we may begin to wonder what sort of novel we are in – an American classic, an Indian soap opera, a postcolonial novel? Meanwhile the truth concerning Chris Dey has still not been discovered. The endless deferral of this main story, with the substitutions of surrogate stories, involves a series of passes to and fro across the field of the novel. Just as the stories Didi tells of her guests are seductive misdirections, so the party itself seduces the reader into a world of obscure connections and murky transactions. There is, however, no way of returning to a primordial identity. That is now extinct. At the centre of the mansion, Tara discovers a traditional Indian joint-family, with grandparents and old retainers, relics of a Calcutta world which has now disappeared. As Dr Kajol Ghosal, her hostess, puts it, the party is about 'the survival of the species' (p. 245). The successful doctors and engineers are part of a world which has adapted in order to survive. Even though 'extinct in their native habitat' (p. 244), Kajol notes their 'marvellous plumage … Wonderful adaptability. A really good captive breeding programme is our only hope' (p. 245). This 'tenacious subspecies' (p. 249) is well represented by Didi, whose previous life in America has involved compromises and deceptions, and whose marriage to Harish (almost as much a proxy-husband as the Tree Bride's) is a cover for a life spent in the gay world. Tara recognises that Didi was not at all traditional; in some ways she is the real American, defiant and path breaking (p. 134), a saleswoman exploiting the past to survive, unconcerned by issues of descent.

In counterpoint to the misunderstandings and evasions of the family-scripted party, with its museumised centre and sense of dying traditions, the modern world appears to offer a straight connection to the truth, courtesy of the efficiency and directness of modern communications technology. Jack sends photos of two potential stalkers by fax and confirms via cell phone that Chris Dey is a member of the Dawood gang, a full-scale criminal cartel controlling crime in Bombay, with major interests in Bollywood movies. Tara may be 'in a movie' in a more sinister sense than she imagines. Jack is convinced that the target is Bish, since 'the biggest thing in India now is high tech' (p. 223). The crime is a priority crime, designed to establish status. The interloper's job is to pull off something big so that the Chinese and Vietnamese gangs (who occupied the Californian stage before the late-arriving Indians) will take the Indians seriously. On the cell phone made possible by Bish's invention, Tara registers 'the joys of globalization' (p. 223.) 'How could it have turned so ugly so fast? We'd unleashed an international crime wave, sitting there doodling codes on napkins in a Stanford pub' (p. 223). Earlier in the novel the cell phone had represented connectivity as security. When her own phone rings, Tara is reconnected to Bish (in a hot tub in Brisbane). Bish appears omnipotent, better protected than half the world heads of state, with 'no end to the technical and human networks he commanded' (p. 256). He has started an assembly plant in Bangalore, a marketing arm in Bombay, and is in discussion with the World Bank over a start-up in Bangladesh. His connections create an empire which overrides national boundaries and hostilities. Indeed he is able to evade the limits of time and space. Flying back from Australia to San Francisco, he will be 'back some time before we leave' (p. 256). Yet in the denouement Bish is seriously injured when a bomb, an Indian signature device, blows Tara's house to smithereens – a bomb probably triggered by a reconfigured cell phone (p. 274). CHATTY's stock value plunges, upsetting the world economy. Bish, however, has fulfilled his traditional destiny. Reunited with Tara, he had revealed that he saw himself as a failure because 'he had failed in his dharma, the basic duty of a man in the householder phase of his life, to support and sustain his marriage' (p. 265). The bomb which destroys Tara's house gives him a chance to save his wife's life and thus complete the task ordained by tradition, his own priority story. In the American media, on the other hand, the wrong stories once again take over the action. Andy is arrested, cast by the press as an insanely jealous ex-lover (p. 274), violent sexual predator and 'hippie laborer' (p. 274), triggering furious Buddhist reaction worldwide. Mukherjee lets the reader enjoy the satire on the American media, creating the impression for us that the reader has superior knowledge, that we know what the real story is. The Chris Dey story, unnoticed by almost everyone, is relegated to the back pages of the newspaper: 'The body of an unidentified Asian male' has 'washed up in the delta' (p. 275).

The reader ends the novel convinced that the target was Bish, that the bomber was part of an international globalised criminal network, and that the aim was financial. The interloper had no family claim at all. The false Chris is the product of a world in which it is easy to make global connections, communications are swift, and no border is impenetrable, a post-9/11 world. Modernity is to blame, and it appears as if the father at the start was right to resist the modern world. But things are not quite so simple. *Desirable Daughters* has a sequel, *The Tree Bride*, which offers a completely different narrative to explain what the story was about. Taken together, the two novels indicate the naïvety of the quest for roots, which backfires spectacularly. Engaging in a roots search, as Tara discovers to her cost, releases energies from the past to trouble the present. The bombing of Tara's house is the result of her naïve belief that in revisiting the past it will remain static, a tourist site with suitable memorials to noble (anticolonial) ancestors, rather than unleashing revenge on behalf of the present Third World. Ironically, in the very last pages of *The Tree Bride*, Tara discovers that she was, after all, at the absolute centre of the tale. The story *was* about her; Bish was irrelevant. Throughout the novel the skeins of plot are woven together via coincidences worthy of Thomas Hardy. The effect is not, however, in any sense retrofit-Victorian. In an information society the role of coincidence is no longer surprising. 'Twenty-first century technology (speed) makes coincidence, or the appearance of coincidence, inevitable. Speed enhances contact, speed shrinks space and time.'[27] The disaster happened because Tara had been telling herself a global story and not a family story. The temptation of the broader stage – a story where she is at the centre – is realised with horrible consequences. When the Tree Bride's father became a dietary traditionalist, he downgraded his Muslim cook to watchman. The marriage of Sameena, his daughter, depended on a promised dowry, the Tree Bride's house, which her family now occupy illegally, as part of the Muslimisation of Hindu estates. Tara's 'roots search' had brought her to that house, awakening in the family the fear that she would reclaim the property, and triggering 'Chris Dey's' activities. As Tara realises, when 'Chris Dey' makes his second attempt on her life, 'It really is all about me' (p. 239). All along the story has been an Indian story of Hindu–Muslim antagonism, a story in which the reconnection to the past (the descent story) is the source of disaster, in which the violence is intimate, the neighbour is the killer, and the return to conservative tradition is the engine of destruction. America cannot expect these antagonisms to play out in their immigrant homelands; Indian history has become American history. Bish's fortune, based on routers, was also his ill-fortune; the cell phone was used against him. But roots are as dangerous to identity as mobility. Tara's desire to have a story of her own, a role in the family drama, is ironically fulfilled. *The Tree Bride* suggests agreement with

Arjun Appadurai's understanding of ethnic violence, rather than offering an explanation based upon the facilitation of crime by globalisation. In Appadurai's account, the worst kinds of ethnic violence are those involving a distorted relation between daily face-to-face activities and the identities produced by modern nation states (pure Hindu and Muslim in this case), a process in which 'large scale identities forcibly enter the local imagination and become dominant voice-overs in the traffic of ordinary life'.[28] Appadurai notes that the primary literature closest to most brutal ethnic violence is shot through with the language of the impostor or counterfeit person, registering uncertainty about categories and intimacy among persons. 'Chris Dey' (Christian–Hindu–Muslim in his different roles) is only one of the impostors of the plot, in which cheater detection is continually impeded by the attempts of individuals to make sense of their disparate and fragmented cultures by syntheses which remain self-centred and inadaptive.

By juxtaposing the two novels, Mukherjee explores the effects of enhanced connections (Utopian or otherwise) both inside the action of the novels and in their relation to each other. *Desirable Daughters* is volume one of a trilogy, in which volume two, *The Tree Bride*, would be conventionally understood as the heir to volume one, inheriting its characters and history. Here the heir refuses to fulfil the conditions of its descent, breaks the rules, revises previous assumptions and places a different story centre stage. And the third volume – potentially diverging and altering the story again – has yet to appear. In this respect the novel sequence is peculiarly contemporary, emphasising a revisionary, lateral model. In the putative trilogy, the second story takes over the stage from the first, dethroning its authority as priority narrative, but is itself vulnerable to the appearance of a third story. The parallel is explicitly familial – specifically with the three daughters of the title. As a result Mukherjee tells a global story without buying into any of the master narratives of globalisation, and without allowing the novel to propagate the phenomenon as unchallengeable. Rather than displaying globalisation as irresistible social evolution, technologically determined, she offers the reader a choice of scenarios, and emphasises the adaptive function of narrative.

Conclusion

It will not have escaped the reader that in the preceding chapters of this study the figure of the surrogate, adopted, illegitimate or transplanted child has been a subtextual or micro-focus, even in novels ostensibly considering macrocosmic or global themes – empire, slavery, biopolitics. In their different ways each of the works considered here appears to have closed the circle – adopting a global structure which turns back upon itself, returning to origins as if in a literary round dance. It is no accident that *The Scarlet Letter* is a key text for transnational analysis; not only because of the Indian background, but also because of the figure of Pearl, the illegitimate, contested child, who moves (in Mukherjee's teasing evocation of her non-European aristocratic crest) from Europe to British America and then to an Oriental destination, choosing the East as her future. Mukherjee's *Holder* reimports Pearl from residence with a rajah, to become the catalyst for the American Revolution; more pessimistically, Updike circles back in the opposite direction, exporting her to Europe again, and to the Dutch location from which her persecuted forebears set out for America. Prager's personal return to the East reclaims another abandoned child as an American citizen; maltreated children are the tragic focus of the neo-slave narrative, with Bradley's Bill Washington extending the story from Africa to Vietnam. Høeg's Isaiah is a child translated (both bodily and linguistically) and carrying within him the seeds of pandemic disaster, the end of the genetic line, as the result of the return to life of a prehistoric organism. McCarthy's 'roots search' also moves back into prehistory, engaging with the sudden 'discovery' that the family of man traces its descent from a violent progenitor, a killer-child, his title invoking an imaginary great circle on the earth's surface passing through the North and South geographic poles. Mukherjee pits desirable daughters against a decidedly undesirable impostor son, reversing her narrative conclusions across the two volumes of her intended trilogy, and transforming her sequel from legitimate heir to rival sibling. Importantly the notion of a vexed inheritance or mysterious line of descent permeates each child's story, with storylines focused on lineage, roots searches and family history, in a structural globality which invokes the circle, the return and the circuit. Lines of descent are no longer clear – or if they are clear, imply disaster. The awareness of the global permeates the fictional at every level.

This study began by asking questions about the role of narrative fiction in a globalised world, particularly its potential for inadvertently propagating the phenomenon which it seeks to interrogate or resist. In the figure of the reclaimed child, transnational fictions appear to register awareness that literature is no longer clearly related to a national 'family'. Its lines of descent are tangled, bastardised or obscured, its filiative patterns no longer self-evident. Fictions thus subliminally evoke a profound unease, a sense that 'our literature is illegitimate, it is not ours'. Less subliminally, in the field of literary history, vigorous culture wars are fought to reclaim the disputed turf. Where do we locate a Bengali-Indian-Canadian-American writer? Or a Danish novel, adulterated by translation, in which the plot turns upon events on a Greenlandic US air base? The economic pressures of a globalised literary world give us literatures jockeying for position in a global 'family' in which some texts are enthusiastically 'adopted' (as in the everyday metaphor for figuring on a college course), while others remain neglected, in the absence of rescue missions by special interest groups. Yet the novel tells a different story of resistance and subversion, clearly indicating that if a new literature is not being born, it is certainly being adopted. The motif of the abandoned child being reclaimed implicitly suggests an awareness that for Americans literature is not just 'ours' but in part belongs to others, or, as Hurston's Native Americans suggest, depends upon the gifts of others – Chinese daughters making America an adoption nation, Africa underwriting its present, India creating its communicative networks. Despite the emphasis on genealogy, sibships are registered as more important than parents and children. Prager abandons the role of mother to become a child again; Bradley sets out to return a brother to the family story; Mukherjee disclaims the 'lost' son in favour of a story of sisters; McCarthy's fable of the harness maker interrogates the status of paternal ancestry. Orphans – Hannah Easton, LuLu, Isaiah – are adopted into surrogate families.

Fictions of America thus register the perception that despite a globalised world, storytelling remains not only unthreatened in its independent power, but has a fertile future as a source of resistance and reparation. Karl Kroeber has drawn attention to the fallacy of modernism, in its blindness to the nature of story as involving endless retelling, endless adaptation. 'Narrative is a repeating form of discourse – in which every repetition is unique.'[1] Narrative may be the way most societies have defined themselves, but narrative is also the means by which sociocultural boundaries can be crossed.

Stories are like plant species that move resolutely but unobtrusively over surprising obstacles, including vast spans of time and space, quietly adapting to foreign environments, and then changing those environments.[2]

As Kroeber argues, the risk for criticism is the tendency to freeze stories to remove the problem of time – of retellings. As critics we may operate as if we were stopping the process of storytelling, offering a final word on how to interpret a narrative, rather than allowing interpretation to open story out to more story, and to stories told after ours. In the novels considered here, retellings loom large, whether intertextually, neohistorically or in recognition of the essentially tentative and contingent nature of existence, and are recognised as both inevitable and desirable. When Bradley's John Washington destroys his research materials and his conclusions, leaving only the original historical clues for the next family descendant to begin investigating the story all over again, he implicitly acknowledges the role of a 'next reader', and leaves a gap for that next reader to fill. That reader will be covering the same ground, circling back to advance forwards, an appropriate image of a globalised reader, imaginatively persistent and unsubdued by modernity. In the familial structures of global fictions the reader recognises him- or herself as a surrogate in an endless chain, not a 'first reader', perhaps, but emphatically not a last reader, either.

Notes

Introduction

1 Amitava Kumar, 'Passages to India', *Nation*, 24 April 2000, 36–9 (p. 39).
2 Later the tactic was popularised by the San Francisco 49ers. See <users2.
ev1.net/%/Ejamrtm/Historyhtm> (accessed 8 November 2005).
3 Bharati Mukherjee, *Desirable Daughters*, New York: Hyperion, 2002, p. 24. (Subsequent page references follow quotations in parentheses.)
4 Dave Welch, 'Bharati Mukherjee runs the West Coast Offense', <www.
powells.com/authors/mukherjee> (accessed 13 October 2004).
5 Paul Harris, 'Fictions of globalization: narrative in the age of electronic media',
PhiN 7, 1999, 26–39 (p. 27).
6 Ibid.
7 James Annesley, 'Market corrections: Jonathan Franzen and the "novel of globalization"', *Journal of Modern Literature* 29, 2, 2006, 111–28 (p. 124).
8 Thomas Peyser, 'Globalization in America: the case of Don Delillo's *White Noise*',
Clio 25, 1996, 255–71 (p. 256). See also Thomas Peyser, 'How global is it?: Walter
Abish and the fiction of globalization', *Contemporary Literature* 40, 2, Summer 1999,
240–62.
9 David Held, Anthony McGrew, David Goldblatt and Jonathan Perraton, *Global
Transformations: Politics, Economics and Culture*, Cambridge: Polity, 1999, p. 2.
10 Anthony Giddens, *The Consequences of Modernity*, Cambridge: Polity, 1990, p. 64.
11 Daniel T. O'Hara, *Empire Burlesque. The Fate of Critical Culture in Global America*,
Durham, NC, and London: Duke University Press, 2003, p. 18.
12 Ibid., p. 19.
13 Stuart Christie, 'Clear and present danger', *Guardian*, 9 November 2002, 15.
14 Mieke Bal, *Travelling Concepts in the Humanities. A Rough Guide*, Toronto: University
of Toronto Press, 2002, p. 25.
15 See Thomas L. Friedman, *The Lexus and the Olive Tree: Understanding Globalization*,
New York: Farrar, Straus and Giroux, 1999; Michael Hardt and Antonio Negri,
Empire, Cambridge, Mass.: Harvard University Press, 2000.
16 Michael Ignatieff, *Empire Lite: Nation Building in Bosnia, Kosovo, Afghanistan*, London:
Vintage, 2003.
17 Chalmers Johnson, *Nemesis: The Last Days of the American Republic*, New York: Henry
Holt, 2006, pp. 81–2.
18 Niall Ferguson, *Colossus. The Rise and Fall of the American Empire*, London: Allen
Lane, 2004.

19 Chalmers Johnson, *Blowback: The Costs and Consequences of American Empire*, New York: Henry Holt, 2000, p. 65.
20 Arvind Rajagopal, 'Technologies of perception and the cultures of globalization', *Social Text* 19, 3, Fall 2001, 1.
21 Arjun Appadurai, *Modernity at Large: Cultural Dimensions of Globalization*, Minneapolis: University of Minnesota Press, 1996.
22 David Nye (1998) 'What should American studies be?'. E-mail (10 December 1998).
23 Arif Dirlik, 'American studies in the time of empire', *Comparative American Studies* 2, 3, 2004, 287–302 (p. 288).
24 Appadurai, *Modernity at Large*, p. 171.
25 Peyser, 'Globalization in America', p. 256.
26 O'Hara, *Empire Burlesque*, p. 163; Bruce Robbins, *Feeling Global: Internationalism in Distress*, New York: New York University Press, 1999; Bruce Robbins, 'The sweatshop sublime', *PMLA* 1171, January 2002, 84–97.
27 Mary E. Virnoche and Gary T. Marx, '"Only Connect" – E.M. Forster in an age of electronic communication: computer-mediated association and community networks', <web.mit.edu/gtmarx/www/connect> (accessed 28 March 2007).
28 <www.email-marketinreports.com/iland/2005_08_01_iland_archive> (accessed 1 April 2007).
29 Johnson, *Blowback*, p. 93.
30 Liam Connell, 'Global narratives: globalisation and literary studies', *Critical Survey* 16, 2, 2004, 78–95.
31 See John Cullen Gruesser, *Confluences*, Athens: University of Georgia Press, 2005, pp. 16–19.
32 Gayatri Chakravorty Spivak, *Outside in the Teaching Machine*, New York: Routledge, 1993, p. 182.
33 Emily Apter, 'On translation in a global market', *Public Culture* 13, 1, 2001, 1–12. See also Amitav Kumar, 'World Bank literature: a new name for post-colonial studies in the next century', *College Literature* 26, 3, Fall 1999, 195–204.
34 See Ruth Mayer, *Artificial Africas. Colonial Images in the Times of Globalization*, Hanover and London: University Press of New England, 2002.
35 Johnson, *Nemesis*, pp. 5–6. See also Chalmers Johnson, *The Sorrows of Empire*, London: Verso, 2004; Mike Davis, 'Bush's Ultimate Thule?', *Socialist Review* February 2003. Available online at <www.socialistreview.org.uk/article.php?articlenumber=8310> (accessed 6 March 2007).
36 Harris, 'Fictions of globalization', p. 2
37 Appadurai, *Modernity at Large*, p. 4.

1 Red letters

1 Bharati Mukherjee, 'A four-hundred-year-old woman', *American Studies Newsletter* 29, 1993, 52.
2 Joseph A. Cincotti, 'Same trip, opposite direction', *New York Times Book Review* 98, 10 October 1993, 7.
3 Francisco Collado-Rodriguez, 'Naming female multiplicity: an interview with Bharati Mukherjee', *Atlantis* XVII, 1–2, May–November 1995, 293–306 (p. 300).
4 See Judie Newman, *The Ballistic Bard: Postcolonial Fictions*, London: Edward Arnold, 1995.

5 Vivian Gornick, 'Playing games with history', *Women's Review of Books* 11, 3, 1993, 15.

6 Bharati Mukherjee, *The Holder of the World*, London: Chatto and Windus, 1993, p. 286. (Subsequent page references follow quotations in parentheses.)

7 Philip Rahv, 'The dark lady of Salem', in *Literature and the Sixth Sense*, London: Faber and Faber, 1970, pp. 55–75 (p. 63).

8 Fakrul Alam, *Bharati Mukherjee*, Twayne's US Authors No. 653, New York: Twayne, 1996, p. 11.

9 Mukherjee, 'A four-hundred-year-old woman', p. 53.

10 On the history of Salem, see James Duncan Phillips, *Salem and the Indies*, Boston: Houghton Mifflin, 1947; and *Pepper and Pirates: Adventures in the Sumatra Pepper Trade of Salem*, Boston: Houghton Mifflin, 1949.

11 Phillips, *Salem and the Indies*, p. 364.

12 Luther S. Luedtke, *Nathaniel Hawthorne and the Romance of the Orient*, Bloomington, Ind.: Indiana University Press, 1989, p. 23.

13 Gloria C. Erlich, *Family Themes and Hawthorne's Fiction: The Tenacious Web*, New Brunswick, NJ: Rutgers University Press, 1984.

14 See Jonathan Arac, 'The politics of *The Scarlet Letter*', in Sacvan Bercovitch and Myra Jehlen (eds), *Ideology and Classic American Literature*, Cambridge: Cambridge University Press, 1986; Walter Benn Michaels, 'Romance and real estate', *Raritan* 2, 1983, 66–87; Lauren Berlant, *The Anatomy of National Fantasy: Hawthorne, Utopia and Everyday Life*, Chicago: University of Chicago Press, 1991; Richard H. Brodhead, *The School of Hawthorne*, Oxford: Oxford University Press, 1986; Eric Cheyfitz, 'The irresistibleness of great literature: reconstructing Hawthorne's politics', *American Literary History* 6, 3, 1994, 539–58; Louise DeSalvo, *Nathaniel Hawthorne*, London: Harvester, 1987; Jay Grossman, '"A" is for abolition?: Race, authorship, *The Scarlet Letter*', *Textual Practice* 7, 6, 1993, 13–31; Charles Lewis, 'The ironic romance of new historicism: *The Scarlet Letter* and *Beloved* standing in side by side', *Arizona Quarterly* 51, 1, 1995, 33–60.

15 Michael J. Colarcurcio, *New Essays on* The Scarlet Letter, Cambridge: Cambridge University Press, 1985, p. 22.

16 Jean Fagan Yellin, *Women and Sisters: The Antislavery Feminists in American Culture*, New Haven: Yale University Press, 1989.

17 Sacvan Bercovitch, *The Office of* The Scarlet Letter, Baltimore: Johns Hopkins University Press, 1991.

18 Claudia Durst Johnson, *Understanding* The Scarlet Letter*: A Student Casebook to Issues, Sources, and Historical Documents*, Westport, Conn.: Greenwood, 1995.

19 Christopher Bigsby, *Hester: A Romance*, London: Weidenfeld and Nicolson, 1994; and *Pearl: A Romance*, London: Weidenfeld and Nicolson, 1995; Maryse Condé, *Moi, Tituba, sorcière ... Noire de Salem*, Paris: Mercure de France, 1986; John Updike, *A Month of Sundays*, New York: Knopf, 1975; *Roger's Version*, New York: Knopf, 1986; *S.*, New York: Knopf, 1988. (Page references for quotations from *S.* follow quotations in parentheses.)

20 Brian Harding (ed.), Nathaniel Hawthorne, *The Scarlet Letter*, Oxford: Oxford University Press, 1990, p. 83. (Subsequent quotations are from this edition and page references follow in parentheses.)

21 Luedtke, *Nathaniel Hawthorne and the Romance of the Orient*, p. 220.

22 Bigsby, *Hester*, p. 189.

23 Erlich, *Family Themes and Hawthorne's Fiction*.

24 Elleke Boehmer, *Colonial and Postcolonial Literature: Migrant Metaphors*, Oxford: Oxford University Press, 1950, p. 53.

25 Gauri Viswanathan, 'The naming of Yale College: British imperialism and American higher education', in Amy Kaplan and Donald E. Pease (eds), *Cultures of United States Imperialism*, Durham, NC: Duke University Press, 1993, p. 93. See also John Guillory, *Cultural Capital: The Problem of Literary Canon Formation*, Chicago: University of Chicago Press, 1993.

26 Viswanathan, 'The naming of Yale College', p. 87.

27 See Fanny Penny, *Diamonds*, London: Hodder and Stoughton, 1906, for an earlier novelist's treatment of Yale.

28 Anthony Ilona, 'Crossing the river: a chronicle of the black diaspora', *Wasafiri* 22, 1995, 3–9.

29 For the accuracy of Mukherjee's portrayal of the Coromandel in the seventeenth century see Sinappah Arasaratnam, *Merchants, Companies and Commerce on the Coromandel Coast 1650–1740*, Delhi: Oxford University Press, 1986; K.N. Chaudhuri, *Asia Before Europe. Economy and Civilisation of the Indian Ocean from the Rise of Islam to 1750*, Cambridge: Cambridge University Press, 1990; Tapan Raychaudhuri, *Jan Company in Coromandel 1605–90*, Verhandelingen van het Koninklijk Instituut voor Taal-, Land- en Volkenkunde, deel 38, 's-Gravenhage: Martinus Nijhoff, 1962.

30 Patrick O'Donnell, 'History without theory: re-covering American literature', *Genre* XXII, 1989, 375–93 (p. 387). See also Peter Carifiol, 'The constraints of history: revision and revolution in American literary studies', *College English* 50, 1988, 605–22.

31 Susan Koshy, 'Review of *The Holder of the World*', *Amerasia Journal* 20, 1994, 188–90 (p. 189).

32 Andrew Delbanco, *The Puritan Ordeal*, Cambridge, Mass.: Harvard University Press, 1989, p. 80.

33 Ibid., p. 221.

34 Northrop Frye, 'Conclusion', in Carl F. Klinck (ed.), *Literary History of Canada*, Toronto: University of Toronto Press, 1965.

35 There is still a distinct lack of information on bibis. The best source, published after Mukherjee's novel, is William Dalrymple, *White Mughals: Love and Betrayal in Eighteenth Century India*, London: Flamingo, 2003. Dalrymple discusses the case of Sir David Ochterlony, born in Boston, who joined the East India Company's army in 1777 and acquired 13 consorts. Bibis were so common a feature of early British India that they are mentioned in one in three wills between 1780 and 1785, and one in four between 1805 and 1810. By mid-century their existence had been suppressed, as an era of racial hierarchising overtook the earlier hybrid intermingling.

36 Modelled on those of William Hedges. See Henry Yule (ed.), *The Diary of William Hedges*, New York: Burt Franklin, 1887.

37 For examples of colonialist discourse as applied to virtual reality see Howard Rheingold, *Virtual Reality*, New York: Summit, 1991, pp. 116, 183; Barrie Sherman and Phil Judkins, *Glimpses of Heaven, Visions of Hell: Virtual Reality and Its Implications*, London: Hodder and Stoughton, 1992, pp. 172ff.

38 Gita Mehta, *Karma Cola*, London: Jonathan Cape, 1980, p. 8.

39 Anne Bower, *Epistolary Responses: The Letter in Twentieth-Century American Fiction and Criticism*, Tuscaloosa: University of Alabama Press, 1997; James A. Schiff, *Updike's Version: Rewriting* The Scarlet Letter, Columbia: University of Missouri Press, 1992.

40 The phrase is itself the product of imperialism, popularised by the accountancy practices of the British empire.

41 John Updike, 'Special Message', for the Franklin Library first edition of *Roger's Version*, 1986, in *Odd Jobs*, New York: Knopf, 1991, pp. 856–8.

42 Phoebe-Lou Adams, 'Review of *S.*', *The Atlantic* 261, April 1988, p. 78.

43 Dell Murphy, *The Rajneesh Story: The Bhagwan's Garden*, West Linn: Linwood Press, 1986. On the Rajneeshees see also Kirk Braun, *Rajneeshpuram, the Unwelcome Society: Cultures Collide in a Quest for Utopia*, West Linn: Scout Creek Press, 1984; Scotta Callister, *For Love and Money: The Rajneeshees: From India to Oregon*, Portland: *The Oregonian*, 1985, first published in *The Oregonian*, 30 June–19 July, 1985; Lewis F. Carter, *Charisma and Control in Rajneeshpuram: The Role of Shared Values in the Creation of a Community*, Cambridge: Cambridge University Press, 1990; Rosemary Hamilton, *Hellbent for Enlightenment: Unmasking Sex, Power, and Death with a Notorious Master*, Askland, Oreg.: White Cloud Press, 1998; Judith Thompson and Paul Heelas, *The Way of the Heart: the Rajneesh Movement*, San Bernardino, Calif.: Borgo Press, 1988.

44 David G. Bromley, Mary Jo Neitz and Marion S. Goldman, *Sex, Lies and Sanctity: Religion and Deviance in Contemporary North America*, Greenwich, Conn.: JAI Press, 1995, p. 148.

45 Hugh Milne, *Bhagwan: The God that Failed*, London: Caliban Books, 1986, p. 137.

46 Ibid., p. 295.

47 Marie Daly Price, *Rajneeshpuram and the American Utopian Tradition*, Discussion Paper Series No. 87. Syracuse: Department of Geography, Syracuse University, 1985, p. 38.

48 Milne, *Bhagwan*, p. 225.

49 Ibid., p. 307.

50 See Matei Calinescu, 'Secrecy in fiction: textual and intertextual secrets in Hawthorne and Updike', *Poetics Today* 15, 3, 1994, 444–65.

51 John Updike, 'Hawthorne's creed', in *Hugging the Shore*, New York: Knopf, 1983, 73–80 (p. 76).

2 In the missionary position

1 Gaby Wood, 'The Chinese girl who calls me mum', *Observer*, 8 July 2001, p. 3.

2 Emily Prager, *In the Missionary Position. 25 Years of Humour Writing from the National Lampoon, Titters, Penthouse, New York Observer, Guardian and the New York Times*, London: Vintage, 1999, p. 21. (Subsequent page references follow quotations in parentheses.)

3 Ibid., p. xv.

4 *The Inn of the Sixth Happiness*. Directed by Mark Robson, written by Isobel Lennart and produced by Buddy Adler. Twentieth Century Fox, 1958.

5 Gayatri Chakravorty Spivak, 'Can the subaltern speak?', in Cary Nelson and Lawrence Grossberg (eds), *Marxism and the Interpretation of Culture*, London: Macmillan, 1988, pp. 271–313 (p. 299).

6 Julia Kristeva, *About Chinese Women*, trans. Anita Barrows, London and New York: Marion Boyars, 1977, p. 83. First published as *Des Chinoises*, Paris: Editions des Femmes, 1974.

7 Rey Chow, *Women and Chinese Modernity. The Politics of Reading between East and West*, Minneapolis: University of Minnesota Press, 1991.

8 Emily Prager, *Wuhu Diary. On Taking My Adopted Daughter Back to Her Hometown in China*, New York: Random House, 2001, p. 3.

9 Howard S. Levy, *Chinese Footbinding: The History of a Curious Erotic Custom*, London: Neville Spearman, 1966, p. 23.

10 Emily Prager, 'A visit from the footbinder', in *A Visit from the Footbinder and other stories*, London: Vintage, 1999, p. 16. First published in Great Britain by Chatto and Windus, 1983. (Subsequent page references follow quotations in parentheses.)

11 Fan Hong, *Footbinding, Feminism and Freedom. The Liberation of Women's Bodies in Modern China*, London: Frank Cass, 1997, p. 289.

12 Levy, *Chinese Footbinding*, p. 2.

13 Ibid., p. 28.

14 Wang Ping, *Aching for Beauty. Footbinding in China*, Minneapolis: University of Minnesota Press, 2000, p. 68.

15 See Pasi Falk, 'Written in the flesh', *Body and Society* 1, 1, 1995, 95–105.

16 Thorstein Veblen, *The Theory of the Leisure Class* [1899], New Brunswick, NJ: Transaction, 1992.

17 Prager, *Wuhu Diary*, p. 150.

18 Ibid., p. 150.

19 James Clifford, *The Predicament of Culture: Twentieth Century Ethnography, Literature and Art*, Cambridge, Mass.: Harvard University Press, 1988, p. 218.

20 Arjun Appadurai (ed.), *The Social Life of Things. Commodities in Cultural Perspective*, Cambridge: Cambridge University Press, 1986, p. 28.

21 Beverley Jackson, *Splendid Slippers: A Thousand Years of an Erotic Tradition*, Berkeley: Ten Speed Press, 1997.

22 Rey Chow, 'Where have all the natives gone?', in Padmini Mongia (ed.), *Contemporary Postcolonial Theory: A Reader*, London: Arnold, 1996, pp. 122–46 (pp. 130–2).

23 Ping, *Aching for Beauty*, p. 68.

24 Emily Prager, *Roger Fishbite*, London: Chatto and Windus, 1999, p. 40. (Subsequent page references follow quotations in parentheses.)

25 Naomi Klein, *No Logo: Taking Aim at the Brand Bullies*, London: HarperCollins, 1999.

26 Katharine Viner, 'Hand-to-brand combat', *Guardian*, 12 September 2000, p. 18.

27 Richard Tessler, Gail Gamache and Liming Liu, *West Meets East. Americans Adopt Chinese Children*, Westport, Conn.: Bergin and Garvey, 1999, p. 8. See also Bruce Porter, 'I met my daughter at the Wuhan Foundling Hospital', *New York Times Magazine*, 11 April 1993, pp. 24–46; Cheri Register, *'Are Those Kids Yours?' American Families with Children Adopted from Other Countries*, New York: The Free Press, 1991.

28 Holly Burkhalter, 'China's horrific adoption mills', *New York Times*, 11 January 1996, p. A 25. See also Human Rights Watch/Asia, *Death by Default: A Policy of Fatal Neglect in China's State Orphanages*, New York: Human Rights Watch, 1996.

29 Karin Evans, *The Lost Daughters of China. Abandoned Girls, Their Journey to America, and the Search for a Missing Past*, New York: Jeremy P. Tarcher/Putnam, 2000, p. 117.

30 Ibid., p. 166.

31 Ibid.

32 Ibid., pp. 119–20.

33 Barbara Tizard, 'Intercountry adoption: review of evidence', *Journal of Child Psychology and Psychiatry* 32, 1991, 743–56 (p. 746).

34 Evans, *The Lost Daughters of China*, p. 166.

35 Ibid., p. 178.

36 Ibid., p. 2.
37 Adam Pertman, *Adoption Nation: How the Adoption Revolution is Transforming America*, New York: Basic Books, 2001.
38 Claudia Castañeda, *Figurations. Child, Bodies, Worlds*, Durham, NC: Duke University Press, 2002, p. 5. See also Claudia Castañeda, 'Incorporating the transnational adoptee', in Marianne Novy (ed.), *Imagining Adoption. Essays on Literature and Culture*, Ann Arbor: University of Michigan Press, 2001, pp. 277–99.
39 There appears to be no reliable evidence for these risks being substantial. See Jay W. Rojewski and Jacy L. Rojewski, *Intercountry Adoption from China: Examining Cultural Heritage and Other Postadoption Issues*, Westport, Conn.: Bergin and Garvey, 2001.
40 Castañeda, *Figurations*, p. 84.
41 Elizabeth Bartholet, *Family Bonds: Adoption and the Politics of Parenting*, New York: Houghton Mifflin, 1993. Castañeda, *Figurations*, offers a full discussion of Bartholet's views. See also Janet Farrell Smith, 'Analyzing ethical conflict in the transracial adoption debate: three conflicts involving community', *Hypatia* VIII, 1996, 1–23.
42 Evans, *The Lost Daughters of China*, p. 13.
43 See Danae Clark, 'Mediadoption: children, commodification and the spectacle of disruption', *American Studies* 39, 2, Summer 1998, 65–86.
44 Evans, *The Lost Daughters of China*, p. 49.
45 Ibid., p. 49.
46 Anon., 'Intelligence report. Your up-to-the-minute guide to summer '97 in the Hamptons', *Vanity Fair*, August 1997, p. 82.
47 *The New Yorker*, 7 July 1997, p. 31.
48 Michel Foucault, *The History of Sexuality*, vol. 1, *An Introduction*, trans. Robert Hurley, New York: Vintage, 1980, p. 137. See Rey Chow, *The Protestant Ethnic and the Spirit of Capitalism*, New York: Columbia University Press, 2002, p. 7.
49 Chow, *The Protestant Ethnic*, p. 21.
50 See Felicity Lawrence, 'Victims of the sands and the snakeheads', *Guardian*, 7 February 2004. Available online at <www.guardian.co.uk> (accessed 19 January 2005).
51 See John Tomlinson, *Cultural Imperialism. A Critical Introduction*, London: Pinter, 1991.
52 An insight resulting from a lunch with Rachel Bowlby, gratefully acknowledged.
53 See Novy (ed.), *Imagining Adoption*.
54 Arjun Appadurai, *Modernity at Large. Cultural Dimensions of Globalization*, Minneapolis: University of Minnesota Press, 1996, Chapter 2.
55 I am influenced in my reading practice here by Rey Chow's discussion of reading texts through details, which she describes as the sensuous, trivial and superfluous textual presences which exist in some ambiguous relation to larger visions, such as reform or revolution, which they displace. Chow discusses the use of feminine detail in the work of Wuhan women writers in the 1980s and 1990s, in *Women and Chinese Modernity*, Chapter 3. Chow acknowledges the influence of the groundbreaking work of Naomi Schor, who sees the detail as the abjected particular, always coded as feminine, whether ornamental or prosaic, but now part of an aesthetic in which the raw, brute, beautiful or even irrelevant detail has a life of its own, rather than being subordinated to the dominant theme of a work of art. See Naomi Schor, *Reading in Detail: Aesthetics and the Feminine*, London: Methuen, 1987,

and 'Introductory note' by the editors of a special issue on the detail, in *differences* 14, 3, Fall 2003, 1–3.

56 For the only study of birth parents' accounts of abandonment see Kay Johnson, Huang Banghan and Wang Liyao, 'Infant abandonment and adoption in China', *Population and Development Review* 24, 3, September 1998, 469–510.

57 Rojewski and Rojewski, *Intercountry Adoption from China*, pp. 105–6.

58 The letter is in a different position in the paperback edition. See below.

59 Nancy Chodorow, *The Reproduction of Mothering*, Berkeley: University of California Press, 1978.

60 Johnson *et al.*, 'Infant abandonment and adoption in China', p. 473.

61 Jonathan Watts, 'China offers parents cash incentives to produce more girls', *Guardian*, 10 July 2004, p. 19.

62 Ibid.

63 Emily Prager, *Wuhu Diary*, London: Vintage, 2002. The American paperback (New York: Anchor, 2002) maintains the original cover and subtitle, though it is noteworthy that it is a trade paperback rather than a popular edition, and is catalogued by Random House under 'academic resources'.

3 Black Atlantic or Black Athena?

1 Ulf Hannerz, 'Thinking about culture in a global ecumene', in James Lull (ed.), *Culture in the Communication Age*, London: Routledge, 2001, pp. 54–71 (p. 57).

2 Eric Williams, *Capitalism and Slavery*, Chapel Hill: University of North Carolina Press, 1944. For a recent discussion, see Kenneth Morgan, *Slavery, Atlantic Trade and the British Economy, 1660–1800*, Cambridge: Cambridge University Press, 2001.

3 One exception is Charles Johnson, who, in *Middle Passage*, New York: Plume, 1991, engages with economic systems by casting his novel as a black-authored supplement to the logbook of a slave ship, transmuting an economic record into a personal story. See Ruth Mayer, *Artificial Africas. Colonial Images in the Times of Globalization*, Hanover and London: University Press of New England, 2002.

4 Martin Bernal, *Black Athena. The Afroasiatic Roots of Classical Civilization*, London: Free Association Books, 1987–91.

5 Alex Haley, *Roots* [1976], London: Vintage, 1991. See Ashraf H.A. Rushdy, *Remembering Generations. Race and Family in Contemporary African American Fiction*, Chapel Hill: University of North Carolina Press, 2001; Alison Landsberg, 'Prosthetic Memory. The Logics and Politics of Memory in Modern American Culture', Ph.D. dissertation, University of Chicago, 1996, Ann Arbor UMI Microform No. 9711252; Helen Taylor, '"The Griot from Tennessee": the Saga of Alex Haley's *Roots*', *Critical Quarterly* 37, 2, Summer 1995, 46–62.

6 Thomas Lask, 'Success of search for roots leaves Alex Haley surprised', *New York Times*, 23 November 1976, p. 40.

7 Manthia Diawara *et al.*, 'Editorial comment: on thinking the black public sphere', *Public Culture* 7, 1994, xi.

8 Paul Gilroy, *The Black Atlantic: Modernity and Double Consciousness*, London: Verso, 1993, p. 28. For a succinct critique of Gilroy see Joan Dayan, 'Paul Gilroy's slaves, ships and routes: the middle passage as metaphor', *Research in African Literatures* 27, 4, 1996, 7–14; Laura Chrisman, 'Rethinking Black Atlanticism', *Black Scholar* 20, 3–4, 2000, 12–17.

9 Toni Morrison, *Song of Solomon* [1977], London: Panther, 1984, p. 322.

10 Paul Gilroy, 'It's a family affair', in Gina Dent (ed.), *Black Popular Culture*, Seattle: Bay Press, 1992, 303–16.

11 Caryl Phillips, *Crossing the River* [1993], London: Collins Educational, 1993, p. 1.

12 Bénédicte Ledent, 'Overlapping territories, intertwined histories: cross-culturality in Caryl Phillips' *Crossing the River*', *Journal of Commonwealth Literature* XXX, 1, 1995, 55–62.

13 Ashraf H.A. Rushdy, *Neo-Slave Narratives. Studies in the Social Logic of a Literary Form*, Oxford: Oxford University Press, 1999, p. 95.

14 Elizabeth Anne Beaulieu, 'Femininity Unfetterd: The Emergence of the American Neo-Slave Narrative', Ph.D. dissertation, University of North Carolina, 1995.

15 Octavia A. Butler, *Kindred* [1979], London: Women's Press, 1988.

16 Gilroy, *The Black Atlantic*, p. 189.

17 Joan Brady, *Theory of War* [1993], London: Abacus, 1994, p. 23.

18 Chrisman, 'Rethinking Black Atlanticism', p. 12.

19 Geoffrey Hartmann (ed.), *Bitburg in Moral and Political Perspective*, Bloomington: Indiana University Press, 1986, p. 6.

20 Maria Lauret, *Liberating Literature: Feminist Fiction in America*, London: Routledge, 1994; Heidi MacPherson, *Women's Movement: Escape as Transgression in North American Women's Fiction*, Amsterdam and Athens, Ga.: Rodopi, 2000.

21 Margaret Atwood, *The Handmaid's Tale* [1985], London: Virago, 1987, p. 93.

22 Michael Foley, 'Satiric intent in the "Historical Notes" epilogue to Margaret Atwood's *The Handmaid's Tale*', *Commonwealth Essays and Studies* 11, 2, 1989, 44–52.

23 Henry Louis Gates Jr (ed.), *The Bondwoman's Narrative: A Novel by Hannah Crafts*, New York: Warner Books, 2002. (Subsequent page references follow quotations in parentheses.)

24 Paul Grainge, 'Remembering the "American century". Media memory and the *Time* 100 list', *International Journal of Cultural Studies* 5, 2, 2002, 201–19 (p. 205).

25 Bob Minzesheimer, 'Novel may be first by escaped female slave', *Chicago Sun Times*, 28 March 2002, p. 32.

26 Jeff Zaleski, 'The Bondwoman's Narrative', *Publishers Weekly* 249, 13, 1 April 2002, 53.

27 David R. Shumway, 'The star system in literary studies', *PMLA* 112, 1, January 1997, 85–100. Shumway, p. 93, draws attention to Adam Begley, 'Black studies' new star', *New York Times Magazine*, 5 June 1988, p. 24, in which dramatic lighting and personal images give the reader a sense of Gates's personal life. It is important to reiterate, as Shumway notes, that 'the quality or value of an individual's work should not be impugned because it has been authorized by the star system', p. 98.

28 Press reports include: Esther Addley and Oliver Burkeman, 'A slave woman writes', *Guardian*, 4 April 2002, pp. 8–9; Fredric Koeppel, 'Gates to sign *Bondwoman's Narrative*', *Commercial Appeal*, Memphis, 21 April 2002, G3; 'Finally slave's story is told', *Seattle Times*, 9 May 2002, Local B1; Diane Roberts, 'Tale captivates, but author a mystery', *The Rocky Mountain News*, 10 May 2002, 29 D; Mia Bay, 'Broken chains', *New York Times Book Review*, 12 May 2002, p. 30; Charles Matthews, 'Gates traces a slave era find', *Sunday Gazette-Mail*, Charleston, 19 May 2002, 1F; Carlin Romano, 'Gates ponders ditching Harvard for Princeton', *Sunday Gazette-Mail*, Charleston, 19 May 2002, 5F; 'Literary notes', *Greensboro News and Record*, 26 May 2002, H5; Roger A. Berger, '*The Bondwoman's Narrative*', *Library Journal* 127, 10, 1 June 2002, 147; Benjamin Soskis, 'Freedoms and fictions', *New Republic*, 3 June 2002, 36–40; Roger Hutchinson, '*The Bondwoman's Narrative* and

Narrative of the Life of Henry Box Brown: Land of inequality', *Scotsman*, 6 July 2002, S2, 8; Ronald Segal, '*The Bondwoman's Narrative*', *Spectator*, 13 July 2002, p. 36; Hilary Mantel, 'The shape of absence', *London Review of Books* 24, 15, 8 August 2002, 3; Douglas Field, '*The Bondwoman's Narrative*', *Times Literary Supplement* 5198, 2000, 28.

29 Wendy Waring, 'Is this your book? Wrapping postcolonial fiction for the global market', *Canadian Review of Comparative Literature* 22, 3/4, 1995, 455–65, is illuminating on paratextual traces, drawing upon Gérard Genette, *Seuils*, Paris: Seuil, 1987.

30 Soskis, 'Freedoms and fictions', p. 37.

31 This comment appears in the abstract of William L. Andrews, 'Hannah Crafts's sense of an ending', on *The Bondwoman's Narrative* website (<www.bondwomansnarrative.com>, accessed 13 September 2002) but has disappeared in the full version of the essay of the same title in the printed *Educational Co mpanion*. The Bondwoman's Narrative: *A XanEdu Educational Companion*, Henry Louis Gates Jr (ed.), Ann Arbor: Proquest, 2002.

32 Graham Huggan, *The Postcolonial Exotic: Marketing the Margins*, London: Routledge, 2001, offers a penetrating critique of the global commodification of cultural difference in the booming contemporary alterity industry. Huggan highlights the homogenisation and levelling out of historical experience as one result of the imagined access to the cultural Other through the process of consumption, in an argument which, while focused upon postcolonial examples, has obvious ramifications for understanding the marketing of African-American literature.

33 Henry Louis Gates Jr and Hollis Robbins (eds), *In Search of Hannah Crafts. Critical Essays on* The Bondwoman's Narrative, New York: Basic Books, 2004, p. xi.

34 Ibid., p. 41.

35 Ibid., p. 293.

36 Ibid., p. 432.

37 Ibid., p. 434.

38 <www.statelib.lib.in.us/> (accessed 25 January 2006).

39 Michele Wallace, 'Who owns Zora Neale Hurston? Critics carve up the legend', in her *Invisibility Blues: from Pop to Theory*, New York: Verso, 1990, pp. 172–87 (p. 174). Wallace refers to Harold Bloom (ed.), *Modern Critical Views: Zora Neale Hurston*, New York: Chelsea House, 1986.

40 Hazel Carby, 'The politics of fiction, anthropology and the folk: Zora Neale Hurston', in Michael Awkward (ed.), *New Essays on* Their Eyes Were Watching God, Cambridge: Cambridge University Press, 1990, pp. 71–94.

41 Gloria Cronin, '*Their Eyes Were Watching God*', unpublished paper, ALA Conference, San Diego, May 1998, p. 4.

42 Franz Boas, *The Social Organization and Secret Societies of the Kwakiutl Indians*, Washington, DC: 1897. Robert Hemenway, *Zora Neale Hurston: A Literary Biography*, Urbana: University of Illinois Press, 1977, p. 63, gives an account of Hurston's relationship to Boas, whom she idolised. He notes that Boas had already discovered that Indians, presumed to be savages, maintained a highly complex, sophisticated belief system, and that the evidence suggested the same was true for illiterate black people. It would therefore be quite logical for Hurston to make connections between Indian and black folklore. On Boas see Melville Herskovits, *Franz Boas*, New York: Charles Scribner's Sons, 1953. Boas was such a notable foe of racism that his 1933 essay 'Aryans and non-Aryans' was circulated clandestinely, printed on tissue paper, by the anti-Nazi underground. Hurston also studied with Melville Herskovits at Northwestern University in 1935–6, but gave up her doctorate and

used her Guggenheim money to write the novel. It is worth noting that Saul Bellow graduated from Northwestern in 1937 with honours in anthropology and sociology, and that he went on to graduate study with Herskovits. Bellow's *Humboldt's Gift*, London: Secker and Warburg, 1975, is also structurally based upon gift exchange. See Judie Newman, 'Bellow's "Indian Givers": *Humboldt's Gift*', *Journal of American Studies* 15, 2, 1981, 231–8. Hurston's 1933 short story, 'The gilded six-bits', *Story* 3, August 1933, 60–70, also involves a poisonous gift, a gold coin which turns out to be merely gilded. Missie May is seduced by a travelling man in exchange for the coin, but discovered by her husband, who forgives her and uses the coin to buy candy in the store.

43 For a later, but comprehensive account see Eli Sagan, *Cannibalism: Human Aggression and Cultural Form*, New York: Harper and Row, 1974. See also Marcel Mauss, *The Gift*, London: Cohen and West, 1954. Originally published as *Essai sur le don*, Paris: Presses Universitaires de France, 1950.

44 Robert Hemenway, 'The personal dimension in *Their Eyes Were Watching God*', in Awkward (ed.), *New Essays*, p. 32.

45 Ibid.

46 Zora Neale Hurston, *Their Eyes Were Watching God*, London: Virago, 1986, 'Afterword' by Sherley Anne Williams, p. 297.

47 Ibid., p. 29. (Subsequent page references follow quotations in parentheses.)

48 Houston A. Baker, 'Ideology and narrative form', in *Blues, Ideology and Afro-American Literature: A Vernacular Theory*, Chicago: Chicago University Press, 1984, p. 57

49 Ibid., p. 58

50 John Lowe, *Jump at the Sun. Zora Neale Hurston's Cosmic Comedy*, Urbana: University of Illinois Press, 1997, p. 174.

51 Peter Messent, *New Readings of the American Novel*, London: Macmillan, 1990, pp. 243–88.

52 Baker, 'Ideology and narrative form', p. 58.

53 Ibid.

54 Trinh T. Minh-ha, *Woman, Nature, Other: Writing Postcoloniality and Feminism*, Bloomington: Indiana University Press, 1989, p. 89.

55 Gail Ching-Liang Low, 'In a free state: post-colonialism and postmodernism in Bharati Mukherjee's fiction', *Women: A Cultural Review* 4, 1, Spring 1993, p. 17.

4 Local life, global death

1 David Bradley, *The Chaneysville Incident*, New York: Harper and Row, 1981, reprinted Edinburgh: Payback Press, 1999, p. 207. (Subsequent page references to the reprint edition follow quotations in parentheses.)

2 Bradley has been well served by some excellent critics; see in particular Cathy Brigham, 'Identity, masculinity, and desire in David Bradley's fiction', *Contemporary Literature* XXXVI, 36, 2, 1995, 289–316; Klaus Ensslen, 'Fictionalizing history: David Bradley's *The Chaneysville Incident*', *Callaloo* 11, 2, 1988, 280–96; Lawrence Hogue, 'Problematizing history: David Bradley's *The Chaneysville Incident*', *College Language Association Journal* 38, 4, 1995, 441–60; Matthew Wilson, 'The African American historian: David Bradley's *The Chaneysville Incident*', *African American Review* 29, 1, 1995, 97–107; Philip J. Egan, 'Unraveling misogyny and forging the new self: mother, lover, and storyteller in *The Chaneysville Incident*', *Papers on Language and Literature* 33, 3, 1997, 265–87; George L. Henderson, 'South of the north, north of the south: spatial practice in David Bradley's *The Chaneysville Incident*', in Gray

Gundacre (ed.), *Keep Your Head to the Sky: Interpreting African American Home Ground*, Charlottesville and London: University Press of Virginia, 1998, pp. 113–44; Ralph Reckley, 'The quest for immortality in David Bradley's *The Chaneysville Incident*', *MAWA Review* 1, 2–3, 1982, 56–9; Missy Dehn Kubitschek, '"So you want a history, do you?"': Epistemologies and *The Chaneysville Incident*', *Mississippi Quarterly* 49, 4, 1996, 755–74.

3 Thomas C. Imier *et al.*, *The Kernel of Greatness. An Informal Bicentennial History of Bedford County*, Bedford County Heritage Commission, 1971, p. 73. Harriette M. Bradley contributed to Chapters VII, X and XIII.

4 Nigel Barley, *Dancing on the Grave. Encounters with Death*, London: John Murray, 1995, p. 132.

5 Ibid., p. 67.

6 Orlando Patterson, *Slavery and Social Death: A Comparative Study*, Harvard University Press, 1982, p. 5.

7 Joseph Roach, *Cities of the Dead: Circum-Atlantic Performance*, New York: Columbia University Press, 1996, p. 35.

8 Ibid., p. 36.

9 Carroll Smith-Rosenberg, 'Surrogate Americans: masculinity, masquerade, and the formation of national identity', *PMLA* 119, 5 October 2004, 1325–35.

10 The history is partly drawn from E. Howard Blackburn and William M. Welfley, *History of Bedford and Somerset Counties, Pennsylvania*, New York and Chicago: Lewis Publishing Company, 1906, though the authors celebrate county patriotism without Bradley's ambivalence.

11 The incident is based on fact. See Emerson H. Loucks, *The Ku Klux Klan in Pennsylvania*, Harrisburg: The Telegraph Press, 1936.

12 On the uses of superstition as a form of social control by the Klan see Gladys Marie Fry, *Night Riders in Black Folk History*, Knoxville: University of Tennessee Press, 1975; on the ways in which the belief in ghosts demonstrated that even the forces of time and death could not block family and community cohesion see Elliott J. Gorn, 'Black spirits: the Ghostlore of Afro-American slaves', *American Quarterly* 36, 4, Autumn 1984, 549–65.

13 Kay Bonetti, 'An interview with David Bradley', *Missouri Review* 15, 3, 1992, 72.

14 For a brilliant account of spatial politics in the novel, which includes a photographic record of the gravesites, see Henderson, 'South of the north, north of the south'.

15 F.H. Pettis advertised widely as a slave catcher. For an example of his advertisements see Emily Catharine Pierson, *Jamie Parker, the Fugitive*, Hartford, 1851, p. 181. Joseph Crawley, John Fidler and Elias Rouse, mentioned in *The Chaneysville Incident*, are listed as major black agents in Bedford County in Charles L. Blockson, *The Underground Railroad in Pennsylvania*, Jacksonville, NC: Flame International, 1981, p. 141. Blockson, citing as his source Harriette Bradley, recounts that the Lester Imes family protected the fugitives.

16 The point is made by Egan, 'Unraveling misogyny'.

17 The point is made by Reckley, 'The quest for immortality'.

18 The case for suicide is argued by Cathy Brigham, 'Identity, masculinity, and desire'. In contrast Klaus Ensslen and Philip J. Egan read the ending in more optimistic terms.

19 David Bradley, 'Our crowd, their crowd: race, reader and *Moby Dick*', in John Bryant and Robert Milder (eds), *Melville's Ever-Moving Dawn: Centennial Essays*, Kent, OH.: Kent State University Press, 1997, pp. 119–46 (p. 139).

5 Going global

1 John North, 'The snow must go on', *Toronto Star*, 16 October 1993, J19.

2 See Eric Cheyfitz, *The Poetics of Imperialism. Translation and Colonization from The Tempest to Tarzan*, New York: Oxford University Press, 1991; Vicente L. Rafael, *Contracting Colonialism: Translation and Christian Conversion in Tagalog Society under Early Spanish Rule*, Durham, NC: Duke University Press, 1988; Tejaswini Niranjana, *Siting Translation: History, Post-Structuralism and the Colonial Context*, Berkeley: University of California Press, 1992. Given the real problems of discussing a translated text, I am grateful to the participants in my master class at the Georg Brandes Skolen, University of Copenhagen, 2004, for the opportunity to test my own reading of *Smilla's Sense of Snow*, and to the editors of *Spring* and the translators who subsequently transformed my lecture into Danish. See Judie Newman, 'Postkoloniale parasitter. Peter Høegs *Frøken Smillas fornemmelse for sne*', *Spring: Tidsskrift for moderne dansk litteratur*, Gaesteredaktion Postkolonialisme, 22, 2004, 9–27. Oversættelse: Morten Gaustad og Sara Koch.

3 Douglas Robinson, *Translation and Empire: Postcolonial Theories Explained*, Manchester: St Jerome Publishing, 1997.

4 Lawrence Venuti, *The Scandals of Translation: Towards an Ethics of Difference*, London and New York: Routledge, 1998, p. 58.

5 Ibid., p. 125.

6 Emily Apter, 'On translation in a global market', *Public Culture* 13, 1, 2001, 1–12 (p. 3).

7 Venuti, *The Scandals of Translation*, p. 93.

8 Peter Høeg, *Smilla's Sense of Snow*, New York: Dell, 1995, p. 119. (Subsequent page references follow quotations in parentheses.) First published as *Frøken Smillas fornemmelse for sne*, Copenhagen: Munksgaard/Rosinante, 1992.

9 Eva Hemmungs Wirtén, 'Smilla rules: exploring translation studies and book history', *SHARP News* 10, 1, Winter 2000/01, 1–4. Wirtén provides an excellent discussion of the details of the novel's translation. The British version is slightly different from the American and is attributed to F. David, a pseudonym for Høeg and his Danish editor.

10 Karin Trolle (ed.), *Miss Smilla's Feeling for Snow. The Making of a Film by Bille August Adapted from the Novel by Peter Høeg*, London: Harvill, 1997, p. 82.

11 Ibid., p. 25.

12 Graham Huggan, *The Postcolonial Exotic: Marketing the Margins*, London: Routledge, 2001, p. 22.

13 E. San Juan Jr, 'Establishment postcolonialism and its alter/native others: deciding to be accountable in a world of permanent emergency', in C. Richard King (ed.), *Post-Colonial America*, Urbana and Chicago: University of Illinois Press, 2000, pp. 171–97. For a reading more receptive to Bhabha's concept of hybridity see Prem Poddar and Cheralyn Mealor, 'Danish imperial fantasies: Peter Høeg's *Miss Smilla's Feeling for Snow*', in Prem Poddar (ed.), *Translating Nations. The Dolphin*, 30, Aarhus University Press, 1999, pp. 161–202.

14 Bill Ashcroft, *Post-Colonial Transformation*, London: Routledge, 2001.

15 J.M. Coetzee, *Waiting for the Barbarians*, London: Penguin, 1982.

16 Ibid., p. 24.

17 Ibid., p. 25.

18 Rey Chow, 'Where have all the natives gone?', in Padmini Mongia (ed.), *Contemporary Postcolonial Theory: A Reader*, London: Arnold, 1996, pp. 130–46 (p. 132).

19 Mary Douglas, *Purity and Danger: An Analysis of Concepts of Pollution and Taboo*, London: Routledge and Kegan Paul, 1966, p. 4. See Judie Newman, *The Ballistic Bard: Postcolonial Fictions*, London: Arnold, 1995, Chapter 6.

20 See Rachel Schaffer, 'Smilla's sense of gender identity', *Clues* 19, 1, 1998, 47–60; Annelies Van Hees, 'Fiction and reality in *Smilla's Sense of Snow*', *European Studies* 18, 2002, 215–26.

21 Trolle, *Miss Smilla's Feeling for Snow*, p. 15.

22 San Juan Jr, 'Establishment postcolonialism', p. 176.

23 Michel Serres, *The Parasite*, trans. Laurence R. Schehr, Baltimore: Johns Hopkins University Press, 1982. See also 'Michel Serres', in John Lechte, *Fifty Key Contemporary Thinkers*, London: Routledge, 1994. Online abstract: <www. uvpress. uv.es/ Acosotextual/serresbio> (accessed 17 February 2004).

24 Serres, *The Parasite*, translator's introduction, p. x.

25 Ibid., p. 7.

26 Ibid., pp. 179ff. The best account of Serres's work remains Steven D. Brown, 'Parasite logic', Paper for Cultures of Information 2, Keele University, 25 November 2001, p. 8. Available online at <devpsy.lboro.ac.uk/psygroup/sb/ parasite> (accessed 17 February 2004).

27 Serres, *The Parasite*, p. 24. Serres makes a careful distinction between predation and parasitism, seeing the former as merely a first stage in human history, p. 10. In his view, human beings live off animals as parasites do, eating them, wearing their skins. Smilla begins as a hunter, but in Denmark, in her kidskin pants, she is already a parasite.

28 Ibid., p. 52.

29 Ibid., p. 66.

30 Steven D. Brown, 'Michel Serres: myth, mediation and the logic of the parasite', p. 3. Available online at <devpsy.lboro.ac.uk/psygroup/sb/Serres> (accessed 17 February 2004). See also Steven D. Brown, 'Michel Serres: science, translation and the logic of the parasite', *Theory, Culture and Society* 19, 3, June 2002, 1–28.

31 Michel Serres, with B. Latour, *Conversations on Science, Culture and Time*, trans. by R. Lapidus, Ann Arbor: University of Michigan Press, 1995, p. 70.

32 I am enormously indebted here to Ruth Mayer, *Artificial Africas. Colonial Images in the Times of Globalization*, Hanover and London: University Press of New England, 2002, Chapter 7. Although she does not discuss Høeg, Mayer examines films, novels and comic depictions of parasitism in relation to Africa, and draws illuminatingly on the work of Serres.

33 Ibid., p. 290.

34 Ibid., p. 260.

35 Serres, *The Parasite*, p. 63.

6 Southern apes

1 Manfred B. Steger, *Globalism: The New Market Ideology*, Lanham: Rowman and Littlefield, 2002, p. 13.

2 Chalmers Johnson, *The Sorrows of Empire*, London: Verso, 2004, p. 260.

3 Christopher Douglas, 'The flawed design: American imperialism in N. Scott Momaday's *House Made of Dawn* and Cormac McCarthy's *Blood Meridian*', *Critique* 45, 1, Fall 2003, 3–24, argues that the novel is an anticreationist, evolutionary novel, setting out to contest any view of American imperialism as a Christian mission. Dana Phillips, 'History and the ugly facts in Cormac McCarthy's *Blood*

Meridian', *American Literature* 68, 2, June 1996, 433–60, also argues that the novel shows that salvation history is played out in favour of natural history.

4 See particularly Robert L. Jarrett, *Cormac McCarthy*, New York: Twayne, 1997.

5 Several critics have drawn attention to a connection with Vietnam: Barclay Owens, *Cormac McCarthy's Western Novels*, Tucson: University of Arizona Press, 2000; Brady Harrison, '"That immense and bloodslaked waste": negation in *Blood Meridian*', *Southwestern American Literature* 25, 1, Fall 1999, 35–42; Richard Godden and Colin Richmond, '*Blood Meridian*, or the evening redness in the east: "itinerant degenerates bleeding westwards"', *Comparative American Studies* 2, 4, 2004, 447–59. The collection of Vietcong ears is noted in Richard Drinnon, *Facing West: The Metaphysics of Indian-Hating and Empire-Building*, Minneapolis: University of Minneapolis Press, 1980; Peter Messent, 'All the pretty horses: Cormac McCarthy's Mexican Western', *Borderlines: Studies in American Culture* 2, 2, December 1994, 92–112, calls attention to the American fear of invasion from the south and the threat of Latino cultural hegemony. John Beck, 'Filibusters and fundamentalists: *Blood Meridian* and the New Right', *Polemics: Essays in American Literary and Cultural Criticism* 1, 2004, 13–26, notes that the novel describes the transformation of a privateer American military into a ragged guerrilla force, as happens in various Vietnam films, and that it appears just as the Republican Party aligned itself with the religious Right. Beck makes the case that we should not ignore the radically conservative undertow to the novel.

6 See Vereen M. Bell, *The Achievement of Cormac McCarthy*, Baton Rouge: Louisiana State University Press, 1988.

7 They are described as 'savages' *passim* in 1858, in John Holland Jenkins, *Recollections of Early Texas*, reprinted Austin: University of Texas Press, 1987.

8 John Rothfork, 'Cormac McCarthy as pragmatist', *Critique* 47, 2, Winter 2006, 201–14.

9 Michel Foucault's concept, after Nietzsche, of genealogy as a method of rediscovering historical struggles as against totalising discourses, in strong opposition to notions of linearity and of the primacy of origins, is quite distinct from the popular uses of genealogy, which emphasise linearity of descent from originals.

10 Cormac McCarthy, *Blood Meridian, or, The Evening Redness in the West*, New York: Vintage, 1992, p. 3. All subsequent page references are to this edition of the novel and follow citations in parentheses. First published New York: Random House, 1985.

11 I am using the term 'man' advisedly, rather than more inclusive language, to reflect the view expressed by ethologists of the male as the norm. On ethology see Robert Ardrey, *African Genesis*, London: Collins, 1961, *The Territorial Imperative*, New York: Dell, 1966, and *The Hunting Hypothesis*, London: Collins, 1976; Desmond Morris, *The Naked Ape*, London: Cape, 1967; Konrad Lorenz, *On Aggression*, London: Methuen, 1966.

12 Ardrey, *African Genesis*, p. 29.

13 Raymond A. Dart, 'The predatory transition from ape to man', *International Anthropological and Linguistic Review* 1, 4, 1953, 201–19 (pp. 207–8). Nadine Gordimer also published a novella, 'Something Out There', satirising ethological beliefs, focusing on Ardrey, Morris and Dart, a year before *Blood Meridian*. This was no coincidence: Dart was in the news. In 1984 there was a world conference of anthropologists in Johannesburg, to celebrate the fortieth anniversary of Dart's discovery. See Judie Newman, 'Nadine Gordimer and the naked

Southern ape: "Something Out There"', *Journal of the Short Story in English* 15, Autumn 1990, 55–72.

14 Robert Locke, 'Fossil remains of oldest ancestor of man found', *Yuma Daily Sun*, 13 June 1982, p. 23, col. 1. See also Rex Dalton, 'Awash with fossils', *Nature* 439/5, January 2006, 14–16. Dalton notes that the work of Tim D. White and J. Desmond Clark was frequently interrupted by wars in an area which he characterises as 'Neolithic with Kalashnikovs', p. 15.

15 Ardrey, *African Genesis*, p. 9.

16 Morris, *Naked Ape*, p. 27.

17 See John Emil Sepich, 'A "bloody dark pastryman": Cormac McCarthy's recipe for gunpowder and historical fiction in *Blood Meridian*', *Mississippi Quarterly* 46, 4, September 1993, 547–63.

18 For a collection of critical views see Ashley Montagu (ed.), *Man and Aggression*, Oxford: Oxford University Press, 1972.

19 Ibid., p. 181.

20 David Pilbeam, in ibid., p. 113.

21 Boyce Rensberger, 'The killer ape is dead', 1973. Available online at <www.alucapatterson.org/APF001973/Rensberger> (accessed 21 March 2006).

22 Ardrey, *African Genesis*, p. 186.

23 As he does elsewhere. Patrick Shaw, *The Modern American Novel of Violence*, Troy, NY: Whitston, 2000, describes McCarthy as 'an aesthetic vivisectionist who refuses to accommodate romantic illusions about Homo sapiens and the place he occupies in nature', p. 133; Owens notes the influence of sociobiological theory and mentions Morris, but concludes that the novel argues that 'mindless atavistic violence is the true nature of mankind, a genetic heritage in common with apes and wolves' p. 4. I would argue that this is the view which McCarthy is attacking in the novel. Duane Carr has also cited Lorenz, Ardrey and Morris as reviving nineteenth-century Social Darwinism, and notes the 'Neanderthal-type figures' in *Outer Dark* and the character of Lester Ballard. In *Child of God*, first published in 1973, Ballard is a serial killer who secretes his victims' bodies in caves, is seen 'gibbering', p. 159, makes a wig fashioned from a dried human scalp, p. 172, and is repeatedly described as ape-like. The cave in which he hides has a room full of bones of bison and elk, and even a jaguar's skull. See Cormac McCarthy, *Child of God*, New York: Vintage, 1993. Commentators have primarily related Ballard, however, to notions of degeneration and 'throwbacks' in Southern poor whites. See Duane R. Carr, 'The dispossessed white as Naked Ape and stereotyped hillbilly in the Southern novels of Cormac McCarthy', *Midwest Quarterly* 40, 1, 1998, 9–20. Carr argues that McCarthy's world vision is a warmed-over nineteenth-century Social Darwinism, widely propagated in the 1960s, and that McCarthy set out to illustrate the thesis shared by Lorenz, Ardrey and Morris.

24 Robert W. Sussman, 'The myth of man the hunter, man the killer, and the evolution of human morality', *Zygon* 34, 3, September 1999, 453–71.

25 Barbara Ehrenreich, *Blood Rites. Origins and History of the Passions of War*, London: Virago, 1998. Ehrenreich's arguments are a focus for Owens, *Cormac McCarthy's Western Novels*, though Owens envisages McCarthy as assenting to the image of man as killer, an image which I argue is being satirised by McCarthy. C.K. Brain had of course preceded Ehrenreich in emphasising man as prey.

26 Ehrenreich, *Blood Rites*, p. 47. It is suggestive that McCarthy's latest novel, *The Road*, New York: Alfred A. Knopf, 2006, focuses on a father and vulnerable young

son crossing a burned-out apocalyptic America in constant fear of being eaten by cannibalistic gangs, hunting human beings for food.

27 Ehrenreich, *Blood Rites*, p. 79.

28 In connection with scalping and its links to menstruation practices, see Claude Lévi-Strauss, *The Origin of Table Manners*, trans. John and Doreen Weightman, London: Jonathan Cape, 1978, pp. 376–432. Originally published as *L'Origine des manières de table*, Paris: Librairie Plon, 1968.

29 Wallis R. Sanborn III, *Animals in the Fiction of Cormac McCarthy*, London: McFarland, 2006, makes this point in his discussion of *No Country for Old Men*.

30 See Elizabeth Rosen, 'The American West through an apocalyptic lens: McCarthy's *Blood Meridian*', *US Studies Online* 3, Spring 2003. Available online at <www.baas.ac.uk/resources/usstudiesonline/default.asp> (accessed 31 March 2003).

31 Owens, *Cormac McCarthy's Western Novels*, p. xii.

32 Jenkins, *Recollections of Early Texas*, p. 65

33 T.R. Fehrenbach, *Comanches. The Destruction of a People*, New York: Alfred A. Knopf, 1974, p. 127. It is worth noting Fehrenbach's comment, p. 3, on the absence of hominid remains in North America, and his insistence that men entered America as experienced killers.

34 Ibid., p. 251. See also Rupert N. Richardson, *The Comanche Barrier to South Plains Settlement*, Glendale, Calif.: Arthur H. Clark, 1933.

35 Fehrenbach, *Comanches*, p. 397.

36 Thomas Pughe, 'Revision and vision: Cormac McCarthy's *Blood Meridian*', *Revue Française d'Etudes Américaines* 17, 69, 1994, 371–82, offers a close reading of this passage.

37 Adam Parkes, 'History, bloodshed and the spectacle of American identity in *Blood Meridian*', in James D. Lilley (ed.), *Cormac McCarthy: New Directions*, Albuquerque: University of New Mexico Press, 2002, pp. 103–24, contests the vision of man as biologically determined, arguing for an emphasis on performative selfhood in the novel. Parkes makes the case that the novel involves a series of performances and thus carries a non-essentialist charge. On Black and White Jackson, see especially pp. 117–19.

38 See Sussman, 'The myth of man the hunter'; Leonard Williams, *The Dancing Chimpanzee*, New York: Norton, 1967; Frank B. Livingstone, 'Did the Australopithecines sing?', *Current Anthropology* 14, 1973, 25–6.

39 I am indebted here to Stephanie LeMenager's discussion of nineteenth-century counter-narratives of Manifest Destiny, generated by apparently empty spaces: Stephanie LeMenager, *Manifest and Other Destinies. Territorial Fictions of the Nineteenth-Century United States*, Lincoln and London: University of Nebraska Press, 2004.

7 Priority narratives

1 James Lull, 'Superculture for the communication age', in James Lull (ed.), *Culture in the Communication Age*, New York and London: Routledge, 2001, pp. 132–63 (p. 138).

2 Manuel Castells, *The Rise of Network Society*, Oxford: Blackwell, 1996, p. 3.

3 Lull, 'Superculture for the communication age', p. 136.

4 Bharati Mukherjee, *Desirable Daughters*, New York: Hyperion, 2002, p. 17. (Subsequent page references follow quotations in parentheses.)

5 Bharati Mukherjee, *The Tree Bride*, New York: Hyperion, 2004, p. 20.

6 Amitava Kumar, 'Passages to India', *Nation*, 24 April 2000, pp. 36–9 (p. 39).

7 Dave Welch, 'Bharati Mukherjee runs the West Coast Offense', <www. powells.com/authors/mukherjee> (accessed 13 October 2004).

8 Edward O.Wilson, *Consilience: The Unity of Knowledge*, Little, Brown, 1998, pp. 77ff.

9 Werner Sollors, *Beyond Ethnicity: Consent and Descent in American Culture*, New York: Oxford University Press, 1986.

10 'Bharati Mukherjee in conversation with Barbara Lane', <www.commonwealthclub. org/archive/02/02-05mukherjee-speech> (accessed 9 May 2002), pp. 1–6 (p. 2).

11 Later the tactic was popularised by the San Francisco 49ers. See <users2. ev1.net/%/Ejamrtm/History> (accessed 8 November 2005).

12 Welch, 'Bharati Mukherjee runs the West Coast Offense'.

13 Paul Harris, 'Fictions of globalisation: narrative in the age of electronic media', *PhiN* 7, 1999, 26–39 (p.28).

14 Manuel Castells, *End of Millennium*, Oxford: Blackwell, 2000, p. 210.

15 Clark Blaise and Bharati Mukherjee, *The Sorrow and the Terror: The Haunting Legacy of the Air India Tragedy*, New York: Viking, 1987. See also 'Bill Moyers interviews Bharati Mukherjee', Transcript, PBS, 20 May 2003.

16 Welch, 'Bharati Mukherjee runs the West Coast Offense'.

17 Dragana Obradovic, 'Older Arts and Newer Technology', BA dissertation, University of Nottingham, 2004.

18 Frank J. Sulloway, *Born to Rebel: Birth Order, Family Dynamics and Creative Lives*, New York: Pantheon, 1996, p. 170.

19 In what follows I draw upon and paraphrase: Frank J. Sulloway, 'Sibling-order birth effects', <www.sulloway.org/Sibling-order-effects(2001).pdf> (accessed 28 October 2005), p. 14059; 'Forum and debate on birth order', <inst.santafe.cc.fl.us?~mwehr/gepsyc/FMBirord> (accessed 29 October 2005); Alfred Adler, *Understanding Human Nature*, Greenberg: New York, 1927. Adler recognised the importance of other factors such as sex order, parental age, cultural, religious and social beliefs, but none the less saw birth order as a very important factor.

20 Sulloway controls carefully for variables such as family size and class, using a meta-analytic methodology, pooling studies to gain statistical power. This is not the place to debate Sulloway's findings. Their enormous popularity says something, however, about a modern tendency to locate oneself less in terms of descent than in terms of lateral links, sibships and friendship groups. Mukherjee's use of birth order is not based upon autobiographical sources. Mukherjee is a middle daughter, with sisters Mira (older), a child psychologist in America, and Ranu (younger) in India. Mukherjee has written several times about the different choices taken by her, an American citizen, and Mira, an expatriate who maintains Indian nationality. See Bharati Mukherjee, 'The road from Ballygunge', in Claudine O'Hearn, *Half and Half: Writers on Growing Up Biracial and Bicultural*, New York: Pantheon, 1998, pp. 71–9.

21 Sulloway, *Born to Rebel*, p. 295.

22 Ibid., p. xv.

23 Arjun Appadurai, *Modernity at Large: Cultural Dimensions of Globalization*, Minneapolis: University of Minnesota Press, 1996, Chapter 3.

24 Ibid., Chapter 2.

25 *Asani Sanket (Distant Thunder)*, directed by Satyajit Ray. Balaka Movies, Sarboni Bhattacharya, India, 1973.

26 *Namaskar, probasi* translates as 'Greetings, diasporan Bengali'.

27 Mukherjee, *The Tree Bride*, p. 13.
28 Appadurai, *Modernity at Large*, p. 155.

Conclusion

1 Karl Kroeber, *Retelling/Rereading. The Fate of Storytelling in Modern Times*, New Brunswick, NJ: Rutgers University Press, 1992, p. 3.
2 Ibid.

Index

192   *Index*